MINNEAPOLIS

City of Lakes
An Illustrated History of

MINNEAPOLIS

by

Joseph Stipanovich

· · ·

Editorial Consultant, Harold Chucker
"Partners in Progress" by Dick Schaaf
Sponsored by
The Greater Minneapolis Chamber of Commerce
Windsor Publications, Inc.
Woodland Hills, California

View of Fort Snelling, *painted in*
about 1850, has been attributed to
E.K. Thomas. Courtesy, The
Minnesota Institute of Arts.

Windsor Publications, Inc.
History Books Division

Publisher: John M. Phillips
Editorial Director: Lissa Sanders
Administrative Coordinator: Katherine Cooper
Senior Picture Editor: Teri Davis Greenberg
Senior Corporate History Editor: Karen Story
Production Manager: James Burke
Design Director: Alexander D'Anca
Art Production Manager: Dee Cooper
Composition Manager: Shirley Leuin
Assistant Composition Manager: Beryl Myers

Staff for *City of Lakes*
Editor: Taryn Bigelow
Picture Editor: Annette Igra
Copy Editor: David Seidman
Editorial Assistants:
   Susan Block, Phyllis Gray,
   Mary Mohr, Susan Wells
Proofreaders:
   Susan Gutierrez, Karen Hartjen,
   Ruth Hoover, Lynn Johnson,
   Jeff Leckrone, Doris Malkin
Designer: Phil Waters
Production Artists:
   Beth Bowman, Pat Bruce,
   Barbara Moore, Shannon Strull

Photo credit abbreviations:
MPLIC   Minneapolis Public Library and Information Center
MHS   Minnesota Historical Society
Color photographs by Phil Waters unless otherwise indicated.

First Edition

Library of Congress Cataloging in Publication Data

Stipanovich, Joseph, 1946-
   City of Lakes.

   Bibliography: p. 377
   Includes index.
   1. Minneapolis (Minn.)—History. 2. Minneapolis
(Minn.)—Description. I. Title
F614.M557S74   977.6'579   81-70496
ISBN 0-89781-048-1   AACR2

CONTENTS

Facing page: *Robert Ormsby*
Sweeny depicted a man and woman
fishing below the falls in his 1856 oil
painting, Minnehaha Falls. (MHS)

PREFACE

The history of Minneapolis is a chronicle of the development of a frontier lumber town into the bustling, metropolitan hub of the Upper Midwest. In the course of that growth, Minneapolis managed to become for varying periods the lumber- and flour-milling center of the United States. The growth of population and industry in the city was rapid and was facilitated by a number of factors. The waterpower of the Falls of St. Anthony which attracted the first settlers, the great forests of central and northern Minnesota, the settlement of thousands of farms in the region, and the timely actions of a group of entrepreneurs all played important roles in the story. *City of Lakes: An Illustrated History of Minneapolis* delineates these salient features as well as the major experiences of the several generations of citizens who have inhabited the city in the course of the last century and a quarter, pursuing the goals of toil and play amidst the ever-changing tribulations of "everyday life."

The title, *City of Lakes*, deserves explanation. While serving as the official label for the city and adorning the municipal signs that are posted on the city limits' major routes of entry, the phrase also symbolizes major themes in the city's progress and history. Other potential symbols vie with the lakes for representing the essence of the city's history. The Falls of St. Anthony come immediately to mind, as they actually propelled, literally and figuratively, the early growth of the city. The falls, however, ceased to be an economic or aesthetic factor in the primary development of the city after 1890. They continued to play a role, of course, but were overshadowed by other developments as they were also overshadowed and covered by the series of dams, sluices, concrete aprons, and river locks built over the years. The same transitory attribute also afflicts the city's sawmills and flour mills, which characterized an important stage in the city's history.

The lakes of the city, however, have an enduring quality which deems them the most appropriate symbols of the city's progress and aspirations. The lakes predate the development of the city and were for a time as much a nuisance as a comfort to the inhabitants. They were transformed by the citizens into beautiful parts of a great park system through dredging and extensive landscaping. The lakes and the parks that surround them, then, reflect the city's effort to retain ties with a pristine, pastoral past in order to increase the livability of the urban environment. Born in the midst of political and social controversy, the lakes and park system also reflect the cleavages that have beset the body politic over the years. And, lastly, the lakes' transformation also symbolizes the faith in technology and its application that has greatly affected the course of the city, especially in the 20th century.

City of Lakes is the story of Minneapolis, but unavoidably it is also the story of the region that has surrounded it and nourished its growth. This fact is reflected in the economic development of the area as the city transformed the produce of the countryside into products that could be marketed throughout the nation and around the world. It is also reflected in the politics of the city as agrarian movements often swept into it. But it was a two-way movement, as ideas from the city also infected the countryside on occasion. The peopling of Minneapolis also reflects the strong ties with the countryside, for in both areas the Scandinavian elements are strong and numerous. Swedes, Norwegians, and New Englanders came to build lives on the farms as well as to make their niches in the city. As time passed and farmland grew scarce, the descendants of the farming immigrants began to come to the city to find the opportunities that eluded them in the countryside. This mingling of urban and rural immigrants in Minneapolis has given the city its strongest human tie with the hinterland.

The story of Minneapolis bears great similarity to the histories of other American cities. There are important differences as well, but the most unique element in the history of the city is the people who have built it. Collectively and individually, the citizens have made the city what it was and what it is—and what it will be. This, then, is the history of the City of Lakes, but a city built by people.

A word of explanation is also in order regarding the structure of this book. Many if not most urban histories are organized chronologically, which is a logical way of telling the story of a city's growth. Certain stories have such distinct elements, however, and such frenetic periods of activity in different spheres at the same time that the chronological narrative is sometimes strained. The singular development of economic activity, political processes, and community in Minneapolis fits this latter type. Consequently the book describes these three areas separately and in as much detail as possible. An additional chapter presents an overview of the city's chronological development to orient the reader to general trends in Minneapolis history. This approach has its pitfalls, but the potential benefits seem to outweigh the risks in presenting the story of the City of Lakes as effectively as possible. A city that has made its success through innovation deserves an innovative history.

Joseph Stipanovich

INTRODUCTION

Minneapolis is a unique community in its beauty, its culture, and its thriving economic activity. But its uniqueness extends beyond that, to the spirit of cooperation among its citizens and to their commitment to improving the quality of the city.

Like other communities, Minneapolis was born because it offered opportunities for concentrated economic activity. As Joseph Stipanovich points out in this volume, those opportunities centered around the Mississippi River and the Falls of St. Anthony, which provided the transport and power to make the frontier village into a major lumber- and flour-milling center for the Northern Plains region.

It took something more than economic opportunity, however, to make Minneapolis endure and grow, rather than shrivel and decline, as did other fledgling communities. That something was an attachment—a tradition of caring—on the part of its citizens, one that gave them a sense of a shared past and future.

It was the people of Minneapolis—first the New Englanders and later the Scandinavians and Germans—who transformed the small frontier community into the center of finance, industry, and culture for a region that extends from Montana to Wisconsin. Their involvement was the fuel that made Minneapolis move forward, overcoming natural and economic setbacks.

It was that involvement of citizens with their community that led to the development of model school, park, and library systems; a nationally recognized symphony orchestra; and theaters and museums. It was involvement, too, by business people, interacting with labor unions and city government to form a "triad" that made Minneapolis work and move forward.

Finally, it is the involvement of citizens from all walks of life in neighborhood associations, community task forces, and citizen and civic organizations that provides constant input for governmental decisions.

Minneapolis, in its history, was not without the conflicts that set labor against business or ethnic and racial groups against each other. But while the "triad" sometimes showed signs of crumbling because of those conflicts, the wounds were always healed and the involvement in the community of those who had been at odds with each other continued in the best interests of the city.

Minneapolis is not without its problems at present. It needs more housing, for instance, and more jobs for its citizens. But the magnitude of these problems is not such that they cannot be overcome, as other problems have been overcome in the past.

The city has a strong base from which to attack its problems. It is the headquarter of more than a dozen national and multinational corporations, a diversified industrial complex, a skilled and educated work force, and a nationally recognized public and private educational system.

It is pride in the city, rather than boosterism, that will continue the involvement of citizens with their community. It is that which made Minneapolis unique among cities, and which will continue to move the community forward.

John C. Bailey, C.C.E. President
The Greater Minneapolis
Chamber of Commerce

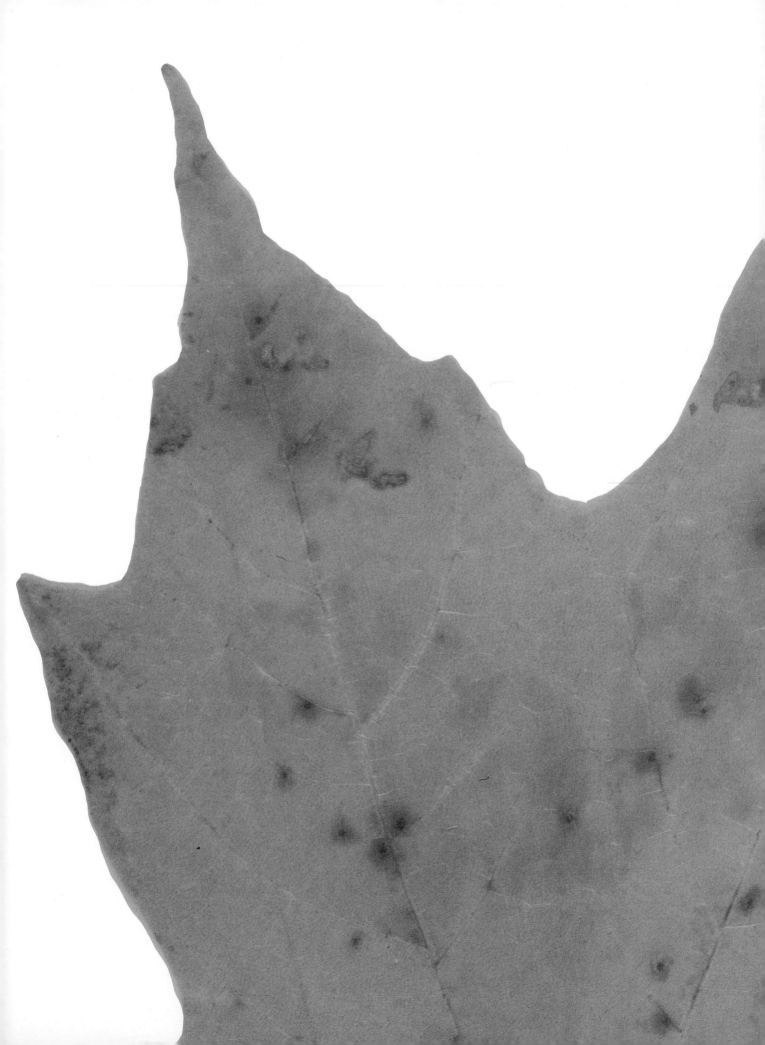

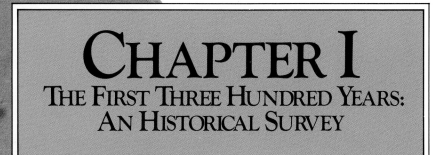

CHAPTER I
THE FIRST THREE HUNDRED YEARS:
AN HISTORICAL SURVEY

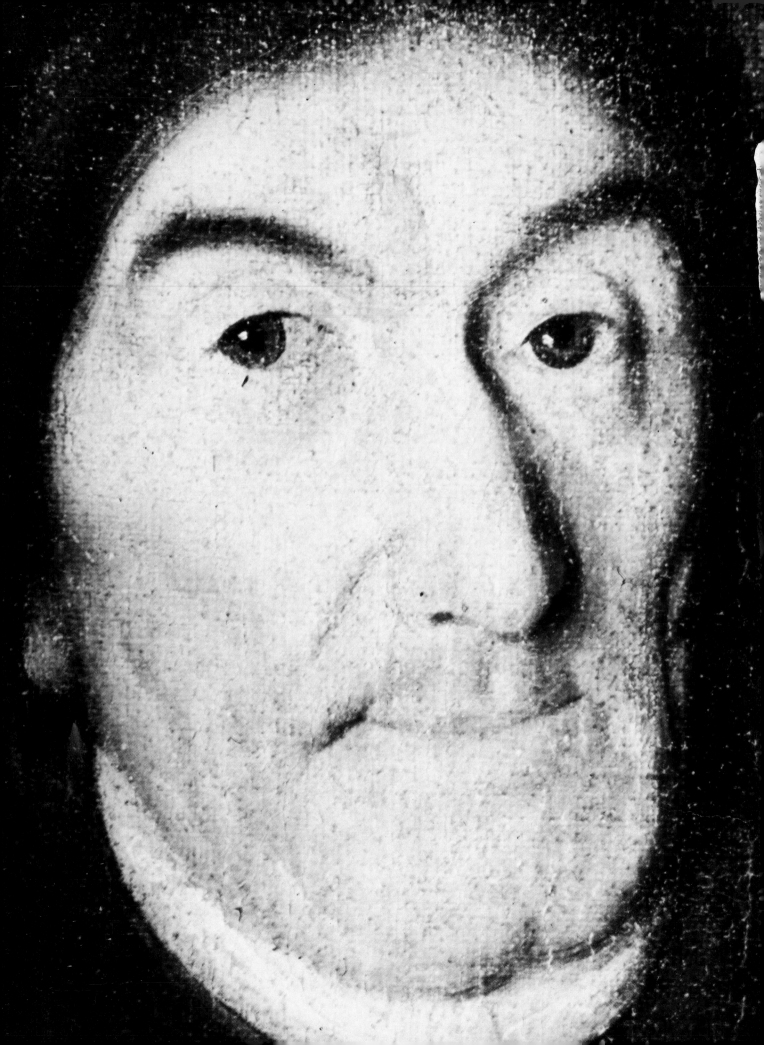

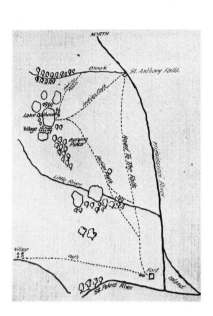

Above: *One of the first maps of the area presently encompassed by the city of Minneapolis shows St. Peter's River to the south, later renamed the Minnesota River, and Little River in the center, now Minnehaha Creek. The area north of Fort Snelling but south of the Mississippi River was part of a large military reservation which prevented legal pioneer settlement until the mid-1850s. From the Minneapolis Star and Tribune Company. (MPLIC)*

Facing page: *Father Louis Hennepin explored and wrote about the Minneapolis area in the 17th century. The county in which Minneapolis is located is named for him, as is a major thoroughfare in the city and an island in the Mississippi River just above the falls. (MPLIC)*

The Mississippi River nurtures many cities on its 2,350-mile trek from the northern lakes to the sea and undergoes many transformations as it winds its way southward through varying terrain created by the passage of epochs. At its southern terminus lies the city of New Orleans with its markets and exotic Creole ambience, while further to the north lie the river ports that stir memories of the Old South when cotton was King: Natchez, Vicksburg, and Memphis. In this part of the river, the banks become lost in swamps and sandbars as the river meanders, searching for its path to the sea. Here Samuel Clemens learned the art of piloting the riverboats amid oxbow lakes and illusory main channels. Further north the river shrinks as one moves beyond Cairo, another of many towns named for places on another river in a different age, and past the confluence with the Ohio. Beyond St. Louis and the point where the Missouri joins in the cascade, the Mississippi shrivels further into itself. Finally, above Lake Pepin and near St. Paul, the Mississippi enters the gorge that drew Southern planters on grand tours and that inspired the poetry of Henry Wadsworth Longfellow.

For it is at St. Paul that the river created high bluffs and promontories as it cut through the glacial debris that formed its bottom from that point to its origin in Lake Itasca in northern Minnesota. The high ground above the river between St. Paul and the Falls of St. Anthony farther to the north was a creation of the river itself. Like a Grand Canyon in miniature, the fast-flowing river in this area crashed over a river bottom that collapsed under the pressure and slowly washed out, leaving a greater and greater gap between the river surface and the land left high above. The Falls of St. Anthony, then, were mobile, moving slowly, mile by mile, further upriver as the crest of the falls continually gave out, washed out, and receded. It is probable that the Falls of St. Anthony moved to a different place between the time that Father Louis Hennepin saw them in 1680 and when American explorer Zebulon Pike traveled past them in 1805.

When Hennepin arrived at the Falls of St. Anthony in the

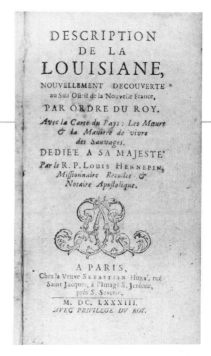

service of God and the French Crown, the area around the falls was primarily the domain of the Sioux family of tribes which included the Mdewakanton ("the people of the spirit or holy lake"), Wahpekute, Wahpeton, Sisseton, Yankton, Yanktonai, and Tetons. Mille Lacs, the holy lake of the Sioux, also known as the Dakota tribes, was the holy center of the group's culture. In the years after Hennepin's departure and his naming of the Falls of St. Anthony after his patron saint, the Sioux received a challenge to their hegemony from the east. Algonquian peoples such as the Chippewa or Ojibwe, Sauk, Fox, Cheyenne, Ottawa, Potawatomie, Cree, and Menominee, were driven westward by the Iroquois peoples and changing economic patterns caused by permanent French and English settlement in North America. In the mid-18th century the Dakota Sioux and the Ojibwe clashed, and the latter established themselves permanently in the areas of central and northern Minnesota, including the area around Mille Lacs. This was the division in effect when the first American military expedition arrived in the area under the command of the intrepid Lieutenant Zebulon Pike.

Pike's command was charged with the mission of finding appropriate locations at which to establish permanent garrisons to maintain American authority along the frontier with Canada. In those days before the War of 1812, the area of Minnesota, while nominally American, was the province of British military officials and operatives of the Hudson's Bay Company who wished to control the lucrative fur trade of that area and beyond towards the Rocky Mountains. Pike was successful in his mission and purchased suitable territory from the Dakota Sioux upon which a frontier fort could be later established. Pike acquired one tract of land at the point where the St. Croix River enters the Mississippi and another nine miles along both sides of the Mississippi from the mouth of the Minnesota up the Mississippi to the Falls of St. Anthony. It was to this latter tract that Lieutenant Colonel Henry Leavenworth led an expedition in 1819 in order to establish a permanent garrison at the junction of the Minnesota and Mississippi rivers.

Above: *The Falls of St. Anthony first received notoriety in printed form in the recollections of Father Louis Hennepin, published in Paris in 1683. Hennepin named the falls after his patron saint. (MPLIC)*

Facing page: *St. Anthony on the East Bank viewed from Hennepin Island is shown here before milling operations covered the area. The slabs of stone debris marked the retreat of the falls up the Mississippi River channel. From the E.A. Bromley Collection. (MPLIC)*

Leavenworth's efforts also were successful and the fort, later named Fort Snelling in honor of a subsequent commandant, became a magnet for settlement in central Minnesota. The Western movement, which characterized American history throughout most of the 19th century, brought the first settlers to the vicinity of the fort. The first settlement that Fort Snelling helped propel into existence was St. Paul, located across the Mississippi River and downstream a few miles. St. Paul had its origins in the entrepreneurial activities of one Pigs Eye Parrant, who had set up shop in a cave near the river flats. The settlement was upgraded when Father Lucien Galtier built a chapel dedicated to St. Paul in the vicinity in the late fall of 1841. The city grew, as it was the northern terminus for steamboat travel on the Mississippi, and it became a bustling center of frontier enterprise as the 1840s passed. When the Minnesota Territory was created in 1849, St. Paul was designated the capital. With territorial status came more settlers, who flowed through the steamboat town and spilled out into the surrounding countryside, establishing farms and small villages. Slowly the hinterland of the town began to develop, along with the trade between countryside and city that has been the hallmark of Western economic development. St. Paul prospered further with the coming of the railroads in the 1860s, and many of them headquartered in the city that was now the capital of the state of Minnesota.

While St. Paul easily and rapidly overshadowed other pioneer settlements, especially those in the St. Croix and Minnesota river valleys, a new challenger appeared in the late 1840s and early 1850s that proved to be more durable. The Falls of St. Anthony attracted interest from the first settlers and soldiers at Fort Snelling, who wasted no time in harnessing some of the abundant waterpower to saw their lumber and grind their flour. The potential of the falls was soon recognized by ambitious men, and by 1849 the first sawmill was in operation in the fledgling village of St. Anthony. Soon squatters were moving into the military reservation across the river in anticipation of its reduction. When the military was pulled back,

Facing page, clockwise from left: *Gideon Pond and his brother, Samuel, were among the first missionaries to work intensively with the Native Americans of the Minneapolis area. On the eastern shore of Lake Calhoun, the missionary brothers established a school and assisted Major Lawrence Taliaferro in his effort to teach the Indians sedentary agricultural habits. The Ponds also studied Native American languages and made numerous translations into Sioux languages. (MPLIC)*

Samuel Pond and his brother were natives of Connecticut who were called to the ministry at a New England revival meeting. Together they came to Minnesota Territory and, after advising the commandant at Fort Snelling, began their work among Native Americans. (MPLIC)

Colonel Henry Leavenworth, the first commandant of Fort Snelling, was in charge of the detail that built the first structures at the junction of the Minnesota and Mississippi rivers. He and his men suffered terrible hardships during their first winter in 1819–1820. Before he could actually begin the permanent construction of the fort, Leavenworth was replaced by Colonel Josiah Snelling, for whom the fort was eventually named. (MPLIC)

In 1857 St. Anthony's riverfront mills and shops lay nestled at the edge of the East Bank Scattered buildings on the West Bank represent the beginnings of Minneapolis. From the E.A. Bromley Collection. (MPLIC)

a new settlement sprang up almost overnight and was named Minneapolis.

Minneapolis and St. Anthony competed for power from the Falls of St. Anthony and also competed for the produce that came to the towns in the form of felled trees and grain. The trees were the products of the great forests to the north, and the sawmills of St. Anthony and Minneapolis were kept buzzing. The towns were booming. In fact, "boom town" refers to a lumber town where a boom has been set up in a river or lake to catch the felled trees that are being floated downstream. Boom Island, the island above Nicollet and Hennepin islands and the Falls of St. Anthony, was so named because it was close to the booms that were set to catch the logs for the St. Anthony mills.

The movement of the logs downriver was something akin to a cattle drive, for each sawmill would send crews to the forests to bring down the trees and move them down the river. Of course, more than one company could be cutting trees at any given time along a given river, so ways had to be developed to sort the lumber when it reached the boom. Thus developed the boom company, a firm that specialized in monitoring log traffic on the river and making sure that the right firms were credited with the right number of logs. Several early Minneapolis pioneers made substantial fortunes as a result of their involvement in such companies, notably the Mississippi and Rum River Boom Company, which operated into the first decade of the 20th century.

While lumbering flourished, St. Anthony became something of a tourist attraction as the fame of the Falls of St. Anthony spread abroad. Steamboats had been making regular runs to St. Paul and Fort Snelling for more than a decade when attempts were made to run them farther upriver to the falls. Early travelers made the journey to the falls overland by stagecoach from St. Paul to St. Anthony, but by the mid-1850s fairly regular arrivals were being made at Cheever's Landing, near the present-day site of the University of Minnesota's East Bank power plant. A fairly fashionable tourist trade was built up from these humble beginnings, catering

Facing page, top: *John H. Stevens, the first settler to build a wooden frame house on the West Bank of the Mississippi River, collaborated with Franklin Steele on several ventures. (MPLIC)*

Bottom: *Colonel John H. Stevens' residence was the first wooden frame structure erected in Minneapolis on the West Bank. Early settlers used the house as a post office, church, meetinghouse, and polling place, and it was here that Charles Hoag first proposed the name "Minnehapolis." The Stevens' house originally stood near where Hennepin Avenue crosses the river, but was later moved to Minnehaha Park. From the E.A. Bromley Collection. (MPLIC)*

primarily to aristocratic customers from the South, although occasional Easterners such as Henry David Thoreau also visited the area. By 1857 the trade had attracted enough interest for the construction of a posh hotel in frontier St. Anthony. Named Winslow House, the hotel was the most prominent structure in the city. Unfortunately for investors rising antislavery feeling in the city's adherents to the Republican party, which included most of the citizenry, helped to discourage the tourist trade as the Southern visitors normally brought their household slaves to attend them, much to the consternation of the local abolitionists. The Civil War halted what little tourist traffic remained in 1860. With its tourist-center aspirations dashed, the citizens of St. Anthony concentrated their attention on the milling of lumber and flour.

Meanwhile, across the river on the West Bank, Minneapolis was growing by leaps and bounds from its hesitant beginning in Colonel John H. Stevens' house. Stevens' house was the first structure built in what is now Minneapolis during the winter of 1849–1850. It was the focal point of all activity in the settlement. It was the post office as well as the general store. It was the church and also the political meetinghouse. Stevens' house was also the Western terminus of the ferry between Nicollet Island and the West Bank. The house has survived to the present, preserved as a symbol of the indefatigability of the early pioneers. Moved from its original location near the Hennepin Avenue Bridge across the river, the house now stands in the park around Minnehaha Falls. (Interestingly, one of the first structures built in St. Anthony has also been preserved. The Ard Godfrey residence, home of the first millwright in the town, stands today in Chute Square at the intersection of University Avenue Southeast and Central Avenue.) Stevens' house is most hallowed, however, for being the place where Charles Hoag, a teacher who was "not unfamiliar with letters," first proposed the name "Minnehapolis" for the West Bank town. The name, a delightfully symbolic combination of the Greek word *polis*, meaning city, and the Dakota Sioux word *minne*, meaning water, caught on and has remained in

Top: *Minnehaha Falls in South Minneapolis reflects the dramatic change of seasons that characterizes Minneapolis weather. Ice and frozen snow encase the falls and frost covers the vegetation in winter. From the E.A. Bromley Collection. (MPLIC)*

Middle: *A major change in bridge construction was made in 1890 where Hennepin Avenue crossed the Mississippi River. Originally spanned by a suspension bridge in the 1850s and replaced by another suspension bridge in the 1870s, the new bridge, still in service, is a steel, arched span. From the E.A. Bromley Collection. (MPLIC)*

Bottom: *Charles Hoag suggested the name "Minnehapolis" for the new settlement on the West Bank of the Mississippi River across from Old St. Anthony. The name stuck, although the "h" was eventually dropped. Courtesy, Minnesota State Agricultural Society. (MPLIC)*

use ever since, although the "h" was dropped almost immediately to make its sound easier on the ear and its pronunciation smoother for the tongue.

Minneapolis and St. Anthony were joined physically for the first time in 1854, when a suspension bridge was built between the West Bank and Nicollet Island. The bridge was one of the first constructed across the Mississippi. It cost $36,000 to build and was designed by Thomas M. Griffith. The linking of St. Anthony and Minneapolis by bridge reflected their interdependence and common social and economic roots. Both were stocked with Yankees from New England and both were sawmilling and growing flour-milling centers. They also were burgeoning trade centers, as were St. Paul and other frontier towns that developed commercial relations with the growing farming communities around them. These bustling agrarian communities were being filled with Scandinavians—Swedes, Danes, and Norwegians—in sharp contrast to the early makeup of Minneapolis but in a definite foreshadowing of future events.

The peaceful years of growth were soon shattered by the rumblings of war as the United States was rent by civil war over secession and the issue of slavery. Abolitionist feeling was strong in territories and new states like Minnesota because of their dedication to individual farming as opposed to the large estates characteristic of Southern agriculture and because of their dedication to the concept of free labor. The rallying cry "free soil, free labor, free men!" was on the lips of the thousands of Minnesotans who marched off to serve the Union cause in the course of the conflict. For the city-dwelling Yankees the war was a moral crusade as well as political conflict. For the newly-arrived immigrants on the farm, issues were seen just as emotionally but in a different context. For them it was an opportunity to display their appreciation and regard for the nation that had offered them free entry and an opportunity to develop their abilities and to acquire property that was undreamed of in their native lands.

Minnesota units served with distinction in a succession of

battles including Shiloh, Chickamauga, a dozen battles in northern Virginia, and, of course, Gettysburg. When the survivors returned they were convinced, immigrant and Yankee alike, that the values they fought for in the Union cause were permanently embodied in the Republican party. This singular attitude was to pervade life in Minneapolis and in the state as a whole until the Great Depression.

While injustices were fought in the Civil War on distant battlefields in the East and in the South, a less noble contest reached its climax in central Minnesota. The Dakota Sioux were treated badly by the Americans from the time that Fort Snelling was first established. Only one man in government service, Lawrence Taliaferro, consistently argued and fought for honorable and decent treatment of the Indian tribes. Taliaferro's efforts were of no avail, and the efforts of missionaries such as the Pond brothers had no effect on government policy. Filled with frustration, the Indians attempted to thwart American policies through armed revolt. The attempt was doomed to failure in the face of the superior armaments and manpower which were mobilized against them. The resulting defeat led to the expulsion of the offending tribes from the state and sped the process of agricultural settlement that had been threatening them with extinction in the longer term.

With the end of the Civil War and the removal of the last Indian threats, Minneapolis and the other towns of central Minnesota continued their prewar patterns of activity. The lumber mills continued to buzz as they turned out greater amounts of lumber with each passing day, week, and year. The lumber was normally shipped to the ever-hungry markets down the Mississippi, but each year more and more of the product was diverted to local use in new furniture factories and shingle shops. The new products were consumed locally at first, but soon some of them were being shipped to outlets in the Minnesota countryside. The coming of the railroads assisted the process as goods were shipped in from the East at lower costs to satisfy every need. Local merchants saw the opportunities in providing some of these goods

Herbert Putnam became the first director of the Minneapolis Public Library and Athenaeum after these library institutions were coordinated in 1886. Putnam, a graduate of Harvard University, systematized the collections and activities of both institutions and went on from Minneapolis to become the Librarian of Congress. Photo by Walter L. Colls. (MPLIC)

Dr. Kirby Spencer's bequest to the Minneapolis Athenaeum on Washington Avenue was the beginning of the present-day Minneapolis Public Library system. Spencer's civic-mindedness characterized many citizens of Minneapolis over the decades. (MPLIC)

locally, and slowly more and more items came to be manufactured in Minneapolis. Farm implements, utensils, furniture, and food items that could not be processed on the farm were the lead items in the trade.

This activity was humble at first, but it laid the solid foundation upon which Minneapolis grew. The continued growth of the countryside also provided the city with an opportunity grander than lumber, and that was wheat. With the energy from the Falls of St. Anthony and a growing amount of wheat grain passing through the city, it didn't take a great deal of imagination to see the potential of flour milling. The problem was milling the wheat into a flour that would sell commercially in a mass market. This problem separated the risk takers from the hedgers quickly. Fortunately for Minneapolis and Minnesota the risk takers were in abundance, and they propelled the city into the forefront of the flour-milling industry.

Flour milling was in harmony with the lumber trade because of the need for wooden barrels to transport the ground flour. This need created a whole new Minneapolis industry, packaging, and helped create more jobs and a more diverse base for the city's growth. By the early 1870s Minneapolis was bustling with enterprise and while, in appearance, it was still a rough-hewn frontier town, visitors and natives alike sensed that it was on the verge of something big.

St. Anthony was merged into Minneapolis by an act of the state legislature effective in 1872. The merger confirmed what everybody living there already knew—that the two towns were bound by common interests, common problems, and a sense of community that could not be contained or restricted by an artificial boundary. This sense of community was primarily the product of the size of the towns. Because the population was relatively small and clustered close to the falls and the river, people depended upon face-to-face dealings in transacting business and in conducting social activities. Because there were few sharp distinctions in income and social status in the early days, equality permeated the city's social atmosphere. A person was judged by peers on the basis of ability and not by other measures.

As fortunes were made and cleavages in the society developed, this openness remained as long as the original settlers remained on the scene. Those who prospered as they and their city aged, and there were few from the early group who did not prosper, saw the city of Minneapolis as the source of their good fortune and with few exceptions attempted to return the favors that had been granted them. It was this spirit that moved Thomas Walker to open his home to the public to allow those who wished to come and view and enjoy the art objects he collected. It was this spirit that led to the creation of the city park system, the city library system, the symphony orchestra, the art institute, and dozens of other institutions that have enriched Minneapolis society ever since.

There were adverse results of this spirit, however, and it would be foolish to ignore them. The problems arose as the city grew and began to fill with strangers, many of whom were as poor when they arrived as had been the first pioneers. These latter-day folk faced different opportunities than had the pioneers, although their ambitions may have been as great. Faced with this influx of aliens and observing them from positions of power, wealth, and influence, the city's old lights adopted a paternal attitude toward them. They knew their city and what was good for it, and in ways that were peculiar to the 19th century, they made sure that their ideas became reality. Labor conflict, breaking out at almost regular intervals, was one of the symptoms of underlying tensions. The problem was not finally resolved until momentous events in the 1930s created conditions for a renewal of civic spirit and involvement on a much broader base.

In the 1880s, however, such problems were distant and not yet dreamt of, for the city was entering its first golden age. Flush with the wealth brought by lumbering, flour milling, and trade, the city began to build structures that reflected its having arrived. A new city hall was built at Third Avenue and 5th Street, and the building's clock tower became the tallest structure

Facing page, top: *After Minneapolis and St. Anthony were consolidated, plans were laid to replace the first suspension bridge linking Minneapolis and St. Anthony with a more durable structure with stone and brick bridge towers. In 1876 the second bridge neared completion, with the span in place and cables secured. From the E.A. Bromley Collection. (MPLIC)*

Bottom: *By 1896 the elaborate concrete apron on the Falls of St. Anthony was in place. Logs and related debris at the base of the apron are evidence of the use of the Mississippi River as a conduit for logging operations. The Minneapolis Exposition Building and the oldest continuously operating church on the East Bank are in the background. From the E.A. Bromley Collection. (MPLIC)*

The Guaranty Loan building, later the Metropolitan Life building, was a 12-story Romanesque structure made of granite and sandstone. Minneapolis' first skyscraper has been demolished. From the A.D. Roth Collection. (MPLIC)

in the city. Then, as now, the building was a favorite of the citizens, reflecting their pride in the democratic process and the wealth of the city. In Old St. Anthony was constructed the Minneapolis Exposition Building on Central Avenue and Main Street. The Exposition Building was the site of many a gala event, but it reached its pinnacle in 1892 when it hosted the national Republican convention. The selection of the city of Minneapolis was something of a coup for the *noveaux riches* entrepreneurs of the city who wished to show off their urban bastion to their Republican peers from the East. As often happens with such events, the convention received mixed reviews from the participants, who were disappointed with city restaurants and adjourned a day early, catching the railroads by surprise.

The building boom of the 1880s also saw the erection of the Masonic Temple and the Lumber Exchange on Hennepin Avenue. The Guaranty Loan building also went up on Hennepin Avenue, followed by the Metropolitan Life Insurance building at Third Street and 2nd Avenue South. This 12-story, Romanesque structure, made of granite and sandstone, was the first skyscraper to be built west of the Mississippi River. Designed by Leroy S. Buffington, the West Hotel was completed in 1884. The Great Northern Railroad built a passenger depot on Hennepin Avenue near the river at this time and also built a stone arch bridge across the river, back when the railroad was still known as the St. Paul, Minneapolis, and Manitoba. Christened "Jim Hill's Folly" by local wags, the Great Northern railway bridge cost $690,000 to build and was the first main line bridge in the Upper Midwest and the second to span the Mississippi, after the Eads Bridge in St. Louis. This sturdy structure, having endured only minor modification, still stands today as a historical monument to the empire builders of the past. The building boom also led to the creation of the first modern complex of buildings on the Minneapolis campus of the University of Minnesota. Eddy Hall and Pillsbury Hall, the work of Leroy S. Buffington, were erected in 1886 and 1889. The central mall of the University was designed by Cass Gilbert, the

In February 1891 the Lumber Exchange in Minneapolis, established to develop orderly marketing routines for Minnesota's lumber and wood products, burned, resulting in extensive damage. Ice on the exterior of the building is frozen water from firemen's hoses. The building was restored and remains standing downtown at 5th and Hennepin. Photo by W.S. Zinn. (MPLIC)

architect of the Minnesota State Capitol in St. Paul.

The building boom of the 1880s led to the erection of major new structures for all of the major public and private institutions in the city of Minneapolis, but there was another equally important side to it. In the 1880s the city grew geographically as it incorporated territory in all directions. Except for another minor addition in the 1920s, the city reached its present boundaries during these years. The proliferation of industry and the influx of people that expansion attracted necessitated the growth, which proceeded with a surprising degree of order. The result was the building of the great grid-like areas of the city which came to serve as the major residential areas, filled with row after row of single-family houses. The expansion also led to the acquisition of the majority of the beautiful lakes that distinguish Minneapolis' inner-city scenery from that of so many other cities of similar size and age.

The geographical growth of the city, the increase in industry, and massive increases in employment led to the first of several mass transportation problems for the city. The solution in the 1880s was to rapidly expand the streetcar, or light rail, transit system. The streetcars enabled workers to live farther and farther away from places of employment and were inexpensive enough to be afforded by blue-collar as well as white-collar workers. This development ended the concentration of population along the river front that had been the rule up to that time. It also caused the kink in the city streets that move away from downtown, first to the southwest and then due south. The early streets were laid out parallel to the river along a northwest-to-southeast axis. When the real estate developers began developing their parcels, however, they laid out their tracts on north-south axes.

While Minneapolis changed radically in physical appearance in the 1880s, a major shift also occurred in its cultural composition. The earliest settlers had primarily been Yankees from New England along with French Canadians. In the 1880s Norwegians, Swedes, Danes, and Germans were entering the city in growing numbers. Some came directly from the old country with urban-oriented skills, while others came via farms in the countryside around Minneapolis and St. Paul. However they got there, they made a lasting impression on the social character of the city. To the east, St. Paul was becoming the ecclesiastical and educational center of the Catholic population of the Upper Midwest as a result of its large Irish and German Catholic immigrant population. In contrast Minneapolis became a Lutheran center as a result of its predominantly Scandinavian and north German immigration. The differences were readily apparent to observers in both cities and contributed to a rivalry that continues, although in a more jocular vein, to the present time.

In the last years of the 19th century, however, the competitiveness led to rancorous exchanges between city newspapers, provincial brawling, and fierce disputes about census tallies. The census of 1890 brought especially bitter news to St. Paul boosters, who saw in the published numbers the ascendancy of the upstart at the falls. The rancor eventually passed but occasional jibes still are loosed. For example, when recently asked to compare Minneapolis and St. Paul, the local guru of Americana Garrison Keillor responded, "The difference between St. Paul and Minneapolis is the difference between pumpernickel and Wonder Bread," a reference to Minneapolis' conservative corporate atmosphere and austere Scandinavian heritage.

With the rapid growth of population and industry came problems that were all too common for Minneapolis and other American cities around the turn of the century. The problems were related to changes in the perceptions of the proper role of urban government and the rise of professional politicians and the political machine. With large-scale immigration city government came to be seen more and more as a provider of services by newcomers who expected to receive the services as well as by those who expected to provide them. The political machine developed as those in power exchanged services and favors for electoral support at the polls. The practice soon spread to other areas of city government and eventually became centered in the police department. By the

Above: *In the 1870s the Minneapolis street railway system experimented with the use of mules. The Number 32 car, with a pair of mules in harness, made the trek from downtown to Lake Street and then back to the downtown area. The use of mules was discontinued in favor of horses and, in turn, horses were replaced by electricity. (MPLIC)*

Facing page, top left: *Looking south from the Mississippi suspension bridge, Minneapolis City Hall stands at the corner of Hennepin and Nicollet avenues in this circa 1888 view. The huge arc lamp pole was erected in the early 1880s in the area in front of the triangular Municipal Building known as Bridge Square. The arc lamps were powered by electricity and could be raised and lowered for maintenance. From the Dewars Collection. (MPLIC)*

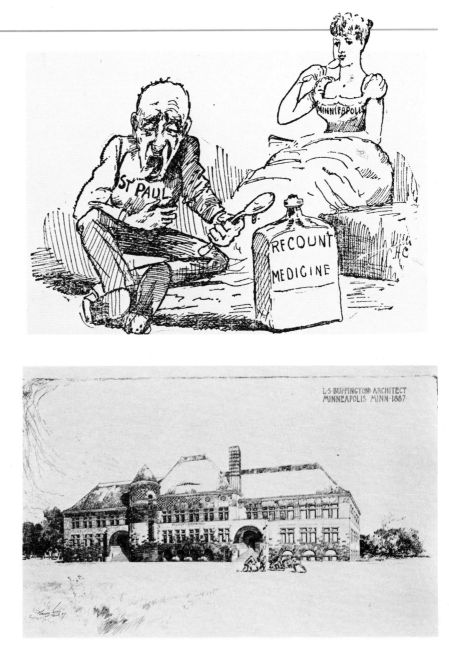

Top right: *The 1890 census reported that the population of Minneapolis had surpassed that of St. Paul, leading to charges and countercharges of falsification of census records between the two cities. A recount confirmed the more rapid growth of Minneapolis and caused much smugness among its citizenry. From the Minneapolis Tribune, August 1, 1890. (MHS)*

Bottom right: *Pillsbury Hall was built in the late 1880s with funds provided by John Sargent Pillsbury with the proviso that the building only be used for scientific investigation. The grant marks a beginning of long-term dependence by the Minneapolis milling companies on the research activities of the university and university graduates. Drawing by Harvey Ellis. From Western Architect, 1913. (MPLIC)*

Minneapolis citizens have experimented with a variety of conveyances, including the tandem bicycle, pictured here with riders outside the Municipal Building on 4th Street at the turn of the century. From the E.A. Bromley Collection. (MPLIC)

early 1900s corrupt city officials were seeking dollars instead of votes. The graft and attendant corruption became so widespread that the muckraking journalist Lincoln Steffens devoted a large part of his *Shame of the Cities* to chronicling the woes of Minneapolis. As Steffens indicated in his writings, activities such as gambling, prostitution, and illegal liquor sales were tolerated and even protected by officials in return for pecuniary considerations. The strict laws developed by the early settlers to control and contain vice provided too many opportunities for gain because of lax enforcement in Minneapolis and the rest of the nation around the turn of the century.

Attempts were made by the city fathers to regain control of the situation, and occasionally scoundrels were given their due. The underlying problems, however, were too much for 19th-century mentalities to overcome, and the problems of corruption became worse as the 20th century progressed. Periods of wide-open activity by lawless elements were followed by periodic efforts at reform in a regular pattern until World War II. The pattern was exacerbated by the institution of prohibition of alcohol at the national level in 1920. The sheer immensity of the failure of prohibition undermined respect for the law and legal processes and spilled over into social areas far distant from the serving of alcoholic beverages. In Minneapolis, for example, the widespread knowledge that the police were regularly bought by bootleggers and gamblers helped make possible the street battles between workers and policemen during the labor unrest of the mid-1930s. These tragic events had their roots in the unsettled growth of the 1890s and the early 1900s.

While city government faltered after 1900, other facets of the city's experience seemed to advance by leaps and bounds. Prosperity became the norm in the city's industries as flour-milling activities continued to expand and a host of new enterprises began to develop. Small businesses, the acorns from which would grow the mighty corporate oaks, found the business and financial atmosphere of the city conducive to them. It should be remembered that most of the major corporations that are headquartered in Minneapolis at present had their beginnings as small businesses. This is true of each succeeding generation of small-business activity. Some prosper and grow and continue to be vital enterprises long after their founders have passed from the scene, whereas others are more transitory. Either way, the large number of small firms has been vital to the economic vitality of Minneapolis from its earliest beginnings.

Between the rapid growth of the 1880s and the Great Depression, which affected Minneapolis in the early 1930s, there was one major interruption in the upward line of growth, and that was American participation in World War I. The declaration of war against Germany caused a mobilization of Minneapolis society and resources that the town had never before experienced. Conscription was implemented, various forms of rationing were instituted, and draconian measures were taken to restrict civil liberties and dissent in deference to the collective war effort. The systematic repression of individuals and groups that opposed or were ambivalent to the war was official state and federal policy and, in Minneapolis, was directed primarily at the pacifist Socialist party, the industrial labor union known as the Industrial Workers of the World, and the agrarian political movement known as the Non-Partisan League. Official harassment of these and other, smaller groups occurred as well as did unofficial vigilante violence. The tarring and feathering of members of these organizations as well as their imprisonment and deportation were common occurrences for the duration of the war. In addition to political excesses cultural antipathies also marked the war period as the large immigrant German population was subjected to attack as a result of the anti-German feelings that often were transformed into near-hysteria. German-language instruction was banned, the German newspapers were proscribed, and persons of German descent were forced from positions of responsibility in the public and private sectors.

As had been the case in the Civil War and the Spanish-American War, Minnesotans went off to fight the enemy in droves.

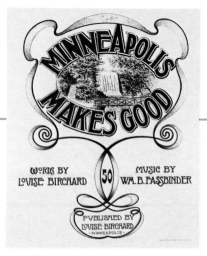

Whole units of Minnesotans distinguished themselves in the engagements at Chateau-Thierry, St. Mihiel, the Argonne Forest, and other places that became as familiar to readers on the home front as cities and towns in Minnesota. Individual Minnesotans served in many different units and branches of service as well. Many of the volunteers were citizens of Minneapolis, including Colonel George E. Leach, who commanded the Minnesota 151st Field Artillery, which served with the 42nd, or "Rainbow," Division, composed of units from all over the United States.

Minneapolis was filled with a variety of war-related activities in 1917 and 1918. Fort Snelling was turned into an officers' training center for more than 2,500 men from Minnesota and neighboring states. The University of Minnesota and other colleges in the city and state organized Student Army Training Corps in the beginning of the 1918–1919 academic year in anticipation of a long conflict. The Dunwoody Institute, a vocational school in Minneapolis, was contracted to train thousands of mechanics, radio and telegraph workers, bakers, and others needed by the various armed services. In nearby St. Paul a special institute was created to train mechanics for duty in the air services, and by the end of armed conflict some 10,000 men had undergone the course of study.

In light of the political and cultural tensions that came with the war and the massive dislocations caused by mobilization of human and material resources for the war effort, it is not hard to understand the relief that was felt when the armistice was announced in November 1918. The end of the fighting caused dancing and partying in the streets of Minneapolis as businesses closed down, church bells rang, and churches held special services of thanksgiving for an end to the bloodshed. Not since the surrender of General Robert E. Lee's army during the Civil War had Minneapolis seen such a massive, popular expression of celebration. The formal celebration was postponed until May 8, 1919, when the 151st Field Artillery was welcomed home in St. Paul by thousands of cheering fellow citizens.

Optimism has generally been a hallmark of Minneapolis citizens. In 1908 Minneapolis celebrated 50 years of urban existence with some lyrical help from Louise Birchard and music from William B. Fassbinder. While the melody has since passed out of memory, Birchard's sentiments live on. (MHS)

In the aftermath of World War I, the citizens of Minneapolis again returned to their pursuit of the American dream. The postwar world was reshaped in two significant ways, as women received the vote and the production and consumption of alcohol were banned by constitutional amendments. Minneapolis women immediately became active at the polls and organized themselves and their voting power in such organizations as the League of Women Voters. A large number of women ran successfully for political offices and several were appointed to state offices.

The establishment of Prohibition was not as successful as women's suffrage, however. Attempts were made to curtail the trafficking in liquor, but from the beginning a large number of citizens defied the law by producing or smuggling the stuff, and a larger number defied the law by consuming it. The opportunities for illicit profits were immense, and organized efforts to control the trade dissipated in the face of immense disregard for the law. Arrests for drunkenness, in fact, more than doubled in the city of Minneapolis between 1920 and 1925, going from 2,500 to 7,000. Illegal stills were in operation all over the city of Minneapolis, but more serious was the flood of imports of Canadian whiskies that were trucked in from Canada almost daily. Because Minneapolis had been a wholesaling center before Prohibition and was a center of the trucking industry, it was easy for bootleggers to hire independent drivers to make the border crossings with their loads of contraband. Much of this cargo was directed at other urban centers, especially Chicago and Kansas City, but most of the hooch was driven through Minneapolis.

With the dollars from the trade, local racketeers found it easier to buy police and city government protection from officials who could not contain their avarice. With other dollars the organized crime elements branched into other areas of activity on a grander scale than ever was contemplated in previous times. Gambling, prostitution, and other "old reliables" were upgraded and expanded, while new areas of endeavor were created such as pro-

viding protection to small businesses through extortion schemes and blackmailing of leading citizens and officials who were observed doing things that they shouldn't have been doing. A rise in gangland murders as the various factions fought over the spoils topped off the sordid situation that continued at varying levels of intensity throughout the 1920s and 1930s.

Minneapolis was also plagued by a surge of intolerance as the 1920s began. Fed by academic and pseudo-academic theories of white racial supremacy and by the heady feelings of power generated by the victory in the war, citizens of Minneapolis joined the resurgent Ku Klux Klan in droves in the early 1920s. Theodore C. Blegen estimates that there were at least ten Klan chapters in the city of Minneapolis by 1923 and there also was a statewide Klan publication. The Klan members carried on the antiradical attitude of the war years in their attacks on socialists, Wobblies, and the new Red, or Communist, menace after the Russian Revolution. They combined with this a rabid anti-Semitism and anti-Catholicism that seem to have been somehow related to the war experience and to a resulting revulsion to the problems of Europe and the Europeans generally. Whatever the underlying causes, fortunately the Klan activity subsided as rapidly as it developed as the national organization disintegrated in the face of scandals surrounding the top leadership, based in Indianapolis. With the organization dissipated, the ideas it represented lost some of their venom and their force.

Tied to the Klan movement was the reaction of fundamentalist Christians to recent developments in science. In the aftermath of the Scopes trial in Tennessee, an effort was made in Minnesota to ban the teaching of evolutionary science at the University of Minnesota in Minneapolis as well as in other public schools throughout the state. The Minnesota state legislature permanently postponed consideration of the measure in 1927, saving Minneapolis and the state the embarrassment of another "monkey trial."

Things were not all glum and raucous in Minneapolis in the 1920s, for great and substantial changes were being effected in other

Students at the Dunwoody Institute, which trained men and women in the trades and skilled crafts, examine a chassis donated by the Dodge Motor Car Company for use in auto mechanics instruction. From the Minneapolis Tribune, *January 1940. (MPLIC)*

Theater and film were the rage in the 1920s. The Lyric Theater at 718 Hennepin Avenue was one of many along that boulevard that drew in throngs from all over the city for the latest movie or vaudeville act. (MHS)

spheres of life. In the area of entertainment the 1920s were of course a watershed as radio, the movies, and music and dance in new, freer forms swept the country. Radio was a technological revolution in entertainment, but it was also revolutionary in its form and content. Events in all areas of human endeavor were brought into the homes of Americans and into their new gadgets, the automobiles, with a swiftness that was unprecedented. News and informational broadcasts, along with sports, theater, musical performances, comedy, the endless episodes of myriad melodramas that became known as the "soaps," and coverage of events overseas flowed into the American consciousness. Minneapolis played a role in the shaping of the new radio medium as Washburn Crosby Company, a forerunner of General Mills, acquired the pioneer radio station WLAG in 1924. Originally established in 1922, WLAG, or "The Call of the North," was given the call letters WCCO, the Washburn Crosby Company's initials, and was used as an advertising arm of the firm's marketing division. The first jingle to go out over the airwaves was for the dry cereal Wheaties, later to become the "Breakfast of Champions." In 1924 the University of Minnesota in Minneapolis inaugurated a program in radio engineering to provide basic research and trained technicians for the growing area.

The movies also captured the interest of the citizens of Minneapolis, and the city's collection of theaters increased rapidly. By 1930 there were 48 movie theaters operating in the city limits. The films of Charlie Chaplin and Douglas Fairbanks, Sr., as well as those of Lon Chaney, Sr., and D.W. Griffith entertained audiences with the assistance of musical accompaniment from either keyboards or full orchestras. The introduction of sound tracks in the late twenties increased the grip of the medium on Minneapolitans.

Literature and music, too, had their moments in the period, and Minneapolis broadened beyond its polka horizons toward increased activity in classical and popular musical forms and an acceptance of new forms best illustrated by the spread of jazz. The acceptance of jazz and blues music, performed exclusively by black musicians in the beginning, was linked to the subterranean social life which developed around the Prohibition speakeasies. Scandalous behavior seemed to increase appreciation for what was viewed by many at the time as scandalous music, and the two flourished in tandem. Minnesota writers such as Sinclair Lewis and F. Scott Fitzgerald described life in Minnesota generally in terms to which the citizens of Minneapolis took umbrage. Works glorifying the pioneer past, such as those of O.E. Rölvaag and William Watts Folwell's filiopietistic *History of Minnesota,* captured the reading public's imagination in Minneapolis to a far greater degree than more current critical works.

As the decade of the 1930s approached, Minneapolis looked forward to even greater prosperity than it had experienced in the 1920s. The signal event closing the decade was the opening of the Foshay Tower in downtown Minneapolis, marked by three days of elaborate celebration that included performances by the band of John Philip Sousa and a specially commissioned march by him to celebrate the occasion. The event was staged in September of 1929 and was marked by endless predictions of future bounty for the city, state, and nation. Ironically the collapse of the financial markets on Wall Street occurred only a few short weeks later and signalled the greatest bust in American history. By 1931 the industrial depression had thrown millions out of work, and the fall in prices was beginning to adversely affect the farmers in Minneapolis' great hinterland. By the winter of 1931–1932 the full severity of the disaster had reached Minneapolis. The Depression and long-festering social problems set the stage for dramatic change in Minneapolis.

The Depression caused a massive change in the political orientation of the citizens of Minneapolis and the state of Minnesota as a whole. In the 1932 elections Minnesota, for the first time in its history, gave its electoral votes to a Democratic nominee for the Presidency. This symbolic event was preceded by decades of activity at the local level, especially in the city of Minneapolis. In the 1920s various coalitions of farmers and workers had at-

Facing page, counterclockwise from top: *Company Q of the University of Minnesota drill team was composed entirely of women who "could drill better than soldiers can, and inspire terror like the Ku Klux Klan," according to announcements of the day. Photo by W.H. Palmer. (MPLIC)*

Lakes and parks bring rustic charm into the heart of Minneapolis' central business district. Loring Park is in the foreground of this view looking north toward the downtown skyline in 1929. The newly constructed Foshay Tower stands to the right, and City Hall's tower peers around its left edge. (MHS)

Movies made their impact upon Minneapolis, and popular figures of the silver screen made periodic visits to the city. Western star Tom Mix and his horse, Tony, visit with Minneapolis Mayor George Leach in the mayor's office in May 1929. Mix later made a personal appearance at the Minnesota Theater. Photo by Norton and Peel. (MPLIC)

The Minneapolis-born Andrews sisters became national stars in the early 1940s. From left to right, Maxene, Patty, and Laverne developed an innovative singing style which characterized their successful career. (MPLIC)

tempted to compete seriously for political office in such groups as the Non-Partisan League and the Farmer-Labor Association, as well as through unrecognized unions. With the Great Depression these various movements found a voice in the person of Floyd B. Olson, a native of Minneapolis' North Side who replaced a corrupt Hennepin County attorney in the early 1920s and went on to the governor's office in January 1931.

Olson supported the candidacy of Franklin D. Roosevelt while being an independent Farmer-Labor leader himself in 1932 and became identified with the New Deal program of FDR. A state income tax to support state education and a holiday for foreclosures of home mortgages were important acts of his second term. The passage of federal legislation that allowed the free organization of labor unions and the removal of restrictions upon them to enter into collective bargaining with their employers gave renewed life to unionization efforts in Minneapolis as well as the rest of the state.

In the spring and summer of 1934, labor and social strife came into the open as workers and those opposed to their newfound rights battled in the streets, in the courts, and in the state legislature. Minneapolis was the focus of this struggle in Minnesota, and the events of that long summer were some of the most dramatic in the city's history. The rise of organized labor, long established in the city's working-class wards and communities, and its entry into the political arena and its challenge to managerial dominion in the workplace marked the end of one era of social relations and the beginning of another.

Minneapolis survived the upheavals of 1934 and continued on an unsteady path through the rest of the hard times that were the 1930s. It was a time when the very bonds of community were tested to the limit as neighbors helped neighbors, and families and friends came together to face the outside threats of loss of livelihoods and also loss of dignity. In many respects the social and psychological blows of the prolonged economic sag were as great as were the financial costs to the people of the city. It is a tribute

Wilbur Foshay, financier and speculator, built the Foshay Tower as a monument to George Washington—hence its replication of the angles in the Washington Monument. The building was completed and dedicated in September 1929, supplanting the City and County Building as the tallest structure in Minneapolis until the IDS Tower was built in the early 1970s. (MPLIC)

to the people of Minneapolis and other great American cities of the time that they did not lose their hope and their belief that the future could be improved. Out of the trauma of the 1930s came a more mature sense of pride in the city than could be contained by the old reflex boosterism, as well as an enduring interest in what later became known as those elements that constitute the quality of life. By 1940 Minneapolis had left preoccupation with disaster behind it and had embarked on a recurrent celebration of its vitality through the establishment of the summer Aquatennial event.

The newspapers of Minneapolis played a major role in the remarkable events of the 1930s as they themselves were rejuvenated and enhanced by new management. The Minneapolis press had fallen on hard times in the 1920s and early 1930s as it abdicated its responsibility to inquire critically into the great issues that faced the city and its people. The vacuum created by this lack of critical activity was filled with scandal sheets that used the endless material provided by what journalist Fred W. Friendly has called "the political corruption in Minneapolis and St. Paul and the truce between bootleggers, gamblers and prostitution merchants and the police and city fathers." Attempts to suppress these entrepreneurial sorties via yellow journalism led to a landmark Supreme Court case, *Near v. Minnesota*, as well as to the murders of an extortionist-editor, Howard A. Guilford, and Walter W. Liggett, editor of the *Mid-West American.*

Guilford was killed by shotgun on Pillsbury Avenue while listening to a Millers baseball game in his car a week before he was to begin a series of radio programs outlining Governor Olson's involvement in the Twin Cities underworld. Guilford was killed in September 1934, and Liggett was machine-gunned in December 1935. The scandal sheets, in addition to covering the sordid aspects of city life, also were purveyors of rabid anti-Semitism and racism generally. The indictment of Isadore Blumenfeld, also known as Kid Cann, for the Liggett murder inflamed such feelings, as did his acquittal despite personal identification by the dead man's widow.

It was in this climate that John and Gardner Cowles acquired the *Minneapolis Star* and in 1939 bought out the competing *Evening Journal*. A new sense of professionalism and social responsibility came to Minneapolis journalism as a result of this new management and in response to the events of the turbulent 1930s. The *Minneapolis Tribune*, founded in 1867 by Colonel William S. King, also found itself in a period of renewal after the low ebb that was reached in that period. The newspapers could not, of course, reverse the deteriorated social situation single-handedly, but their new activism played an important role in the development of a reform climate that was finally effective politically with the mayoral election of 1945. The process was greatly aided by the repeal of Prohibition in 1933 and the elimination of this source of revenue for the underworld element.

Minneapolis was in the midst of economic recovery and efforts to clean up its city government when the Japanese attack on Pearl Harbor brought the United States into World War II. As happened in World War I and the Civil War, Minneapolis threw its resources and spirit into the national war effort. Minnesota's 151st Field Artillery again saw active service as it was assigned to the European theater of operations and went through the campaigns in North Africa, Sicily, and Italy. Units of the Minnesota National Guard were dispatched to the Aleutian Islands for garrison duty while others saw action in the Pacific. On the home front, Minneapolis organized its civil defense network and organized drive after drive for the sale of war bonds to aid the financing of the war effort. The city developed innumerable assistance activities under the Red Cross and developed specialized aids for servicemen in the USO, or United Service Organization.

The University of Minnesota in Minneapolis also played a major role as its specialists contributed invaluable services to a variety of activities, including the Manhattan nuclear project, medicinal advances, military nutrition, and the development of new technology for weapons systems. Dr. Alfred O.C. Nier of the University first isolated the uranium isotope, while Professor I.M.

Facing page, clockwise from top left: *Striking truck drivers attack special deputies of the Citizens' Alliance, some clad in jodhpurs and polo hats, in the Minneapolis City Market on May 22, 1934. Photo by Dave Silverman, Minneapolis Star and Tribune Company. (MHS)*

After it became apparent that the Minneapolis Police and Citizens' Alliance would not be able to halt the mounting violence of the 1934 truckers' strike, Governor Floyd B. Olson intervened by declaring martial law and sending in the Minnesota National Guard to restrain both sides. Here, members of the Minnesota 151st Field Artillery await instruction before moving about the city. Photo by Dave Silverman, Minneapolis Star and Tribune Company. (MHS)

Several battles between police and strikers occurred during the 1934 truckers' strike when police attempted to allow nonstriking truck drivers to operate in the city while strikers attempted to enforce picket lines. As the strike dragged on, these skirmishes escalated in violence and finally led to bloodshed as the police resorted to the use of firearms to control crowds of striking workers. (MHS)

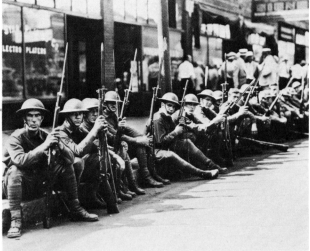

Kolthoff assisted in the development of synthetic rubber. Dr. Owen Wangensteen of the medical school developed a surgical technique for dealing with intestinal obstructions and Dr. Ancel Keys helped develop the K-ration, perhaps viewed dubiously by GIs more concerned with palate than nutrition.

Minneapolis businesses contributed greatly to the war effort in ways as diverse as the city's economy. Honeywell developed new aeronautical systems and weapons, while the Northern Pump Company manufactured naval gun mounts, and Minneapolis Moline produced artillery ordnance. Crown Iron Works developed portable bridges and floating devices while the Onan Corporation, long a supplier of electrical goods to farmers, manufactured electric generators, power plants, and radio equipment for the military services. General Mills produced a variety of food products for the war effort, plus gun sights, torpedoes, and other mechanical devices. The Munsingwear Company and the North Star Woolen Mills produced great quantities of underwear and blankets for the various services. The diversity of these contributions to the war effort revealed that the underlying infrastructure of the Minneapolis economy was intact despite a decade of depression and that it was capable of producing goods aplenty in a revived economy. The technical sophistication of its firms also revealed a side of the city's economic potential that few knew existed in earlier years. High productivity and advanced technological skill boded well for the future of the city. •

As the war neared its conclusion, the citizens of Minneapolis became concerned about the nature of the postwar world. Remembering that they had thought of World War I as the "war to end all war," they hoped to avoid a repetition of events that had undone the promise of that struggle. Thinking was provoked initially by Wendell Wilkie's wartime book *One World* which argued for American acceptance of the notion of common interests uniting the race in more ways than they were divided. Harold Stassen, Republican politician from South St. Paul, echoed such sentiments and, after service in the Navy in the Pacific with Admiral William

Facing page, top: *William S. King, an early settler in Minneapolis, was one of the founders of the Minneapolis Tribune. He was among the first of the leading citizens to settle and build a magnificent residence on the shores of the city's lakes. (MPLIC)*

Middle: *Early Minneapolis Aquatennials included the "pushmobile" derby. Contestants tense as they await the starting whistle at the 1940 derby. From the Minneapolis Star and Tribune Company. (MHS)*

Bottom: *Fireworks over Lake Calhoun signal the end of the 1954 Minneapolis Aquatennial Celebration. From the Minneapolis Star and Tribune Company. (MHS)*

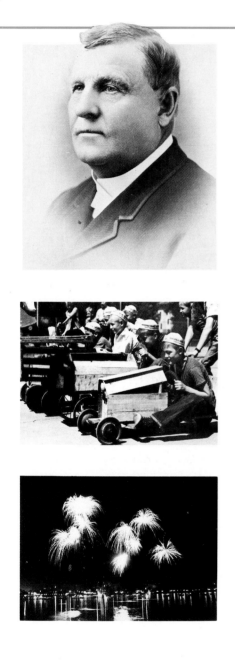

F. Halsey, served as a delegate to the United Nations conference in San Francisco in April 1945. Citizens of Minneapolis became interested in the United Nations concept and by the end of the war came to support American involvement in it wholeheartedly.

In the summer of 1945, after the defeat of Germany and before the surrender of Japan, Minneapolis was temporarily drawn away from world events by a mayoral election. Hubert H. Humphrey, a reform candidate who had been instrumental in the alliance between the Democratic party and Floyd B. Olson's Farmer-Labor party, was elected mayor of the city. Humphrey had been defeated two years earlier by Marvin L. Kline, but he persevered with his program and ran again in 1945. The campaign was marked by the murder of another Minneapolis area publisher, Arthur Kasherman, who was in addition a convicted extortionist and who admitted a few days before his death to having seen money pass between criminals and city police officials. The murder incensed the city population, and Humphrey was swept into office with a mandate to end corruption and to bring city government into the 20th century. Ably assisted by Minneapolis-born and bred Orville Freeman and Arthur Naftalin, Humphrey embarked upon his term with the vigor and cheer that made him a unique political personality for three decades.

Humphrey worked feverishly to bring honor and self-esteem back to law enforcement in the city and to focus the energies of the citizenry upon struggling for a better future rather than dwelling upon the animosities of the past. A champion of civil liberties from his childhood in the Dakotas, Humphrey established the first equal employment commission in the United States in the city of Minneapolis. Stung by the charge made by sociologist Carey McWilliams that Minneapolis was the most anti-Semitic city in the United States, Humphrey made strenuous efforts to make the city government and the city itself places for open opportunity. Humphrey was reelected mayor in 1947 and in 1948 made an impassioned speech before the Democratic party's national convention, pleading for inclusion of a civil rights plank in the party platform.

Humphrey's performance at the convention made him the Democratic nominee for the U.S. Senate in the 1948 elections. Being elected to the Senate, Humphrey resigned as mayor and was replaced by Eric G. Hoyer.

In postwar Minneapolis people were busy readjusting to peacetime after four years of war. Thousands of returning servicemen flocked to the University of Minnesota in order to take advantage of their educational entitlements under the GI Bill of Rights. The student population soared and makeshift arrangements were made to handle the torrent. Former army barracks were converted into classrooms and were immediately filled by former servicemen. Prior to World War II, because of the Depression and the costs at private colleges, college education had been unavailable to many people. After the war and beginning with the GI Bill students, university training became accessible to a growing segment of the city population. Housing was another problem that faced the city as the population became swollen with new workers and new businesses. This crisis in space began the development of the suburbs of the city in earnest.

In 1950 the population of Minneapolis reached 521,718, the highest total in its history. After that time, however, the population of the city began to drop as younger, upwardly-mobile couples moved out of the city and settled in adjacent towns such as Bloomington to the south; Edina, Golden Valley, Minnetonka, Plymouth, St. Louis Park, and Brooklyn Park to the west; and Fridley, Roseville, Coon Rapids, and Anoka to the north. The same process occurred in neighboring St. Paul with slightly different timing. With the development of automobiles and a network of roads and highways to move them, the flight to the suburbs was made possible.

The shift in population from the central cities to the suburbs was accompanied by overall population growth that presented problems for the traditional government forms at the local and county levels. In response the state government created the Metropolitan Planning Commission in 1957 to coordinate efforts to

Facing page, clockwise from top left: *Cyrus Northrop, president of the University of Minnesota from 1884 to 1910, supervised the development of the professional schools and the graduate school. Photo by Huebner. (MPLIC)*

Hubert H. Humphrey, former mayor of Minneapolis and senator from Minnesota, later to become Vice-President of the United States, and Orville Freeman, governor of Minnesota and, later, Secretary of Agriculture in the cabinet of John F. Kennedy, take in the last baseball game played by the Minneapolis Millers at old Nicollet Ball Park in Minneapolis in 1955. Photo by Kruger, Minneapolis Star and Tribune Company. (MHS)

Folwell Hall, located at 15th Street SE and University Avenue, is used today as the center of language instruction on the University of Minnesota campus. The building was named after William Watt Folwell who was president of the university from 1869 to 1884 and later wrote a multi-volume history of Minnesota, published in the 1920s. From the A.D. Roth Collection. (MPLIC)

deal with housing, water, transportation, sewage, and industrial development in the Minneapolis-St. Paul area. In 1967 the planning commission was transformed into a regional governing body, the Metropolitan Council, with decision-making powers in the areas that had been formerly researched.

The 1950s were another exciting period for economic development in Minneapolis and the surrounding area, as a flood of new small businesses was created in a host of traditional and new areas of activity. Air transportation came into its own in the postwar years, and Minneapolis became the home of North Central Airlines, which primarily served the Upper Midwest. The computer industry had its origins in the area in an unused Northwest Orient Airlines hangar in St. Paul, where Engineering Research Associates assembled an early prototype. From that beginning several major firms have sprouted, including Control Data Corporation in Bloomington, a division of Sperry-Univac spread around the metropolitan area, the systems division of Honeywell in Minneapolis, and a host of other firms. Medicine also became an important new area as developments in medical science at the University of Minnesota and elsewhere created a need for firms that could manufacture complex medical devices and instrumentation. The traditional food industries headquartered in Minneapolis, such as Pillsbury, General Mills, Cargill International Multifoods, and Peavey, adjusted to the changing market conditions in the United States and around the world and upgraded their products and selling activities to remain competitive. Agribusiness continued to be a major facet of Minneapolis' economic vitality.

In the 1960s Minneapolis was affected by the social tensions and transformations that swept the rest of the country, but the decade began on a note of high culture as Minneapolis was selected by Sir Tyrone Guthrie as the location for his repertory theater. The selection of Minneapolis involved independent actions by Frank Whiting, director of the University of Minnesota theater, and John Cowles, Jr., of the Minneapolis Star and Tribune, that led to the formation of an informal committee com-

Following pages, top: *The University of Minnesota is shown in 1904, with the armory to the far left and Pillsbury Hall to the right front of it. The Old Main is the second building from the far right. The elm trees that cover the grassy plain in the center were decimated by Dutch elm plague in the 1970s, but the gateway and walkways are still recognizable. Photo by H.W. Wilson. (MPLIC)*

Bottom: *University of Minnesota in Minneapolis has experienced a great deal of growth in the last 100 years. Here, the class of 1909 poses for a group portrait in front of Burton Hall on the East Bank campus. Photo by Johnson and Company. (MPLIC)*

posed of themselves and Phil von Blon, Roger Kennedy, Pierce Butler III, H. Harvard Arnason, Otto Silha, Louis Zelle, and Justin Smith. The Thomas B. Walker Foundation gave $400,000 and land for the theater building in order to convince Tyrone Guthrie that Minneapolis would nourish the planned theater and give it every possible chance for success.

In May 1960 the informal theater committee, along with Richard Gale and Boris Sokoloff, flew to New York City and gave a presentation to Guthrie's agents, Peter Zeisler and Oliver Rea. The committee informed them of the Walker grant and land, the $400,000 in cash, and promised to raise another $1.5 million. On May 31, 1960, the decision to locate Guthrie's theater in Minneapolis was announced on the lawn behind the Walker Art Center at a press conference attended by Rea and Zeisler. Afterward Lou Gelfand was appointed administrator of the nonprofit Tyrone Guthrie Theater Foundation, and the fundraising drive was successful. Additional assistance was provided by the Ford Foundation, and in 1963 the first season began with performances of William Shakespeare's *Hamlet,* Moliere's *The Miser,* Anton Chekhov's *Three Sisters,* and Arthur Miller's *Death of a Salesman.* Hume Cronyn, Jessica Tandy, George Grizzard, Rita Gam, and Zoe Caldwell were the feature players in the company during the first season. In the second season in 1964, the program included works by Shakespeare, George Bernard Shaw, Tennessee Williams, and Ben Jonson. Charles Cioffi, Paul Ballantyne, Ed Flanders, Ellen Geer, and John MacKay joined the distinguished ranks of Guthrie alumni in the course of the second season. The theater's survival and even prosperity were assured by this time.

While Minneapolis basked in the radiance of the cultural jewel of the Guthrie Theater as the newest addition to a diadem that already included the Minneapolis Public Library, the Minneapolis Institute of Art, and Walker Art Center, events from the national scene forced the citizenry to take up more complex problems. The civil rights movement among America's black population was reaching a peak of activity in the mid-1960s under the

leadership of the Reverend Martin Luther King, Jr., and other black leaders as they pursued the attainment of equality of opportunity and full access to the political process. Although small in comparison to those of other major urban centers, Minneapolis' black population was active in the struggle both locally and nationally.

The black movement was soon overshadowed in Minneapolis by the controversy surrounding the prosecution of the war in Vietnam. The war was viewed ambivalently by a large part of the population and especially by the young males who would be expected to wage it. The University of Minnesota in Minneapolis became a center of discussion and criticism of the war locally and as the fighting dragged on became a center of war protest. Conscription became a particular object of protest, as did manufacturers of war materiel and college officer-training programs. Protest and discussion about the war were escalated after the launching of the Communist Tet offensive in February 1968, which indicated that a successful conclusion to the war would require a protracted and massive effort. The assassinations of Martin Luther King and Robert F. Kennedy and the challenge to President Lyndon B. Johnson mounted by Minnesota Democratic Senator Eugene McCarthy made Minneapolis a turbulent center of political activity. The situation was further complicated by the fact that the Vice-President, Hubert H. Humphrey, was also from Minnesota and, after Johnson's withdrawal from the Presidential race in April 1968, sought the Democratic Presidential nomination as well.

While these turbulent events were unfolding, Minneapolis was proceeding with more basic activities such as urban renewal and the revitalization of the central business district as part of the Great Society's program for the cities. The old Gateway district along Washington Avenue in Minneapolis had degenerated into a skid row that was targeted for demolition and revitalization, while Nicollet Avenue, the retail center of the Upper Midwest, was transformed into a pedestrian mall by eliminating automobile traffic and refurbishing the avenue's structures. In addition a massive

Facing page: The "Old Main" building of the University of Minnesota was completed in 1858 and served the university for 46 years. It was destroyed by fire on September 24, 1904. From the E.A. Bromley Collection. (MPLIC)

housing program, initiated under public auspices and supported by private financial institutions, enabled citizens to maintain their high rate of personal home ownership. Twin City Federal, Midwest Federal, First Federal, and Minnesota Federal led this private effort, aided by the F and M Savings Bank.

Despite these improvements the social tensions generated by the Asian war and the civil rights agitation that often turned violent after the death of Martin Luther King captured the attention of Minneapolis citizens as they headed for the polls in the 1969 mayoral elections. In a dramatic turn of events from the mid-1940s, an independent candidate from the Minneapolis police department, Charles Stenvig, ran for mayor, promising to bring law and order back to the city. After eight years of tenure by liberal Democrat Arthur Naftalin, a close personal friend of Hubert Humphrey, the city voters overwhelmingly endorsed Stenvig in an election that was viewed by the rest of the nation's cities as an omen of things to come in other areas as well. Stenvig's election was more symbolic than substantive, however, and served primarily to politicize police department relations with the city government over the following decade. Stenvig served two consecutive terms, returned to active police duty, and then was elected to another term in 1976–1977 before finally returning to the police department again.

The 1970s began with Minneapolis still embroiled in the issues of the 1960s with campus unrest reaching a peak in the tumultuous events of 1971 and 1972, years marked chiefly by the bombing of Hanoi and the mining of Haiphong harbor. After the end of American involvement in the Vietnam hostilities in 1973, however, as well as the end of conscription, large-scale turmoil subsided. Racial issues remained high on the city agenda but were broadened significantly by the organization of political, cultural, and economic bodies among the large Native American population in the city.

In 1972 a 52-story structure was raised on the Nicollet Mall between 7th and 8th streets. The Investors Diversified Services building, or IDS, marked a new trend in Minneapolis development

Above: *The entire faculty and student body of the University of Minnesota pose in 1888. University president Cyrus Northrop is seated in the first row, the ninth from the right. This was the year in which the* university awarded its first Ph.D. (MPLIC)

Following pages: *The Minneapolis Symphony Orchestra, shown in the auditorium of the Northwestern Building, made its debut* in 1903 under the leadership of conductor Emil Oberhoffer. Today it is known as the Minnesota Orchestra, and its home base is Orchestra Hall. (MPLIC)

as its large office space reflected the growing importance of services to the local economy. Since 1972 a large number of buildings have joined the IDS in a downtown building boom that, in the entire history of the city, was equalled only by the 1880s' construction activity. The new Government Center, designed by architect Joseph Carl Warnecke of San Francisco, was built adjacent to the City Hall building, and Northwestern Life Insurance built a new headquarters, using a design by Minoru Yamasaki, in the old Gateway area. In addition the First Bank of Minneapolis built itself another headquarters in one spire of the two-towered Pillsbury Center, with the Pillsbury headquarters occupying the other spire. The Lutheran Brotherhood, an institution which evolved from immigrant insurance activities, also built itself a new headquarters, and International Multifoods is in the process of doing the same as part of the City Center project, which will also house retail and office space for the Donaldson's store. Orchestra Hall, the new permanent home of the Minnesota Symphony, and the Hyatt Regency Hotel were also constructed on Nicollet Mall, as were several groups of condominiums near Loring Park and also at the other end of the mall near Gateway Center. The Minneapolis Institute of Art received significant additions when the buildings for the Minneapolis College of Art and Design and the Minneapolis Children's Theater, designed by Kenzo Tange, were constructed next to it. A large number of other buildings, large and small, were also added to the city's stock of new structures.

In addition to this flurry of construction, there has also been a good deal of restoration. The old Butler Brothers warehouse, for example, has been restored and converted into offices, retail shops, and restaurants. An old mill building on Nicollet Island has been in the process of being transformed into a plush hotel, and an old warehouse complex has been converted into an array of shops, restaurants, and boutiques known as St. Anthony Main, on Southeast Main Street. In its 10th decade of civic use, City Hall also has been undergoing refurbishment, along with a host of other buildings around the city, both downtown and else-

Facing page, clockwise from top left: *Located on First Avenue North in downtown Minneapolis, the Butler Brothers warehouse was an elegant edifice for a warehouse as seen in this 1907 photograph. In recent years the interior of the building has been completely redone to make room for shops, boutiques and restaurants in one of Minneapolis' best examples of intelligent preservation and restoration of an old but valuable structure. Photo by Sweet. (MPLIC)*

The first Minneapolis Public Library was an attractive structure located at 10th Street and Hennepin Avenue in downtown Minneapolis. In the early 1960s the library was moved to a new facility on the Nicollet Mall where it has continued its tradition of community service. Its humanities and social science collections are especially impressive. (MPLIC)

Tenth Avenue's foot and rail bridge connected Southeast Minneapolis with South Minneapolis for many years. This view shows the East Bank and the omnipresent lumberyards. From the E.A. Bromley Collection. (MPLIC)

where. The official work of monitoring the overall restoration effort has been coordinated by the Minneapolis Heritage Preservation Commission, which has designated several historic districts and which has sponsored the restoration of the workers' housing district along Milwaukee Avenue in South Minneapolis.

Despite the many changes that have swept through Minneapolis since the first settlers arrived in St. Anthony in the late 1840s, Minneapolis has maintained a remarkable diversity among its component communities. In Northeast Minneapolis, for example, one finds an exotic Southern and Eastern European flavor with the large numbers of Polish, Ukrainian, Czech, and Italian surnames and business enterprises. *Pirogis* and authentic *kielbasa* can be purchased over the counter in delicatessens in the area (and, for the more sedentary, can be brought to the table) at a variety of ethnic restaurants.

Near North Minneapolis one finds a different setting in the apartment dwellings that mark the center of one of the city's black communities. Soul food restaurants and clubs set the area off from the more working-class neighborhoods further north. The jukeboxes' contents move from rhythm and blues to polkas and country-western music as one moves through the area. The churches are predominantly Baptist and Lutheran, and the streets are crowded with a multitude of diners and small ma-and-pa stores as well as myriad small businesses catering to wholesale and retail needs. In Southeast Minneapolis, in contrast, one finds the telltale signs of a large student population, with theaters showing films never advertised on television and the eateries displaying a rough-hewn charm that reflects limited student budgets and an avoidance of atmosphere born of emphasis upon appearance rather than content. Dinkytown, across from the main entrance to the University of Minnesota, has almost the storybook look of a collegiate place of congregation, with its bookstores, movie houses, diners, gift shops, bakery, drugstore, fast food outlets, and other services. A mixture of apartments and houses, the area has some of the oldest homes in the city and a good portion of its

Above: *Prospect Park's "witch's hat tower," positioned on one of the three highest elevations in the city limits, is a familiar sight to the citizens of Minneapolis. The lovely park around it is part of the city system developed by the Minneapolis Park Board over several decades, and the residential area around the park, also known as Prospect Park, is one of the few areas that has winding streets rather than the developer's grid that predominates in other parts of the city. Photo by A.F. Raymond. (MHS)*

Facing page: *Looking south in this photograph one sees the lakes in western Minneapolis as they appeared in 1932. Lake of the Isles in the foreground, Lake Calhoun in the middle, and Lake Harriet in the distance are the three largest lakes in the city and provide a variety of opportunities for year-round enjoyment. (MHS)*

history. On the border between Northeast and Southeast stands Our Lady of Lourdes Catholic Church, the oldest Catholic parish in the city and one of the oldest buildings in the city. Southeast is complemented by the Prospect Park residential area, which presents an aura of solitude in the midst of the industrial activity that swirls about it in the Midway district to the north and east.

South Minneapolis is primarily marked by the Scandinavian immigrant experience, with some major exceptions. The West Bank area, or Cedar-Riverside, has the feel of the 1960s, with cooperative restaurants, theater, and housing, and a string of saloons where Bob Dylan once attempted to find acceptance for his music before fleeing to New York City. Even here the Swedish and Norwegian past echoes, as the Snoose Boulevard festival was centered here for years in celebration of the tobacco-chewing immigrants who once populated the place. Further south along Franklin Avenue is the center of the Native American community in Minneapolis. Faced with severe problems, these Native Americans have persisted in remarkable efforts at developing a livable community amenable to their culture in the midst of a city undergoing constant change. The fact that other groups have made the transition from the same area, although not the same circumstances, encourages one about the prospects for their eventual success.

Further to the west, around the great chain of large lakes, the city puts on airs as its fine homes blend gracefully with the well-manicured shores of the lakes. In winter the area takes on a fairyland aspect as the houses and grounds are covered with an ermine blanket and the lakes freeze into huge, shimmering crystals. The scene conjures an image of peace and prosperity that one somehow associates with the main imagery of the American dream and the American reality. There are other areas with greater incomes and finer homes than South Minneapolis, but for an inner-city environment it is truly remarkable to see in late 20th-century America. Minneapolis, through the accidents of history as well as the energies of its citizens, has been, truly, a fortunate city.　　•　　•　　•

Efforts were made to allow hiking and walking in the rustic areas of the Minneapolis park system, including the area around the Minnehaha Falls. A footbridge across Minnehaha Creek was installed and a wooden stairway was added for easy access. (MPLIC).

Left: *Hotel Lafayette at Minnetonka Beach is depicted in this circa 1883 lithograph by an unknown artist. (MHS)*

Below left: *Ferdinand Reichardt, a Danish immigrant, painted St. Anthony Falls in 1857. The falls are shown between St. Anthony and Hennepin Island, with Winslow Hotel in the background. (MHS)*

Facing page, top: *In about 1875 Alexander Loemans painted St. Anthony Falls in 1842 from below the falls. Loemans, a resident of St. Anthony from 1873 to 1880, did not include any people, houses, or other signs of development in his oil painting. (MHS)*

Bottom left and right: *The Falls of St. Anthony were depicted in a series of lithographs by Henry Lewis published in Das Illustrirte Mississippithal in 1854–1857. (MHS)*

Page 51: *Frederic Calhoun, a native Minneapolitan, painted Lake Calhoun in 1923. The clear blue lake was once a swamp. (MHS)*

Left: Joseph R. Meeker painted Minnehaha Falls in 1879. A footbridge and wooden stairway have been built to allow hikers access to the falls. (MHS)

Facing page: Louis Haugg made this lithograph of the Washburn mill complex in about 1890, showing the railroad in the foreground. (MHS)

CHAPTER II
FROM MILLS TO MICROCHIPS:
THE TRIUMPH OF ENTERPRISE

Above: *As was true for many Midwestern cities in the 19th century, Minneapolis was the creation of real estate entrepreneurs and speculators. Snyder and Macfarlane, two early operators in Minneapolis, had an office in the vicinity of what was later Bridge Square, circa 1855. From the E.A. Bromley Collection. (MPLIC)*

Facing page: *Entrepreneur John H. Stevens, an early settler, built the first wooden frame house on the West Bank of the Mississippi River. Thomas Wood painted his portrait. (MHS)*

As is true of many urban centers, the story of the economic development of Minneapolis hinges upon the development of the surrounding countryside. But the hinterland of Minneapolis provided only opportunities— opportunities that could have been squandered as well as utilized to the fullest. The crucial element in the process was the human one. The people who saw the potential of the opportunities that presented themselves and acted upon them were the agents of action. Some of these men and women grasped very large opportunities indeed and amassed very large fortunes. In the late 19th century such financial success was more often than not the result of practices that are frowned upon today but were the logical result of unbridled market competition and illicit combination, which were the orders of the day in the dawn of American industrialization. But while some few reached for and grabbed fortunes, others, the great masses, attempted to take advantage of more humble opportunities and rewards. For every financier who took a seat on the Minneapolis Grain Exchange, there were tens of thousands of farmers and their families who labored for months to sow and harvest the hard, red spring wheat, while thousands of others labored to move the wheat to the mills and grind it, package it, and move it on to the consumers. The story of the entrepreneur and the laborer is, then, part and parcel of the same epic.

The first systematic development of the Minneapolis hinterland by Europeans began with the intrusion of the French fur interests in the 17th century. With advance groups of explorers and missionaries, the French systematically explored the Mississippi River system and most of its major tributaries in their hunt for souls and furs. Father Louis Hennepin, who first observed and named the Falls of St. Anthony in 1680, was one of many missionaries who accompanied these French expeditions. The French engaged in some fur trapping on their own, but a great deal of it was actually undertaken by the indigenous tribes of Dakota Sioux and Ojibwe who lived in the areas to which the French came. The French traded weapons, gunpowder, iron utensils, cloth, and myriad other products to the Indians, who gladly exchanged their furs to acquire them. European weapons made hunting easier, iron utensils improved culinary operations, and cloth increased the diversity of apparel, so the exchange tended to improve the life-style of the Indians in the short run. In the long run, however, the Indians suffered in the exchange, as they were made dependent on the superior technology of the Europeans without acquiring the means to master that technology and fashion it for use with their own resources. Consequently the Indians had to continue making their exchanges, or their rifles would be without powder, their utensils would wear out, and their cloth would need to be replaced. The products of the trade became indispensable to their survival. This dependence made it relatively easy for later intruders to displace the Indians and appropriate their ancestral lands.

As is well known the French and the English competed for hegemony in the North American wilderness, and their competition led to a series of wars in the course of the 18th century, which led to the expulsion of the French from the continent. After the French and Indian War, or the Seven Years' War as it was known in Europe, ended in 1763, the English emerged as the masters of the continent and of the fur trade of the interior. The English were not long without rivals, however, as the American War of Independence ended with the new republic controlling the Mississippi River system so recently wrested from the French. Between the end of the Revolutionary War in 1783 and the end of the War of 1812 in 1815, however, American control of its domain was not effective. The Hudson's Bay Company agents and fur traders roamed at will over the American Northwest, as did officers of the British army, who negotiated treaties and alliances with the indigenous tribes. It was these violations of American sovereignty that led to the direct settlement of Minnesota.

In 1805 the United States dispatched Lieutenant Zebulon M. Pike, intrepid explorer and frontier soldier for whom the mountain in Colorado is named, to the upper Mississippi River area to establish contact with the dominant Indian tribes in the area and

Colonel Josiah Snelling ordered the construction of the first lumber mill and gristmill on the West Bank to meet the needs of the detail assigned to construct Fort Snelling. From the E.A. Bromley Collection. (MPLIC)

to establish an American presence, however temporarily. Pike passed by the Falls of St. Anthony and into the interior of what is today Minnesota, and signed a treaty with Little Crow, a Sioux chief. The treaty transferred land from the tribe of Little Crow to the United States government, including nine miles on both banks of the Mississippi River from the point where the river was joined by the Minnesota River to the Falls of St. Anthony. The U.S. government paid Little Crow 1¼ cents per acre, but actual payment was not forthcoming for some time.

The American government did not follow up on the Pike expedition until after the War of 1812 when, in 1817, Major Stephen H. Long was dispatched to the area to reconnoiter and make recommendations for future action. Long recommended that a U.S. military garrison be established on the upper Mississippi. In the summer of 1819 a military detachment under the command of Lieutenant Colonel Henry Leavenworth was ordered to the area to establish the fort. The following year, Colonel Josiah Snelling arrived to take command of the post, and he proceeded to establish the fort, which exists in part to the present time.

During the construction of the fort, Snelling required lumber, and in order to meet that need, he ordered the construction of a sawmill at the Falls of St. Anthony. The sawmill was built on the West Bank of the river and was soon joined by a grist mill which Snelling ordered constructed to grind fresh flour to aid in the provisioning of his troops. The flour mill was erected adjacent to the sawmill and remained under military jurisdiction until 1849. It was these mills that later attracted the interest of Illinois Congressman Robert Smith. The irony of the military post created by the United States, later called Fort Snelling to honor its perspicacious commandant, was that it was originally intended to provide protection for American fur interests in the region. The long-term effect of the fort was, however, to open the region to diversified exploitation and to demonstrate the potential of the waterpower at the Falls of St. Anthony.

The direct development of the area that is today Minneapolis was the consuming project of entrepreneur Franklin Steele. Steele came to the upper Mississippi region to participate in lumbering activities in the St. Croix River Valley. The St. Croix River today forms part of the boundary between Wisconsin and Minnesota and in the late 1830s was beginning to be developed on a large scale by lumber interests. Steele helped organize the St. Croix Falls Lumbering Company, which acquired the waterpower of Taylor's Falls on the St. Croix, but Steele left the St. Croix to become the sutler at Fort Snelling and to pursue opportunities in that region. He recognized the potential of the Falls of St. Anthony and successfully laid claim to the area on the East Bank of the falls.

It was Steele who built the first private commercial sawmill at the falls with the assistance of the skills of Maine millwright Ard Godfrey. It was also primarily Steele's efforts that attracted sufficient capital to propel the infant lumbering industry forward. Unfortunately, for Steele at least, he had the habit of overextending himself beyond his access to capital, and that flaw ultimately explains his inability to accrue the same fortunes that others acquired with less acumen and timing. Steele's other major achievement was in helping to open the West Bank area of the falls to settlement through his efforts with the military ferry service and the establishment of the John H. Stevens claim.

Steele was a colorful character and had the singular fortune to acquire Fort Snelling in 1858 and, later, to charge the government rent for it when it was again used after having been deactivated for service in the Civil War. Steele's major failure, however, was in not acquiring the water rights to the power of the falls on the East Bank. If Steele had been able to acquire these rights he would have had a monopoly on the power generated by the falls, but this loss was not the essence of his failure. The problem for Steele was the great capability and competitiveness of the men who managed to gain control.

Robert Smith was connected with the Washburn interests

Facing page: *Settlement in Minneapolis and Old St. Anthony was linked to the early efforts of the garrison at Fort Snelling to harness the power of the Falls. A lumber mill and gristmill were built on the West Bank of the falls in the 1820s and were used to grind flour and cut wood for construction of the fort and victuals for the garrison during the early winters. The mill structures survived long after they passed out of the hands of the army and are shown here circa 1870. From the E.A. Bromley Collection. (MPLIC)*

Facing page: Ard Godfrey, a native of New England as were most of the early lumber entrepreneurs in Old St. Anthony, came to the Falls of St. Anthony in the late 1840s and directed the construction of the first mill on the East Bank of the river. Godfrey was also the first postmaster in St. Anthony. (MPLIC)

Top right: After his involvement in the development of the first mill on the East Bank of the Falls of St. Anthony, Ard Godfrey attempted to harness the power of the Minnehaha Falls in South Minneapolis and establish his own independent milling operation. Shown here are the ruins of the Godfrey effort located between the falls and the Mississippi River, into which Minnehaha Creek flows. The venture apparently failed because of the irregular flow of Minnehaha Creek. (MPLIC)

Bottom right: Ard Godfrey's house is shown here in its original location before it was moved to a park in Southeast Minneapolis. One of the first structures in Old St. Anthony, the house was built from lumber produced in a lumber mill that Godfrey himself helped build in the 1840s. From the E.A. Bromley Collection. (MPLIC)

which through a remarkable family extended throughout the Midwest from their base in New England. In 1855 Smith formed the Minneapolis Mill Company with several partners in order to develop the waterpower on the East Bank and turn a profit from it. Among Smith's partners was Dorilus Morrison, who acted as business agent for Cadwallader Colden Washburn, a Wisconsin lumberman and later a governor of that state. Between 1855 and 1865 Smith and Morrison bought out their other partners and in the latter year C.C. Washburn and his brother William became partners in the firm. Robert Smith died in 1867, and his heirs sold the Smith interest in the Minneapolis Mill Company in 1869. C.C. Washburn thus gained controlling interest in the company.

This process of acquisition was detrimental to Franklin Steele because of the capital resources which this group could draw upon in their efforts to develop the falls waterpower on the West Bank. Steele had formed his own power company to develop the falls' energy on the East Bank, the St. Anthony Falls Water Power Company, with capital provided by Eastern investors. By 1868, however, Steele's distant partners sold out and were replaced by local businessmen, including John S. Pillsbury. With chronic capitalization difficulties, Steele's power company was bothered by problems associated with the islands located in the river just above the falls. The problems were not physical but stemmed rather from conflicting claims to the islands and the rights to the river power that flowed past them. These conflicting claims precipitated a nearly total disaster in 1869 and were primarily the result of Franklin Steele's approach to the business as a real estate developer rather than as a manager and planner.

The Minneapolis Mill Company on the West Bank developed its operation, in contrast to Steele's, with surprising foresight and clarity of purpose. In 1857 the company began a canal along the riverbank which would carry the river water diverted from the flow over the falls. Along this canal sawmills could be located, and water would be furnished to them at specified amounts for specified charges. Later flour mills would be accommodated along the canal

Above: *John Sargent Pillsbury, the first of the major milling family to arrive in St. Anthony, was active in retail trade before he became involved in milling. His nephew, Charles, began operations in flour milling, and John invested in the enterprise. It was John who granted funds to the University of Minnesota to construct Pillsbury Science Hall on the East Bank campus. (MPLIC)*

Facing page: *East River Channel, between Hennepin Island and the East Bank, was the cradle of St. Anthony's industry. The area soon became congested as firms competed for river frontage and access to the power of the falls. Shortage of space helped spur the development of the milling area on the West Bank, where the nucleus of Minneapolis developed. From the E.A. Bromley Collection. (MPLIC)*

as well. Steele's operation on the East Bank was never able to achieve the same degree of orderliness in its operations and so was unable to accommodate as many customers for its waterpower.

Another problem with the East Bank was geographical. The river bends to the southeast just above the falls, so open space does not grow wider as one moves away from the riverbank. On the West Bank the opposite holds true: there was more room there for the expansion of supporting facilities such as transportation and the development of the central business district as well. Along the interior lines of the East Bank residences, commercial areas, and industrial operations crowded together in competition for restricted space. The crowding is reflected in the nature of the area to the present day.

The vast increases in the number of logs being brought to Minneapolis for conversion to lumber necessitated expansion of the mills, and because of better management, more space, and more capital and know-how, the West Bank absorbed the bulk of the expansion that occurred. By 1869, in fact, the operations supplied by the Minneapolis Mill Company were turning out twice as much lumber as the Steele complex on the opposite shore. The disparity between the development of the two operations was made even more acute with the rise of flour milling in Minneapolis and St. Anthony.

The growth of flour milling was the result of the incredibly rapid agricultural migration into Minnesota that caused a population explosion there. From 6,000 people in 1850 Minnesota's population soared to 172,000 in 1860, with 156,000 of these people living in rural areas. The number of farms soared. By 1870 the population increased again, two and a half times, to 440,000 people, of whom 370,000 were rural—and again the number of farms rocketed.

This growth in the agricultural population naturally caused a great increase in the output of farm produce and the number one farm commodity produced was wheat. Until 1870, however, the bulk of the wheat produced in the state was ground into flour

Above: *Cataract Flour Mill was the first flour mill built on the West Bank of the river in Minneapolis. Its owners were W.W. Eastman, who later dug the tunnel that almost caused the Falls of St. Anthony to wash out, and Paris Gibson. From the E.A. Bromley Collection. (MPLIC)*

Facing page: *Hennepin Island became a major center of milling operations because of its proximity to the Falls of St. Anthony. Congestion on the river front was already clearly a problem in 1866. From the E.A. Bromley Collection. (MPLIC)*

outside of the state. In the early years St. Louis attracted much of it, as it was very easy to float the crop downriver on rafts made of lumber that was destined for the same market. Later as the railroads penetrated into southern Minnesota, where the majority of the agricultural population was centered in these early decades, the terminal wheat centers of Milwaukee and Chicago also began to attract the crop. Some wheat was, however, shipped to Minneapolis and St. Anthony even in the early years.

The first flour mill was constructed in the vicinity of Minneapolis in 1851 when R.C. Rogers built a rude grist mill at the end of a row of St. Anthony lumber mills. Rogers' mill did custom work; that is, the wheat would be hauled in by the owner of the grain, it would be ground into flour for a fee paid to the mill owner, and then the owner of the flour would cart it off. Commercial milling was initiated in 1854 when John Eastman, John Rollins, and Rufus P. Upton built a mill in St. Anthony and engaged in the purchase of wheat, its processing, and also its distribution. Flour milling slowly expanded from this beginning. In 1858 the mill owned by Eastman and others, known as the "Minnesota" or "Island Mill," shipped 125 barrels of flour to Boston—the first flour produced in Minneapolis that was not locally consumed. Although flour milling was first instituted on the East Bank, by 1869 the West Bank was producing five times as much flour as was the East Bank. It was after 1869, however, that flour milling began to expand into national and international significance.

The lumber industry, however, was the main engine of growth in the first three decades. William D. Washburn, Cadwallader's brother, was very active in the industry, especially in the Rum River area. He established a sawmill at Anoka, where the Rum flows into the Mississippi, and was active in other operations in Minneapolis. Another prominent lumberman, Caleb Dorr, was—like the Washburns, Ard Godfrey, and most other lumbermen—a native of New England. Dorr spent most of his career in service to the Mississippi and Rum River Boom Company, which monopo-

Caleb Dorr, one of the earliest settlers in Old St. Anthony, spent the greater part of his career active in the lumber industry. In later years Dorr was boom master of the Mississippi and Rum River Boom Company, which held a virtual monopoly on river logging operations between Anoka and Minneapolis. Dorr also held various elected offices in Minneapolis, such as alderman, and was active in the cultural and social affairs of the community. (MPLIC)

lized the control of the movement of logs on the two rivers throughout the second half of the 19th century. But the Mississippi and Rum River Boom Company operated only as far north as Brainerd, and when the logging industry expanded further northward, Dorr helped create the Northern Boom Company to control the log traffic on the northern portion of the river. Other prominent Minneapolis businessmen who made substantial fortunes in the lumber industry included Dorilus Morrison, who was involved in many Washburn enterprises; Thomas B. Walker, who later became a major patron of the arts in Minneapolis; Thomas H. Shevlin, who later was a patron of the University of Minnesota; and Richard Chute, after whom is named the park where Ard Godfrey's house now stands in the Old St. Anthony district.

The lumber industry had two long-term effects on the growth of the city of Minneapolis. First, it provided a great amount of capital in the form of profits, capital which was available for investment in other industries; and secondly, it caused industries related to lumbering to develop and concentrate in Minneapolis. Much of the capital generated by lumbering was used to finance flour milling in Minneapolis as well as related industries, especially railroads. The activities of the Washburns provide the best single example of this pattern of investment. As early as the 1850s lumber-related industries began to appear in Minneapolis. In 1854 Orrin Rogers opened a sash and door factory. In 1855 E. Broad began making edged tools for use in the mills and in factories, tools that would finish the lumber and transform it into other products. In 1857 H.C. Butler began production of manufacturing tools and mill picks. These examples reflect a process of diversification that was based on technological development, a process that has continued with periodic halts and sudden spurts ever since.

The first major technological challenge that confronted the entrepreneurs in Minneapolis was that of how to extract the greatest amount of power from the Falls of St. Anthony. The West Bank interests, controlled by the Washburns, extracted more power from

Facing page, clockwise from top left: *Thomas B. Walker, lumber magnate, was active in the development of the major social and cultural institutions in Minneapolis, including the Minneapolis Institute of Arts, the public library, the symphony orchestra, and the park system. Walker is best remembered as the creator of the Walker Art Gallery, which now operates in conjunction with the Guthrie Theater. (MPLIC)*

Thomas H. Shevlin, a prominent Minneapolis lumberman, was a munificent benefactor of the University of Minnesota, and Shevlin Hall on the East Bank campus bears his family name. (MPLIC)

William W. Eastman directed the digging of the tunnel that almost led to the washing out of the Falls of St. Anthony. Eastman was also active in real estate development and supervised the building of the rowhouses on Nicollet Island that became known as Eastman Flats. (MPLIC)

West Bank lumber mills required extensive works to keep their operations running smoothly. Causeways carried wastes for dumping into the river and materials, such as logs, downriver for further processing or direct shipment to other markets, such as St. Louis. From the E.A. Bromley Collection. (MPLIC)

the falls than did the Steele group on the East Bank, and they received a far greater return for their efforts. The demands on the falls, however, continually increased as planing mills, furniture factories, a paper mill, more flour mills, and more sawmills located around them. The crisis was brought to a head when East Bank entrepreneur William W. Eastman began a tunnel under Nicollet and Hennepin islands in order to divert river water for use in his operations. The tunnel was a disaster. It collapsed and river water diverted into it immediately began to erode the soft sandstone that lay beneath the hard, limestone river bottom. The falls began to wash away and disintegrate into rapids. This calamitous development threatened the entire supply of power from the falls.

The tunnel gave way on October 4, 1869, and the reaction of the city populace was immediate. Most of the able bodied population rushed to the river to begin to fill in the collapsed tunnel. Feverish efforts over several weeks saved the falls, but it was apparent that more permanent action would have to be taken, and the aid of the federal government was enlisted in the effort. The federal government responded with assistance after a drawn-out process of supplication, and between 1870 and 1884 the government spent some $615,000 to build a concrete apron over the falls, two low dams above the falls, and a bypass channel to carry floating logs around the falls. The federal expenditures were justified as necessary "to insure navigation on the Upper Mississippi." The Falls of St. Anthony were thus preserved as a source of inexpensive power for the city's fledgling milling interests.

There were, however, indirect consequences of the falls disasters. First, the capital improvements required on the East Bank forced Franklin Steele out of the waterpower business, and in 1875 he sold his interests to the Chute brothers, Richard and Samuel, and to Frederick Butterfield. Steele left Minneapolis to reside in Washington, D.C., but on a journey to Minneapolis in 1880, he died in the city he had founded. Another effect of the falls disaster, albeit an indirect one, was the merger of St. Anthony with Minneapolis in 1872. By that time the population and industry of

On October 4, 1869, a tunnel under the eastern edge of the Falls of St. Anthony collapsed, causing a great deal of destruction to mills located in the area. While the immediate threat to the city's waterpower was averted, it took decades to permanently protect the falls. From the E.A. Bromley Collection. (MPLIC)

In the aftermath of the tunnel collapse of October 1869, workmen from companies along the river attempt to halt the collapse of the falls by filling in the tunnel. The Minneapolis skyline and first suspension bridge can be discerned in the distance. From the E.A. Bromley Collection. (MPLIC)

Cadwallader Colden Washburn was the prime mover behind the development of the Washburn Crosby Milling Company, which eventually developed into General Mills. Washburn, a Wisconsin resident, served as governor of that state and never maintained any formal residence in Minnesota. Photo by E.R. Curtiss. (MPLIC)

Minneapolis had far outstripped the city on the East Bank, and the near disaster at the falls reminded St. Anthony's citizens of their inferior situation, helping them to overcome their remaining reticence at the prospect of joining their fortunes with the future of the West Bank city.

As has been mentioned the 1850s were a period of boom in the lumber industry and the period when flour milling took its first hesitant steps. Also in that decade related industries in the fashioning of wood products and the manufacture of woodworking tools developed in proximity to the sawmills. In the 1860s further expansion of the city's industrial base occurred as larger flour mills were constructed, railroads made connections with the city, and farm implement dealers and manufacturers were developed. The largest of the flour mills constructed in the 1860s was the mill built by Cadwallader Washburn in 1866. Six stories high and built at the cost of $100,000, the new Washburn mill was the largest in the United States west of Buffalo and had the capacity to grind 840 barrels of flour daily. Cadwallader Washburn made another wise move in the decade when he engaged George Henry Christian, a native of Alabama who had come to Minneapolis to operate as a flour broker, as manager of his Minneapolis interests and also took Christian on as a junior partner. Christian soon proved his abilities as manager as he wrestled with the growing technological problems which the Minneapolis mill industry was encountering. Railroad connections, in the meantime, were made with the terminal markets at Chicago and Milwaukee, and much wheat grown in Minnesota was shipped directly to these centers.

As had occurred with lumbering, the flour industry created related industries as it began to develop. A large cooperage industry grew as coopers were set to work fashioning barrels in which the flour could be shipped. Minneapolis also began to develop as a merchandising center for the agricultural countryside that surrounded it. Much merchandise was simply imported to the city and then reshipped for sale in rural areas, but in 1860 the Monitor Plow Works was established in Minneapolis to craft plows locally, and

Southerner George Henry Christian came to Minneapolis to work with the Washburn interests. Attuned to the need for technological innovation in the flour milling industry, Christian introduced the "middlings" purifier in the early 1870s, which greatly expanded productivity in the mills. (MPLIC)

in 1873 the Minneapolis Harvester Works was established to fashion equipment for the harvesting of crops.

As the 1870s began Minneapolis was making slow progress towards its development as a center of the flour-milling industry. Lumbering, of course, continued to grow in importance, but the numbers of jobs created by the new industry declined each year as technological improvements increased the productivity of the workers. The millers of Minneapolis and their managers faced severe obstacles in their efforts to capture a greater share of the flour market. The basic problem was with the wheat variety that was grown by the Minnesota farmers in their northern climate. Hard, red spring wheat was their main wheat variety, and when this wheat was ground with the traditional grist wheels, the hard wheat produced flour that was coarser and darker than that produced by winter wheat grown and ground elsewhere in the nation. The flour that was produced by the millers in the 1870s, then, commanded a lower market price and was less in demand than the flour produced in other milling centers such as St. Louis and Chicago. Minnesota flour was usually mixed with the whiter and finer flours as an additive when it was shipped to the East.

Also during this era a squeeze began to be felt concerning the waterpower available from the Falls of St. Anthony. Sawmills and flour mills were competing in earnest for the available waterpower, and the flour interests, which controlled the West Bank Minneapolis Mill Company operation and had sizeable interests in Steele's St. Anthony Water Power Company on the East Bank, gradually forced the sawmills to seek new sources of power to sustain their operations. The Minneapolis Mill Company began after 1876 to ease out the lumber mills that had previously contracted to the company for waterpower. The Mill Company made the freed waterpower available to the flour millers, notably the Washburn interests. By 1880 the great majority of sawmills on the West Bank were utilizing steam power in their operations instead of waterpower from the falls, and by 1887 the last sawmill operated by waterpower was closed down. A young Austrian engineer named William de la

Facing page: *The construction of the apron over the Falls of St. Anthony and related works on the river required the reconstruction of conduits to and from major mills still utilizing waterpower from the falls. The work shown here was required for the Pillsbury A Mill on the East Bank in Old St. Anthony, circa 1888. From the E.A. Bromley Collection. (MPLIC)*

Barre, who became agent and engineer for the Minneapolis Mill Company in 1883, directed the final phase of this process and managed the power needs of the flour-milling interests from that time until the industry began to decline.

Minneapolis millers beginning in the 1870s and for some time afterward were plagued by the problems of seasonal fluctuations in their need for credit. They purchased the wheat from the farmers in the fall during and after the harvest and sold their flour the following year. This timing of their market activity meant that they required huge outlays of cash in the fall in addition to the money needed for their year-round operating expenditures. The milling interests took the step in 1872 of creating a national bank in Minneapolis that would be sensitive to their peculiar financing needs. The bank also hoped to attract sufficient deposits from lumbering interests in Minneapolis to free the entire business community from dependence upon correspondent banking institutions in the East. Another action taken by the milling interests in this regard was to form the Minneapolis Millers' Association. Incorporated in 1876, the organization was the brainchild of financier William H. Dunwoody, who also helped organize the millers' bank. The purpose of the association was to concentrate the needs of the millers in a single purchasing pool. Dunwoody sought successfully to control the activities of all the millers' purchasing agents operating in the agricultural countryside. Dunwoody, from his offices in Minneapolis, in effect dictated the prices that the buyers should pay to the farmers. The wheat thus purchased then would be shipped to Minneapolis, where it would be distributed to the millers according to their capacity to process it. The organization was in fact a collusive monopoly that allowed the millers to determine the price of wheat in the region rather then allow the price to be determined by the normal processes of the free market. The monopoly was successful because the major millers, such as the Washburns and the Pillsburys, fully supported the Dunwoody system.

The existing rail transportation routes also conspired against

the success of Minneapolis millers. The early rail routes tied the Minnesota agricultural areas only to the terminal markets at Milwaukee and Chicago, and so competition with milling interests in these areas was very great. In 1872 some relief was gained by the millers when Minneapolis was connected to the rail line between St. Paul and Duluth, a port on Lake Superior. With this connection the millers were able to ship their wheat and flour out of Duluth, bypassing the Milwaukee and Chicago terminals. But in order to break into the Eastern and international markets, the millers needed direct access to the seaports on the Eastern Seaboard. The millers also recognized that they would soon need to capitalize on the continuing expansion of the agricultural frontier to the West into the Dakotas. As a consequence of these needs—the grain supply in the West and the markets in the East—the millers became actively involved in the planning and financing of railroad construction.

In the 1870s the milling community was joined by the Pillsbury family. John S. Pillsbury had been involved in retail activity in Minneapolis and St. Anthony from the 1850s, but in the early 1870s his nephew, Charles, came to Minneapolis to explore opportunities in the flour-milling industry. By 1874 Charles decided to enter the industry and formed the Charles A. Pillsbury Company. Charles' uncle, John, invested in the enterprise, and so did Charles' father, George A. Pillsbury, who migrated to Minneapolis from New England at the age of 68. The Pillsburys made slow progress through the 1870s as Charles systematically investigated the technology of the industry in the United States and in Europe and made plans for future expansion.

Despite the Pillsbury family's competition, Minneapolis milling continued to be dominated by the Washburn interests. In 1874 Cadwallader Washburn completed his massive A Mill on the West Bank. The Washburn A Mill had the largest daily capacity of any mill in the city. Because it was the pride of the city and represented a large percentage of the city's flour capacity, it caused an even greater shock when the mill exploded, leveling itself and

Above: *Jacob Koontz Sidle was the first president of First National Bank of Minneapolis, an early major banking institution in the area. Sidle had previously directed his own private banking operation in the city. (MPLIC)*

Facing page, top left: *Northwestern National Bank was created in the early 1870s to meet the need of flour milling and lumbering interests for a local source of capital. Northwestern Bank Corporation, or Banco, is currently the largest banking firm headquartered in Minneapolis and like its rival, First Banks, serves much of the Upper Midwest. From the E.A. Bromley Collection. (MPLIC)*

Top right: *First National Bank at the intersection of Washington and Nicollet avenues was Minneapolis' second largest banking operation in 1870. The bank no longer needs to share space with tonsorial parlors or furniture stores. From the E.A. Bromley Collection (MPLIC)*

several adjacent mills, on May 2, 1878. Fortunately the explosion occurred in the evening when reduced crews were at work, so loss of life was kept lower than it might have been. Eighteen people did die in the explosion, however, and in a few seconds a third of the city's milling capacity was destroyed. Mills adjacent to the Washburn A Mill—including the Humboldt, Diamond, Pettit, Zenith, and Galaxy—were also destroyed or severely damaged by the explosion, as was a machine shop, a wheat elevator, a railroad roundhouse, some planing mills, a couple of lumberyards, and even a few residences.

Washburn A Mill (center) was the major mill of the Washburn interests in Minneapolis in the late 1870s. It is shown here a few days before an explosion demolished it in 1878. From the E.A. Bromley Collection. (MPLIC)

The explosion and fire, which continued afterward, was the worst single industrial accident in the history of Minneapolis flour milling and caused considerable consternation. Other fires and small calamities had afflicted the city's industries previously, but the swiftness and force of this disaster created a real hardship. The flour millers had more immediate reason for discomfort, however, because insurers of the mills were refusing to pay claims resulting from the explosion. Dust had long been considered a danger in the mills, and it was vaguely sensed that there was a link between the presence of dust in the larger mills and the occasional explosions that had occurred previously. While the relationship between dust and explosions had not been precisely defined in the 1870s, insurance companies refused to insure mill properties against the dangers of explosions. The question arose in the destruction of the Washburn A Mill, then, as to whether the explosion had occurred and caused fires to break out or a fire had precipitated the explosion. The millers, for reasons of economic survival, held to the latter view.

The question attracted the interest of two instructors at the University of Minnesota. Louis W. Peck of the physics department and Stephen F. Peckham of the chemistry department sought to determine the cause of the Washburn A Mill explosion. The physicist, Peck, experimented with dust to determine the nature of its explosive capability. Once Peck was able to produce controlled dust explosions, Peckham attempted to estimate the force of the explo-

Washburn A Mill exploded and burned on May 2, 1878. Built in 1874, the Washburn A Mill was the largest mill at that time, and when it blew up, 18 people were killed and one-third of the city's entire milling capacity was destroyed. From the E.A. Bromley Collection. (MPLIC)

sion that had occurred at the Washburn A. Peck and Peckham determined that the dust present in the mill had exploded after being exposed to an open flame. In reviewing the operations of the mill, they speculated that the flame was produced when the feed of grain to the grist stones was interrupted. The stones then ground each other, producing sparks, great heat, and flame, touching off the grain dust that filled the air of the building. From the ruins and the debris of the fallen walls, the two also determined that a series of very rapid explosions had actually occurred, rather than a single blast.

As a result of the work of Peck and Peckham, the flour-milling industry made dust control and fire prevention high priorities in the design of their mills. Some time after the scientists reported their findings, the insurance companies involved in the coverage of the disaster area began making payments on their policies. Later there was also speculation that there were other possible causes of the dust explosion, such as bare electrical connections or the inadvertent striking of a match by a mill worker. Despite the possible error in their explanation of the origin of the flame that sparked the explosions, Peck and Peckham did establish the cause-and-effect chain between dust, fire, and explosions.

Several other major technical innovations in flour milling occurred in the 1870s that had important consequences. The middlings purifier was introduced into the mill operated by George H. Christian around 1873 and led to a great increase in productivity, as an increased amount of flour was produced from a smaller amount of wheat. Without the purifier milling produced flour as well as many particles that were "middling" in size, between the grains of wheat and the fine flour particles. The middling particles, with the purifier installed, would be removed from the flour for regrinding or for alternative uses through the mechanism of sieves and air currents. Another technical innovation resulted from the travels of Charles A. Pillsbury to Budapest, Hungary, at the end of the 1870s. Pillsbury had formed his milling company earlier in the decade, but he went to great lengths to insure that his primary facilities would

Above: *Charles A. Pillsbury, a native of New England, was the "brains" behind the development of the Pillsbury flour company and fortune. Charles, a meticulous manager, traveled to Budapest to research the latest milling innovations, which he improved upon. He established a research and development attitude that has since characterized the Minneapolis milling interests. (MPLIC)*

Facing page: *The Crown Elevator at 9th Street and Second Avenue Southeast burned on July 28, 1927. At this time explosions and fires were still major hazards in the storage and processing of grain. (MPLIC)*

be the most modern and the most productive possible, and so he strove to equip his mills with the most advanced equipment available. Pillsbury journeyed to Budapest for two basic reasons: first, the Hungarian wheat crops were of the hard variety similar to those grown in the Upper Midwest, and secondly, because Hungarian flour had a superior reputation in European flour markets because of the methods for grinding the wheat. Pillsbury wished to investigate the Hungarian process and determine why it produced superior flour from hard wheat when the Minneapolis millers could not do the same.

The Washburn interests also investigated the Hungarian process. In 1874 George H. Christian installed a set of rollers in the mill he managed, rollers similar to those used in the Budapest mills, and in 1878 C.C. Washburn established a mill totally equipped with rollers as an experiment with the new system as well. It was Charles Pillsbury, however, who implemented the Hungarian roller mill system on the largest scale, as a result of his direct observation of the process in Europe. The Pillsbury A Mill, constructed at a cost of one million dollars and completed in 1881, utilized the roller milling process exclusively and had a daily capacity of 5,000 barrels. From the introduction of the middlings purifier and the roller milling process, the day of large-scale production had come to American flour milling.

The process of gradual reduction was introduced with the roller method of flour milling and it too greatly increased the productivity of the new mills. In old stone milling the flour had been ground in, basically, a one-step process. In the gradual reduction process of roller milling, the wheat passed through series after series of matched rolling bars that gradually reduced the wheat to flour. The gradual reduction process, with some other minor technical improvements, greatly increased the productivity of the Minneapolis mills and, more importantly, increased the ability of the millers to control the quality of their flour products. "Patent" flours, the flours of the highest grade were developed as a result and were primarily represented by Pillsbury's "Best XXXX" and Washburn's

Above: *In addition to the A and B mills, the Pillsbury Company also developed facilities for packaging and storing their products prior to shipment to markets throughout the world. Photo by F.L. Mortimer. From the Dewars Collection. (MPLIC)*

Left: *The 1889 tenth business annual of the Minneapolis Saturday Evening Spectator was filled with advertisements for flourishing businesses. John Sargent Pillsbury is listed in two of the firms' ads, reflecting his own diverse business interests. (MPLIC)*

Facing page: *Erected in 1881 at a cost of one million dollars, Pillsbury A Mill, the pride of the Pillsbury milling operations, was designed by Leroy S. Buffington. Located on the East Bank in the Old St. Anthony Main area, the mill is still used as a warehouse by the Pillsbury Company. The old Phoenix mill is at the left. Photo by F.L. Mortimer. From the Dewars Collection. (MPLIC)*

"Gold Medal" flours. In a relatively short period of time, Minneapolis flours became the premium flours in the American marketplace, being much in demand and commanding 10 to 20 percent more in price than the closest competitors. Minneapolis flour had risen from the bottom of the barrel to the top of it.

The technological innovations of the 1870s revolutionized the flour-milling industry and caused a certain amount of reorganization. In 1879 the Washburn interests were reorganized as Washburn Crosby Company. That firm had three massive mills in operation in 1880 and the equally large Pillsbury Company had five mills (including the new Pillsbury A Mill) in operation by the following year. In 1869 there had been 13 mills in Minneapolis and St. Anthony, and each had a separate owner or group of owners. In 1880 there were 25 mills in Minneapolis, and eight were owned by Pillsbury and Washburn Crosby, whose mills produced more than one half of the entire Minneapolis flour output. The earlier financial activities of William H. Dunwoody strengthened the position of the Minneapolis millers further as they maintained their monopoly on grain purchases through the agency of their buying pool and through their development of banking institutions in Minneapolis to finance their massive operations. In the 1880s the Minneapolis milling industry expanded even further and began to eliminate other obstacles to growth and control.

During the 1880s the agricultural hinterland of Minneapolis continued to grow and expand at a phenomenal rate. From an 1880 farm population of 632,000 people, the Minnesota numbers expanded to 867,000 in 1890. In the same period of time, the population of Minneapolis increased from 46,887 to 164,738. While the farm population of Minnesota continued to grow, the farming frontier in North and South Dakota also expanded rapidly. The amount of wheat flowing into Minneapolis from the north and west was great enough to propel Minneapolis wheat and flour marketing into an international sphere.

The transportation problem, however, had to be settled before the international expansion could be undertaken most

William Hood Dunwoody, a Philadelphia native with extensive training in flour milling, joined the Washburn Crosby Company in 1877. Dunwoody rationalized the marketing activities of flour millers in Minneapolis through the establishment of a cartel and opened up the European market for processed Minneapolis flour products. Dunwoody Institute, which is dedicated to vocational education in the Minneapolis area, is named for the financier. (MPLIC)

Since its inception the Minneapolis Chamber of Commerce has played a central role in the development of agribusiness in the city, and it housed the Minneapolis Grain Exchange until after World War II. The Chamber continues to pursue long-term goals to improve the area's economy. (MHS)

profitably. To solve the problem the Minneapolis millers built their own railroad. The railroad was called the Minneapolis, St. Paul, and Sault Ste. Marie, and it connected Minneapolis with the Canadian railhead at Sault Ste. Marie, where Lake Superior, Lake Michigan, and Lake Huron meet. The connection at Sault Ste. Marie linked the Minneapolis millers with the Canadian Pacific Railroad, and through that line their products were cleared to the ports of Montreal and Boston. The "Soo Line," as it was called, freed the Minneapolis millers from the domination of the Chicago railroads. The railroad was completed in 1887, and by its second year of operation the Soo Line was carrying more wheat to the East than was any other railroad. Interestingly enough, the first president of the new railroad was William D. Washburn, independent miller and lumberman as well as brother to Cadwallader, the major owner of the Washburn Crosby Company. The major investors in the railroad were, of course, other millers in Minneapolis, as were the majority of the railroad's board of directors.

The determination to build the Soo Line had received a great boost in the early 1880s from the Minneapolis Chamber of Commerce. The chamber was organized and incorporated in 1881 by a group of grain merchants whose primary interest was the purchase of grains in the Upper Midwest for transshipment to milling operations in the East. These grain speculators were resented by the Minneapolis millers and their financial agents, led by William Dunwoody, who saw the grain traders as a threat to their supply of wheat for their local mills. Their purchasing activities also disrupted the monopoly of the Minneapolis Millers' Association, which Dunwoody had established to reduce competition and keep grain prices down. The organization of the Chamber of Commerce was an effort on the part of the grain traders to break the millers' monopoly. The resistance of the millers to the organization soon dissipated as members of both groups began to realize that there were more advantages to cooperation than existed in competition, and so the Minneapolis Millers' Association was dissolved, and the millers joined the Chamber of Commerce.

The Chamber of Commerce label was something of a misnomer, for in reality it was a grain exchange. It retained the name of Minneapolis Chamber of Commerce, however, until after World War II, when it was formally changed to the Minneapolis Grain Exchange. The milling interests and the grain speculators were both quite satisfied by the new arrangement, and the milling interests soon achieved a dominant position within the exchange. Between 1883 and 1894, in fact, all of the presidents of the chamber were chosen from the ranks of the millers.

The development of the grain exchange, or chamber, further stimulated the development of Minneapolis in several ways. First, it increased the importance of Minneapolis as a terminal grain market, as it could establish prices for wheat sold to local interests as well as wheat destined for distant markets. Secondly, the exchange increased the importance of Minneapolis as a financial center, for the exchange paved the way for speculation in grain futures (that is, future harvests could be bought and sold at fixed prices as financial instruments in the form of paper issued by the large milling firms and grain elevator and shipping companies). The cash market for currently-sold crops also continued on the exchange. During the 1880s the role of futures grew, but after 1890 sale and resale also became an important part of the market activity on the exchange.

The establishment of the grain exchange had an immediate impact on the Upper Midwest. In 1881 less then 200,000 bushels of wheat had been shipped East from Minneapolis. In 1882 shipments rose to two million bushels, in 1884 to four million, and in 1886 to six million. By 1891, 21 million bushels of wheat were moved to Eastern destinations and overseas.

The tremendous upsurge in the wheat traffic reflected the growth during the 1880s of the storage capacity in Minneapolis. The grain storage elevators of Minneapolis could accommodate two and a half million bushels in 1883; in 1890 the capacity rose to 16 million bushels as a result of increased construction. The wheat was

The Chicago, Milwaukee, and St. Paul Railroad Station, shown here in 1902, is located at Third and Washington avenues in South Minneapolis. It has not been used for some time as a railroad depot, and plans are underway to convert the structure to new use as office space and/or apartments. From the E.A. Bromley Collection. (MPLIC)

gathered in Minneapolis through a complex system of elevators located near railroad lines throughout the entire Midwest. It was at these elevators that farmers sold their wheat to milling companies and speculators through the agents of the exchange, at prices established in Minneapolis. The elevator companies were resented by the farmers of the Midwest for a variety of reasons, but primarily because of the system of grading imposed upon them. As early as 1858 the Chicago Wheat Exchange had created three grades in which all wheat purchased would be placed and which would command three different prices. If a farmer's wheat was graded in the lowest category, he would receive 20 to 30 cents less per bushel than if his wheat were in the first or second category. Because the elevators were not operated competitively and because they were controlled by the large milling interests either in Minneapolis or a center in the East, the farmer had no recourse if his wheat was declared inferior. Eventually the farmers attempted to solve the problem by establishing their own elevators through a system of cooperatives that they owned and operated on their own. By the 1920s wheat farmers in Minnesota were storing one-half of their annual crop in their own cooperative elevators. Even at that time, however, they were still marketing their wheat primarily through the Minneapolis Chamber of Commerce.

As the 1880s drew to a close, the Minneapolis millers began another project which enhanced their position in the national flour-milling industry. Intensive merchandising of their products at home and abroad was the essence of the milling interests' new activity. To develop the national market, the various milling companies hired specialists in retail trade and advertising to complement their corporate staffs. The most successful of these individuals was James S. Bell, who joined Washburn Crosby Company in 1888. At the same time, William H. Dunwoody journeyed to London for an extended stay to help establish markets for Minneapolis flour and Upper Midwestern grain in Europe. The efforts paid handsome dividends in a relatively short period of time and, by the end of the 1890s, Minneapolis was the flour-

Top: *Minneapolis companies produced agricultural machinery for farmers in the Upper Midwest. Minneapolis Harvester Works boasted that the Appleby twine binder they manufactured had an "automatic packer trip" that "prevented the binder from clogging, whatever the condition of the grain."*

Bottom: *Minneapolitans celebrated the completion of James J. Hill's Great Northern Railroad in 1890. The railroad linked Minneapolis and St. Paul with the Pacific Coast and opened up new markets on the Dakota and Montana plains for farming wares manufactured in the city. Windmills were among the products that Minneapolitans eagerly hoped to sell in this large marketplace. (MHS)*

James S. Bell, a marketing specialist, instigated the national promotion of Washburn Crosby Company products in 1893. Bell's efforts were later developed and imitated by General Mills and Pillsbury. (MPLIC)

milling center of the United States and of the world. In the course of the same decade, the milling companies diversified their product lines further when they began producing animal feeds. Agriculture in Minnesota was diversifying as the years passed, and dairy and cattle enterprises were becoming more important in the farm economy, especially in southern Minnesota.

From the early 1880s the tendency toward concentration in the flour-milling industry had become more and more pronounced. In 1889, however, the largest of the milling concerns was created when William D. Washburn (not to be confused with Cadwallader, whose interests were concentrated in the Washburn Crosby Company), Charles Pillsbury, and some English investors merged their various interests to create the Pillsbury-Washburn Flour Mills Company, Ltd. Aside from becoming one of the largest milling concerns in the world, the new corporation achieved additional fame by buying the two companies that controlled the waterpower of the Falls of St. Anthony, the Minneapolis Mill Company and the St. Anthony Water Power Company. The millers had long controlled the falls companies separately, but the combination of the two companies under central management made possible the development of the falls as a major hydroelectric power station. Electricity had been produced at the falls since 1882, but only a small amount of the falls' power was actually used for the generation of electricity. William de la Barre, who had been agent and engineer for the Minneapolis Mill Company from 1883, was made directing officer for both the falls companies by Pillsbury-Washburn, which kept the identity of the two companies intact because of long-term leases which both companies had let to power consumers. De la Barre had seen the potential for hydroelectric power development at the falls and he proceeded to develop it in the following years.

In 1908 the Pillsbury-Washburn Flour Mills Company, Ltd., suffered a major reversal when it became involved in a massive and disastrous grain speculation deal. Coupled with the financial crunch brought on by the Panic of 1907, the corporation found itself in receivership. In the aftermath of the debacle, the

newly formed Pillsbury Flour Mills Company leased all the mills of Pillsbury-Washburn, and the waterpower companies at the falls were kept under the management of Pillsbury-Washburn so that its income and the income from the leases could be used to pay off the corporation's debts. Eventually, in 1923, the waterpower companies were sold to Northern States Power Company for three million dollars, ending the association between the milling interests and the falls, which had begun when the army built the first mills at the falls in the 1820s.

While the flour-milling industry was becoming predominant in Minneapolis, other diverse industries also began to develop in the city. In the 1880s, for example, the production of jute and cotton flour bags began in the city. For the first few decades the city millers had packaged their product in wooden barrels that were fashioned by the large number of coopers who had come to Minneapolis. Differences arose, however, between the coopers and the millers over the price to be paid for the barrels, and in the face of union organization and strikes, the milling management sought an alternative and cheaper product. So it was that flour came to be shipped in bags instead of barrels. The refusal of the millers to bargain with the coopers set the tone of labor relations in Minneapolis, until violent upheavals in 1934 brought abrupt changes. It is ironic that the millers, whose major successes in the marketplace stemmed from their willingness to collude and act in unison, refused to afford the same rights of combination to their employees who wished to form unions. The pattern was set nonetheless, and Minneapolis was known as an employers' town, a "bastion of the open shop," for more than half a century.

Retail trade in Minneapolis also grew very rapidly at the end of the 19th century, serving both the growing population of the city, which reached 202,000 in 1900, and the surrounding hinterland. By 1900 the rural population of Minnesota exceeded 1.1 million, and Minneapolis wholesalers and retailers were competing to provide this population with the goods it required and desired.

Strikes initiated by coopers, or barrel makers, in the 1880s began the move to package flour products in paper and cloth. Vehement antiunionism marked early industrial and financial leadership in Minneapolis and remained in force until the 1930s. The switch to paper and cloth forced the coopers out of the marketplace but created a wealth of new jobs as the paper container and cloth container industries expanded beyond the needs of the flour industry. From the E.A. Bromley Collection. (MPLIC)

In the 1870s the state capital, St. Paul, had dominated the wholesale and retail trades in Minnesota. In 1878, for example, the wholesale trade in Minneapolis was only one third of that of St. Paul. By 1890 the volume of wholesaling in Minneapolis exceeded that of St. Paul, and by 1900 Minneapolis was doing almost twice as much wholesale business as its neighbor. In the retail area, large retail operations began to emerge in the 1880s, when William and L.S. Donaldson acquired Colton and Company in 1884 and when George D. Dayton acquired the Goodfellow and Eastman establishment in downtown Minneapolis. The Donaldsons' "Glass Block" on Nicollet Avenue was the most elegant store in Minneapolis during this period. Another important addition to Minneapolis retailing was the establishment of Young-Quinlan in 1894. Opened by Fred C. Young and Elizabeth C. Quinlan, the store was the first purveyor of ready-to-wear women's clothing in the city. Young-Quinlan was all the more remarkable a success, as the cofounders were both ex-clerks, and Quinlan, an Irish immigrant, steered the firm to success after the death of her partner during the first year of their operation. A multitude of other retail outlets in downtown Minneapolis opened throughout the period, and by 1900 the city was the major retail center in the state.

The late 19th century also saw the development of Minneapolis as a major insurance center. Because of the city's prominence in other aspects of finance, it was natural that insurance would also develop in the area. The large concentrations of industrial property and residences, to a lesser extent, also were important factors, especially because the industries were specialized and were located quite a distance from other insurance centers. The Northwestern National Life Insurance Company of Minneapolis was established in 1885, and several other large firms that specialized in wholesale trade coverage, farmers life insurance, and fire insurance soon followed.

Construction trades flourished in Minneapolis after 1880 as a result of massive construction in the city, residential and commercial as well as industrial. The construction of railroads throughout

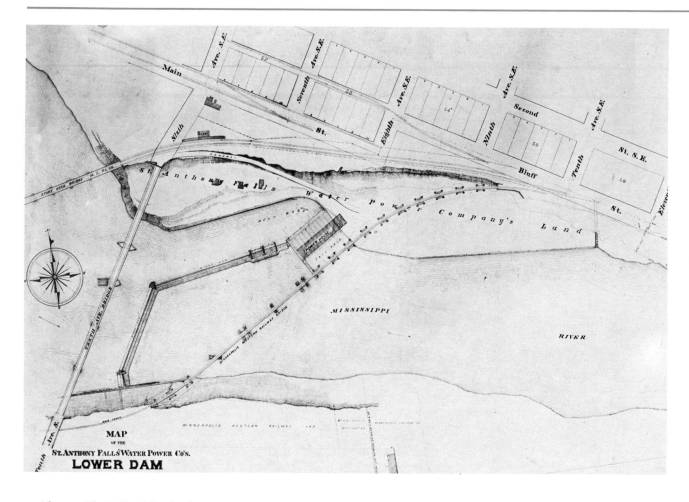

MAP
OF THE
ST. ANTHONY FALLS WATER POWER CO'S.
LOWER DAM

Above: *The Falls of St. Anthony provided waterpower for lumber and flour mills. After William de la Barre was appointed manager of the St. Anthony Falls Water Power Company in the 1880s, the falls also were turned into a source of hydroelectric power. Here is the complex that operated in the late 1890s. (MHS)*

Facing page, left: *The early*

Minneapolis business district resembled that of other cities with the possible exception that streets remained unpaved longer than elsewhere in the country. Barrels, shown here in great supply in 1888, were once a major Minneapolis product. Strained labor relations between barrel makers and buyers caused the use of the barrel as a flour container to be replaced by innovations in paper and cloth

packaging. Photo by F.L. Mortimer. From the Dewars Collection. (MPLIC)

Right: *Dayton's Department Store came to Nicollet Avenue in the 1880s and over the years became the largest single store on the street. Its original building is shown on the southwest corner of the intersection of 6th Street and Nicollet in the late 1890s. (MPLIC)*

Facing page: *Donaldson's Glass Block, shown here at night in 1931, was the first major department store established in Minneapolis on Nicollet Avenue. Opened for business in 1881, Donaldson's is still located on Nicollet Mall. From the Graphic Arts Studios Collection. (MPLIC)*

Following pages, left: *Workers lay wooden paving blocks on Third Avenue South between 22nd and 24th streets, circa 1905. Minneapolis streets remained unpaved for the first 40 years of the city's existence. When paving was finally instituted, a variety of materials was used including bricks and mortar material. The impressive structure in the right background is the William D. Washburn residence. (MPLIC)*

Right: *By the early 1900s most city streets were paved, and wide boulevards and well-trimmed parkways at the foot of Lowry Hill reflected replacement of horses and wagons by automobiles as primary means of transport. St. Mark's Episcopal Cathedral can be seen at left. Photo by C.J. Hibbard. (MPLIC)*

the state contributed to this boom, as did the building of the vast elevator system in the wheat-growing areas. Street paving and sidewalk construction also began in Minneapolis in 1880, as did the construction of the street railway system on a large scale. At the same time the development of the Minneapolis telephone system began. The first telephone link was established in the city in 1877.

In 1884 another new industry came on the scene when Albert Butz patented a device to control furnace dampers and thus regulate heating in homes, businesses, and factories. Butz put his device into production after founding the Consolidated Temperature Company. In 1899 Willard Sweatt acquired Butz's company and changed the name to the Electric Heat Regulator Company. In 1927 the company was in turn acquired by the Honeywell Heating Specialties firm. When Butz began producing his heat regulating devices in the 1880s, few dreamed or imagined that he was laying the foundation for the firm that would be Minneapolis' largest employer a century in the future.

As flour milling moved into its greatest period of activity, as the city's industrial base grew and diversified, as finance became a major facet of Minneapolis economic life, and as the city became a distribution center for the Upper Midwest, lumbering, which had played a prominent role in the city's early development, also reached its apex of expansion. The exploitation of the Minnesota forests reached its peak in the last years of the 19th century and the first years of the 20th. The output of the sawmills in Minneapolis grew phenomenally as a result of this intensive logging. In 1860 the Minneapolis mills turned out 18 million board feet of lumber, by 1865 the output had increased 62 million board feet and, incredibly, by 1870 the annual output reached 118 million board feet. The next 30 years saw even more fantastic expansion as the sawmills developed steam power to power their operations. By 1899 the Minneapolis sawmills were turning out 590 million board feet of lumber a year. In addition to developing the raw lumber, mills in Minneapolis and assorted factories turned the wood into construction lumber, doors and sashes, frames of various types, furniture,

shingles, laths, and a variety of other products.

The intensive exploitation of the Minnesota forests could not continue forever, however, because they were not limitless, and in the years after 1900 the lumber industry began a decline that was even more spectacular than its growth had been. The peak of sawmilling was reached in 1899 and by 1919, only 20 years later, all the sawmills in Minneapolis were closed and out of operation. The related factories producing the various wood products continued in operation but had to secure their lumber from other sources. This difficulty restricted their growth somewhat as other centers nearer the working forests gained advantage over them.

The decline of sawmilling was soon followed by the gradual decline of the Minneapolis flour-milling industry. Fortunately for Minneapolis, the decline was gradual and not precipitous as was the case with the lumbering industry. The lumbering industry employed a relatively small part of the city's work force even at its peak, and other industries were able to absorb the excess. The loss of the revenues and employment provided by the flour-milling concerns posed a much greater challenge to the Minneapolis economy. The downward trend in Minneapolis flour milling was caused by several factors.

The first factor was the development of other hard wheat-growing areas in the United States and Canada. After the technological innovations of the 1870s and 1880s and the resulting premiums placed upon Minneapolis flour in the world market, other wheat growers began to switch to hard wheat varieties from the soft varieties they had previously cultivated. Kansas, formerly a major producer of soft winter wheat, was the first major area to produce hard winter wheat in the lower Midwest. Technological improvements in the milling and preparation of the hard winter wheat, similar to those which had improved the marketability of Minnesota's hard spring wheat, soon made Kansas City a major milling center that was beginning to rival Minneapolis. A decline in the demand for various wheat products, which began to set in

Elizabeth Quinlan, right, chats with Frances Cranmer Greenman at the opening of the Minneapolis Symphony season in 1932. Elizabeth Quinlan cofounded Young-Quinlan, a retail store on Nicollet Avenue specializing in ready-made clothing for women that reflected the work styles of the late 19th century. From the Minneapolis Times. (MPLIC)

after 1900 in the United States, further reduced Minneapolis' competitive edge, as Kansas City was better located to reach the major markets at lower prices.

The development of the Canadian wheat-growing areas had a twofold effect upon Minneapolis' flour industry. First, the wheat the Canadians put on the market reduced prices generally, and secondly, the Canadians gained control of the export trade that Minneapolis once had dominated. The loss of the export trade resulted when Buffalo flour millers began large-scale "milling in bond," using Canadian wheat. The Canadian wheat would be shipped to Buffalo, imported into the United States, milled, and then exported out of the United States to a foreign destination. As a result of this development the Canadians were able to export their high-quality flour more cheaply than could the millers in Minneapolis.

The rise of Buffalo as a major milling center, however, did not catch the Minneapolis millers by surprise. In fact the Minneapolis millers controlled the rise of Buffalo and owned 85 percent of the milling capacity in Buffalo when that city's flour production actually surpassed that of Minneapolis. The Washburn Crosby firm had, in fact, established a major mill in Buffalo as early as 1903. The Minneapolis milling interests did not control the Kansas City milling industry to the same extent as they did in Buffalo, but they did own 25 percent of the mill capacity in that city. As the 20th century progressed the Minneapolis share of the market gradually declined as Buffalo and Kansas City rose to preeminence. Buffalo finally surpassed the Minneapolis output in 1929 and produced double the Minneapolis output by 1953. Kansas City never surpassed Minneapolis before 1950, but the Kansas City hinterland mills out-produced Minneapolis and its hinterland mills by 50 percent in 1930.

After 1900, then, both lumbering and flour milling began to decline in importance in the Minneapolis economy. Lumbering was in the process of disappearing, leaving a residue of woodcraft industries. Flour milling was declining at a slower rate, losing

Minneapolis Heat Regulator Company, located at Fourth Avenue South and 28th Street, began operation as a manufacturer of home thermostats. The firm, shown here circa 1930, manufactures thermostatic devices and has grown and diversified into the Honeywell Corporation, which designs and produces computerized heating and cooling systems. From the A.D. Roth Collection. (MPLIC)

production to competing centers in Buffalo and Kansas City. With flour milling, however, a subtle transformation was occurring: the large flour millers continued to maintain their headquarters in Minneapolis and were actually gaining control over their rivals. As time passed more and more flour mills in Minneapolis ceased to function as mills and were either dismantled entirely or left intact and put to different uses. The most famous mill to survive to the present from the golden era of Minneapolis milling is the Pillsbury A Mill, which has a very minute milling capacity presently. It is in its 100th year of existence and is used primarily as a warehouse and packaging center.

Thus while Minneapolis began to lose jobs in the mills, it began to acquire other jobs in management, financial administration, advertising, market research, product research and design, and other mid-level management and administrative positions. The effect was to upgrade the work force in Minneapolis and the surrounding region as the transformation was effected. The process of dismantling the Minneapolis mills was not totally achieved until the 1960s.

As the role of flour milling declined in Minneapolis, the milling interests headquartered there began to acquire operations elsewhere. The growth of Washburn Crosby Company into General Mills reflects this expansion. Washburn Crosby Company, with deep roots in Minneapolis' earliest history, and as the creator of Wheaties and Betty Crocker, was the keystone of the giant General Mills corporation formed in 1928. When General Mills was organized it included the holdings of Washburn Crosby in Minneapolis, Buffalo, and elsewhere, as well as the Royal Milling Company and Rocky Mountain Elevator Company of Great Falls, Montana; the Kalispell Flour Mill Company, also of Montana; the Red Star Milling Company of Wichita, Kansas; the El Reno Mill and Elevator Company of Oklahoma; the Kell Milling Company of Texas and Oklahoma; and the Sperry Flour Company. The process of concentration of holdings in the milling industry obviously continued well into the 20th century. Pillsbury enjoyed similar expansion and

International Milling, a less well-known Minneapolis firm, also expanded and later became International Multifoods.

The importance of Minneapolis as a financial center, meanwhile, received national recognition when the city was made the headquarters of the Ninth Federal Reserve District. The Federal Reserve System was created in 1913 by Congress to provide the nation with a central and independent monetary agency which could also provide the services of a national bank, something the United States had not had since the early 19th century. The federal system was to be decentralized, however, so that a measure of balance and autonomy in financial matters could be acquired by various regions throughout the country. The location of one of the new Federal Reserve's 12 district headquarters in Minneapolis reflected the fact that the city was the banking center of the region. The location of the Federal Reserve brought additional advantages to the city and attracted more financial intermediary institutions to the area.

As the 20th century progressed the economy of Minneapolis became more diversified. The Census of Manufacturers, taken by the U.S. government in 1929, indicated, for example, that while flour and grain-mill products were still the most valuable products in the city's economy, printing and publishing came second. The products crafted in the city's foundries and machine shops were the third most valuable items produced in the city, while railroad car construction and repair, the assembly of electrical machinery and related apparatus, furniture making, the processing of butter, and the preparation of spices and coffee all ranked in the top 10 most valuable activities, measured by the worth of output.

The development of electrical machinery was particularly rapid in the 1920s. Since Albert Butz had started making his heating regulators, other electrical enterprises had also begun operations in the city. In 1922 D.W. Onan began making electrical devices for use in the repair of automobile engines. In 1925 Onan's firm needed more shipping boxes in which to transport its products to markets, and the staff developed an engine-driven

Minneapolis was an established banking and financial center for the Upper Midwest when the Federal Reserve Banking System was created by Congress before World War I.

Consequently, Minneapolis was chosen as one of the district headquarters of the Federal Reserve System. The Ninth Federal Reserve District building in Minneapolis was

first located at 5th Street and Marquette Avenue in 1925, but has since been moved to a new facility on Nicollet Mall just off Washington Avenue. (MPLIC)

Ornate detail characteristic of the late 19th century decorates the First National Bank of Minneapolis. Brass spittoons reflect the widespread use of chewing tobacco during this period. (MPLIC)

Left: *Minneapolis grew as the financial, merchandising, and transportation center for a large agricultural area encompassing the entire Upper Midwest. As a result, Minneapolis became a major producer and distributor of farm-related goods and equipment. The Deere and Webber Company became a giant in the industry, and its headquarters, shown here in the late 1920s, was located at 800 Washington Avenue North. (MPLIC)*

Facing page: *Meter readers pose to exhibit the uniforms of the Minneapolis General Electric Company in August 1918. From the Records of the Women's Bureau.*

Minneapolis General Electric Co.
Meter Readers.

circular saw which could be used to build inexpensive crates. The saw also became one of the firm's products. In 1926, in response to the demand of farmers who lived beyond the reach of existing power lines, Onan developed a battery-less direct current generating plant which they could use to create their own electricity. As the radio became more and more popular, however, the firm had to develop a power source that generated alternating current. By 1929 Onan was marketing a small AC set known as the Ten-Lite, which could generate sufficient electricity to power 10 incandescent lights in the farmhouse and the barn and still power the AC radio in the farmer's living room. Onan survived the Great Depression, and during World War II the firm produced nearly half of all the electric plants used by the American military during the conflict. After the war the company continued to specialize in the manufacture of portable electric plants and standby electric plants for use during emergency power interruptions.

The experience of this firm reflected the general trend in Minneapolis industry after 1900. Businessmen in established endeavors and entrepreneurs with more resourcefulness than capital responded to changes in the economy and acted to meet new sources of demand created by the changing conditions. In the case of the Onan firm, for example, the general introduction of electricity as a new power source throughout the United States created a whole new market potential throughout the country, but the opportunity that presented itself to Onan stemmed from the peculiarities of the large agricultural expanse of the Dakotas, Montana, and Minnesota. Because these regions were sparsely populated, the construction of power lines in many rural areas was long delayed. At the same time the population of the area could afford the products that electricity could power, and these products were desired. Minneapolis was the wholesale and retail center of the region, and it was logical that entrepreneurs there would develop products that could satisfy the rural needs and turn a profit in the process.

The diversification of Minneapolis industry was greatly

With the completion of the Nine Foot Channel and a series of locks and dams up and down the Mississippi River in the post World War II period, Minneapolis became heavily involved in the barge traffic on the river, at least in the ice-free warmer months. Here a dredge is at work on the channel, across from the University of Minnesota River Flats area. (MPLIC)

aided not only by the investments in basic research by various firms tackling particular problems in the market but also by research carried out at the University of Minnesota. The university had grown slowly during the last half of the 19th century, emphasizing a liberal-arts curriculum as its core program. The first doctor of philosophy at the university, Charles Burke Elliott, received his Ph.D. in history in 1888. But while liberal arts continued to play a major role in the university's overall activities, they soon became overshadowed by the science and engineering programs, the latter concentrated in the Institute of Technology, and by the professional programs in law, medicine, and dentistry.

The regents of the university in the late 19th century always included representatives of the Minneapolis milling interests in their ranks, and their influence was instrumental in the development of applied research. When Pillsbury Hall was built on the campus in 1889, for example, at the behest of and with the funds of John S. Pillsbury, the only stipulation made was that the building be dedicated to scientific research. There was nothing conspiratorial or sinister in such activities, but the tackling of industrial research problems by the university greatly aided in the development of the economy of the entire state.

The university's role grew more and more important as the 20th century rolled along, for basic research and experimentation grew more complex and costly as time went by. It is not too strong a judgment to conclude that industry, agriculture, and mining in the state could not have progressed as they have without the beneficial activities of the faculty of the University of Minnesota.

The automotive age, arriving with the clatter of pistons and the chattering of valve lifters, also had a great impact on the economy of Minneapolis. As an established wholesale and retail center, the city leaped at the opportunities offered by the commercial truck and soon was flooded with them. Trucks were hauling agricultural produce to city markets as well as to processing centers. They hauled the products of the furniture factories to the outlets in the hinterland, as well as myriad other products that the rural

Above: *Professor E.W. Davis, the "Father of Taconite Mining," was a professor at the University of Minnesota's Institute of Technology for many decades. In the course of his research, Davis developed methods for refining the taconite reserves of northern Minnesota which were essential for the continuation of the Minnesota iron-mining industry after iron ores were exhausted in the 1950s. Davis' work created 20,000 jobs that will last well into the 21st century and hundreds of millions of dollars of potential revenue for the state's economy. (MPLIC)*

Right: *Burton Hall was constructed in 1906 and served as the main library at the University of Minnesota for many years, until library functions were taken over by Walther Library. In the background is Shevlin Hall, erected in 1895 and financed in part by the lumbering family of the same name. (MPLIC)*

Facing page: *Brewing was not a major industry in the grain center of Minneapolis. Shown here in 1941, the Grain Belt Brewery, constructed in 1891 and located in northeast Minneapolis next to the Mississippi River, was one of the few breweries built and operated in the city. From the Minneapolis Star and Tribune Company. (MPLIC)*

Above: *Thomas Lowry, who made a fortune in the urban transit system industry in Minneapolis and St. Paul, resided in this estate on the edge of Lowry Hill. Lowry Hill was formerly known as the Devil's Backbone. From the E.A. Bromley Collection. (MPLIC)*

Facing page: *Thomas Lowry made his fortune through the development of the streetcar system in Minneapolis and, later, in St. Paul as well. (MPLIC)*

population sought to acquire. They hauled coal around the city to residences, factories, and power stations. By the early 1930s there were more than 5,000 commercial trucks registered in Minneapolis. As the truck thus superseded the horse as a source of motive power, the automobile reworked the transportation patterns of the city in a way that is familiar to all American cities.

The streetcar, electrified after 1889, had been the primary source of rapid transit in the city until the 1920s, when the mass-produced automobile began to find its market. In 1920 Minneapolis streetcars carried 140 million passengers, the peak in the system's operations from its beginning in 1875 to its demise in the mid-1950s. After 1920 the number of streetcar passengers rapidly declined as the automobile became more accessible and convenient for growing numbers of citizens. Before being undone by the car, however, the streetcar system made substantial fortunes for its investors. The company went into decline and in the early 1950s the decision was made to switch to buses. Eventually the transformed system became a publicly subsidized government transportation agency.

The Great Depression came upon Minneapolis in the aftermath of the stock market collapse as it did upon other American cities. Minneapolis weathered the storm remarkably well, however, when viewed in light of the experience of other industrial cities. The major financial institutions in the city survived the trauma, as did the major industrial enterprises. Unemployment levels in Minneapolis reached record highs in the early 1930s, but recovery was more sustained in the city after that than was true of many other parts of the country. Unemployment continued to be a major problem until World War II, but after 1933 the employment level inched slowly upward and did not suffer violent reversals as a result of the recessions of 1937 and 1940.

The most important change to occur in the city during the Depression was the rise of organized labor as a major force in the economy as well as in politics and social life. This development reversed 80 years of labor relations that had been dominated en-

tirely by the city's employers. Although many, perhaps the majority, of the city's business leaders thought the recognition of unions would lead to the "Bolshevization" of the city government and the total destruction of the city's economy, they were ultimately induced by the force of federal as well as state intervention to allow workers to organize unions where they wished and to bargain collectively over their conditions of work and remuneration. The dire consequences of this development, predicted by some business observers, did not materialize, and a new era in relatively benevolent industrial relations between management and labor has existed since.

With World War II, prosperity finally returned to Minneapolis as the industries geared up for full production and as thousands of workers were drawn into the military services. Unemployment was ended rapidly and the only problem many workers had was how to spend their money in a period of rationing. Women entered the work force in manufacturing and other areas in Minneapolis during the war because of the manpower shortage caused by military service, and most families saved a large amount of their income for postwar purchases of homes, autos, and other consumer goods that were not to be had during the war.

Minneapolis industry, both large and small firms in all areas, rose to meet the demands of the war effort as one. General Mills and Pillsbury developed special food products for use by the armed forces and stepped up production to feed liberated populations as well as the troops themselves. North Star Woolen Mills and Munsingwear filled contracts for uniform items, blankets, and underclothing for the millions under arms. Crown Iron Works developed portable bridges and pontoon platforms for use in the Pacific and European theaters of war. Honeywell developed flight systems for army aircraft as well as some new types of bombs, while the Onan Corporation developed most of the radio and electrical power plants used by all the armed services. A thousand smaller firms filled lesser contracts for items as small as paper clips to ones as large as fabricated metal structures, while others did

Rigorous winters required that Minneapolis develop innovative solutions to basic problems such as heating. One such innovation was the development of central heating systems for clusters of large buildings. The University of Minnesota, for example, has a history of providing central heating for its many campus structures, and one of ten boilers in the university's central heating plant is shown here in 1938. Many large cities, including St. Paul, Minnesota, have considered applying the central heating concept to their entire central business districts. (MPLIC)

The Lyndale and Minnetonka Motor Line was a response to geographical growth and dispersion in the Minneapolis area. Reinstitution of the system, abandoned for many decades, has been discussed in the late 20th century. From the E.A. Bromley Collection. (MPLIC)

specialized contract work, performing tasks for the larger firms that smaller firms could perform more efficiently and more cheaply. After World War II this trend continued to develop in new industries as well as in old.

World War II reflected the underlying potential of the Minneapolis economy for rapid change and the development of new, technologically-oriented products. The University of Minnesota, with its Institute of Technology and Medical Sciences departments, served as a basic source of exploration in pure research, exploration that was necessary for technological advance. Only government-sponsored activities could provide the resources necessary to achieve initial massive breakthroughs in the new areas that were developing. Thus the first contract for a computer manufactured in the area was issued by the Bureau of the Census. Additional demands were made by the Department of Defense for complex new aerospace systems and various components for missile systems. Spurred by this initial demand, technological breakthroughs were achieved that made the electronics revolution possible.

While several larger firms in Minneapolis dominated the production of the computers themselves, hundreds of smaller firms produced peripheral devices and specialized software services. Once the computers were designed entrepreneurs developed thousands of different, specialized applications that generated a whole new set of marketable goods and services. The small business in the computer-related industry was the one that carved a niche and then managed to change as the basic trends in the industry as a whole shifted. The shifts could be very rapid, requiring large and small businesses to maintain up-to-date skills and well-trained, innovative managerial personnel in order to survive. The development of word-processing systems, computers specially designed to deal with clerical and accounting demands in offices, and computerized medical devices and equipment were important subareas that developed rapidly out of the computer environment. The shift from relatively simple furnace-control devices to complex

environmental control systems was another. By the late 1970s computers and related products and services accounted for some three and a half billion dollars of Minneapolis-St. Paul's annual production.

While manufacturing in high-technology areas became an important part of the post-World War II Minneapolis economy, two other areas became of marked importance also. Wholesale and retail trade grew rapidly as the general volume of consumption increased along with people's incomes. The restaurant business, for example, skyrocketed as people's life-styles were revolutionized by changed habits of work and recreation. Service-area jobs, a relatively unimportant area before the Depression, also exploded in the postwar period. Between 1960 and 1980, employment in Minneapolis in the service sector trebled. This jump, reflecting a trend that was occurring nationally as well, is even more remarkable when one considers that it does not take into account a similar jump in the growth of finance, insurance, and real estate in the city during the same period of time. The general thrust of these figures indicates that small business, as measured by numbers of employees, experienced a real boom in the years after the war. This contention is borne out by the fact that 5,000 of the estimated 9,000 firms in Minneapolis in 1977 had 10 employees or less. By their very nature services and financial activities can generate large numbers of firms with relatively small staffs and relatively high outputs. The generally low level of capital investment required for such businesses, which are normally dependent upon human capital represented by professional skills and specialized knowledge, explains how education, formal and informal, has come to play a more central role than ever before in the Minneapolis economy.

Another interesting aspect of Minneapolis' economic growth in the 1960s and 1970s has been the maintenance of downtown as a major retail center in the growing metropolitan area. This is all the more remarkable in light of the Dayton Hudson Corporation's lead in developing the enclosed suburban shopping mall. Southdale, the first enclosed suburban shopping mall in

Above: *Wilbur Foshay was a successful securities broker and Minneapolis businessman until the stock market crash of 1929 wiped out his assets and those of his investors. Angry investors demanded an investigation of Foshay's business practices, and Foshay was indicted, tried, and convicted for various violations. Although he was sent to prison, the builder of the Foshay Tower was eventually pardoned by President Franklin D. Roosevelt. (MPLIC)*

Facing page: *After Wilbur Foshay's securities empire collapsed in the early days of the Great Depression, his assets, including the Foshay Tower, were auctioned off in order to partially satisfy his creditors. The auction was effected in the foyer of Minneapolis City Hall, with the statue of the Father of Waters looking on impassively. (MHS)*

Facing page: *Deflation brought hard times to Minneapolis during the Great Depression and affected banks as well as individuals. Located at 115 South 4th Street, the Farmers and Mechanics Savings Bank, the only mutual savings bank in the state, managed to survive the bleak times. In March 1982 Marquette National Bank acquired F & M Savings. Photo by Lee Brothers. (MHS)*

the United States, was built by Dayton's, later to become Dayton Hudson in the mid-1950s. Soon a ring of similar "dales" and other malls were in place around both Minneapolis and St. Paul, seemingly threatening the continued vitality of the retail operations in the central business district. The downtown Minneapolis retail area, however, held on to the premier position it had enjoyed since the 1880s, as the Nicollet Mall concept was implemented and the large retailers upgraded their facilities and dug in for the long haul. The retail census of 1977 reflected the success of their efforts, as it indicated that Minneapolis downtown retailers still sold 15% of all retail goods sold during the year—the largest single share of any retail cluster in the 10-county area surveyed.

As Minneapolis proceeds through the last quarter of the 20th century, then, its economy is based firmly upon several independent sectors. Agribusiness products and services continue to be major sources of jobs, while high-technology goods and services provide even more employment and the greatest single percentage of Minneapolis output as measured in dollars. Printing and publishing is another major area of activity in Minneapolis and involves not only newspaper and magazine endeavors but also massive production for the retail and wholesale trades to satisfy their print needs, as well as myriad other demands made by the manufacturing, financial, and transportation sectors. Financial, insurance, and real estate services are another major sector of the economy that has increased the importance of Minneapolis as a financial center. First Bank Minneapolis and the Northwestern Bank of Minneapolis have grown as the demands for banking services have grown in the postwar years, while savings and loan institutions have also provided major services in the area of housing finance. Home-grown investment firms such as Piper Jaffray & Hopwood and Dain Bosworth, Inc., along with Investors Diversified Services and large numbers of smaller firms, round out this picture. Transportation, communications, and utilities also are major elements of the Minneapolis economy, as direct links with Europe have been established by Northwest Airlines and Republic Airlines has emerged as

a national air carrier, while the communications and utilities sectors have increased their productivity over the past 20 years.

As a result of this configuration, Minneapolis is in an excellent position to enter the changing economic arena and maintain its leadership in promoting innovation and change. The absence of a major heavy-industry base in Minneapolis and the metropolitan region means that the city can make rapid shifts without losing massive capital investment locked into areas that cannot easily be transformed into other types of economic activity. The small scale of business endeavor in Minneapolis, with thousands of firms producing various goods and services around a nucleus of 200 or so very large firms, and the concentrations in trade, services, and financial activities both suggest that large numbers of entrepreneurs could easily make the transition to the wholly new areas of enterprise that may present themselves as technology continues to revolutionize the world at a pace that is growing ever more rapid. Diversity, scale, and entrepreneurial innovation have made Minneapolis successful in economic endeavor in the past and seem to ensure success in the future.

•   •   •

Above: *Bridgeman Ice Cream and Fountain Shops have been a feature of Minneapolis for more than half a century. The shop at 621 Hennepin Avenue, shown here in December 1937, was the first opened in the chain. (MPLIC)*

Top: *Nicollet Avenue, "Fifth Avenue of the West," shown in 1926, was kept free of streetcars for shoppers' convenience and safety. Nicollet Mall is now off limits to automobile traffic. Photo by C.J. Hibbard. (MPLIC)*

In 1847 millwright Ard Godfrey moved to Minneapolis from Maine to build a sawmill at the Falls of St. Anthony, and in 1848 he built a Greek Revival house that became a meeting place for residents of the new settlement and their guests. The Ard Godfrey House, located at 28 University Avenue Southeast, is now owned by the Minneapolis Park Board and has been restored under the administration of the Women's Club of Minneapolis. Visitors to the historic site tour rooms filled with authentic items from the Godfrey family, such as the Chickering piano, which has a six-octave keyboard and is made of rosewood. The instrument, purchased by Ard's brother-in-law Hiram Emery and shipped from Boston, was played both by Ard and by his daughter Helen. Helen's dolls are displayed in her room. Passing through the rooms, one can sense the time in which the Godfrey family inhabited the house . . . clothes hang on pegs (because actual closets were taxed as rooms) and an 1852 Farmers' Almanac hangs in the kitchen. The Ard Godfrey House stands as a symbol of Minneapolitans' proud sense of their past. Photographs courtesy of the Women's Club of Minneapolis/Ard Godfrey Project.

CHAPTER III
POLITICS IN THE CITY OF LAKES
· · ·

Above: *Activists in the women's suffrage movement organized a white elephant sale in 1915 to raise funds for political activity. Suffrage came to Minnesota with the passage of the Constitutional amendment in 1920, but some state laws restricting the rights of women had been rescinded prior to that time. (MHS)*

Facing page: *Charles Hoag, a teacher, suggested that the new settlement on the West Bank of the Mississippi River be called "Minnehapolis." Courtesy, Hennepin County Historical Society.*

P olitics, simply defined, is a process through which decisions are made. In American history decision-making has not occurred in a vacuum, and the history of politics in Minneapolis follows the trend of the national experience. National and state issues, the status of the economy and its prospects, the goals and aspirations of a population divided occasionally by ethnic and religious differences, and the charisma and energy of individuals are various forces which have shaped and often intruded upon the city's political activities.

The central observation that one can make about the history of Minneapolis politics, and American national politics generally, is that change over time has been the rule and not the exception. Change has occurred in the structure of the political process as well as in the population and environment which were involved in it and were shaped by it. The increase in the number of people who have access to the political system has been a hallmark of the change of the political structure. The franchise, once the exclusive reserve of propertied white males, has been extended over the years to include women and minorities. The use of the ballot has also shifted over time, changing from a statement of personal preference or narrow group interests to allegiance to a political philosophy competing with others in the form of political parties to shape the city's destiny. The rise of diverse political parties has been an important part of that process in Minneapolis and Minnesota. Third parties in Minneapolis and Minnesota, as well as fourth and fifth parties, have been the order of the historical day, unlike the national experience. The very nature of the voting process has also changed. The Australian ballot, or secret ballot as it is better known contemporarily, is an innovation which was introduced only in the last years of the 19th century. The channels of political power have also changed. Minneapolis, for half of its history, was the object of direct intervention by the state legislature and only achieved its independence in 1920. It is this complex of technical issues and substantive ones, then, that have characterized the political history of the city.

Political decision-making that affected Minneapolis predated the actual establishment of the city and was undertaken at the highest levels of the federal government. The nature of the activity was actually to open the area that was to become Minneapolis to settlement. The opening of the East Bank area, which became the core of Old St. Anthony and later Northeast and Southeast Minneapolis, was a relatively easy affair, and the establishment of claims there followed the pattern of the frontier generally. The settlement of the West Bank, today North and South Minneapolis, proved to be much more complicated, however. The essential problem was that the area was a part of the Fort Snelling Military Reservation and settlement on military areas was prohibited. The economic potential of the area along the Falls of St. Anthony was early established when the army had built the grist mills and sawmills in the 1820s. In a frontier region tied to rivers as sources of transport and with energy sources few and far between, the falls were a plum that attracted the interest of powerful political interests.

Franklin Steele and his associate John H. Stevens first broached the military reserve when Stevens established the ferry service above the falls for the military. It was Illinois Congressman Robert Smith who made the dramatic coup with the War Department when he obtained the lease to the military mills on the West Bank and in 1853 purchased them outright. The premise of Smith's lease was that he intended to settle in Minnesota and live at the mill site. After obtaining the mill lease, Smith went to lengths in his correspondence to indicate that he was actually maintaining a residence at the site. The result of Smith's subterfuge was that the East Bank was opened to surreptitious settlement, and the falls' power on that bank passed into the hands of Smith and Cadwallader Washburn, one of the major forces in the flour-milling industry that soon became established.

The presence of the Stevens and Smith claims on the East Bank opened the area to illegal settlement because it quickened rumors that the military was soon going to withdraw the area from

military control and make it available to settlement. Settlers, anxious to be in place when that occurred, began crossing the river and establishing themselves on claims they hoped to legalize in the future. The withdrawal of the military and the reduction of the size of the Fort Snelling reservation, however, did not materialize as rapidly as the squatters had hoped. The army, therefore, began forcibly moving the over-eager pioneers from the reservation. Eventually, however, the military relented and the squatters were either given permits or ignored.

The problem was that until the settlers could register their claims legally, the claims were not valid. To protect their shaky title, they formed claim protection associations that guaranteed that the members would respect each other's claims and would assist each other in protecting their claims against interlopers. The Equal Right and Impartial Protection Claim Association was the first of several claim associations founded on the West Bank and marked the beginning of city government in the area. John H. Stevens' home, the first private residence built on the West Bank, served as the meeting-place for the larger claim associations and also functioned as a hotel, church, theater, bank, and land office.

On the East Bank, meanwhile, the city of St. Anthony had been formally organized in 1849. Originally, on the plats, the town had been designated as St. Anthony Falls, but the name was presently shortened. St. Anthony was not incorporated as a city, however, until 1855, and the first city elections were held that year, with Henry T. Welles becoming the first mayor. Six aldermen were also elected that year, and among them were Caleb D. Dorr, later the boom master of the Mississippi and Rum River Boom Company, and Daniel Stanchfield, an associate of Franklin Steele who had performed timber surveys on the Rum River in order to attract Eastern capital for Steele's logging and sawmill operations.

Political activity had begun even before the city elections were held, as the majority of the settlers were from New England and were quite aware of national political issues and quite opinionated about them. Abolitionism was widespread among the transplanted New Englanders, as well as was a distrust of the Democratic party and a hostile attitude toward the slaveholding South. Such political views were of more than passing importance in the 1850s, when national debates were raging concerning the extension of slavery to the territories, of which Minnesota was one until 1858. Northern pioneers were dedicated to the principle of yeoman farmers settling the western lands and looked with horror at the possibility of slave labor being introduced with plantation systems to compete with the settlers for land.

On July 4, 1854, an antislavery convention was held at the Congregational Church in St. Anthony and was organized and led by John North, Reverend Charles Secombe, and Reverend C.G. Ames. The convention narrowly missed becoming the founding convention of the Republican party, for though the organizers had considered establishing a new political party, they decided, finally, to defer that action until the following year. Meanwhile, on July 6, a similar meeting held in Jackson, Michigan, and another subsequent meeting in Ripon, Wisconsin, did lead to the formal creation of the new Republican party.

The new party combined two basic themes to make itself immediately attractive to the settlers in Minnesota. First, its antislavery stand welded sentiments of "free soil, free labor, and free men" among the New Englanders and others. Also, the party preached temperance in personal behavior, including abstinence from liquor, and this made the party attractive also to Scandinavian immigrants, who were beginning to come into the farming areas in significant numbers. Temperance became an early issue in St. Anthony also, and in 1852 a city newspaper reported proudly, "There is not a gambling institution, or a drinking saloon, or a whiskey grocery, or a grog shop in town. We have no room for those who frequent such places." Unfortunately for the strong temperance people, business interests overcame strict adherence to moral rigidity, and in 1855 a liquor licensing system was established, primarily to regulate establishments catering to lumberjacks who

A fire company races down Cedar Avenue in response to an alarm in 1907, with Holtzermann's Store in the background, a landmark building in the Cedar-Riverside area. Fire was a major threat in Minneapolis, and the city fire department grew over the years, constantly improving its equipment. (MPLIC)

began to frequent the town in their free time.

Republicanism also caught hold in Minneapolis, and feeling for it was greatly enhanced by difficulties surrounding the land-ownership issue. In 1852 the reduction of the Fort Snelling reservation was ordered by President Millard Fillmore, but the registration of claims was not accomplished until 1855. Hennepin County was formed in the interval in 1852, as was a Temperance Society in Minneapolis in 1854 to insure that no "drunkard makers" be allowed to prosper in the environs of the village. By 1856, with the land claims finally settled to the relief and satisfaction of the squatters, the town of Minneapolis was authorized by the state legislature. Formal government was slow in development, however, and it was not until 1858 that a town council was organized. Interestingly, the first president of the Minneapolis town council, Henry T. Welles, had the unique qualification of having also served as the first mayor of the city of St. Anthony. The four other members of the council, or board of trustees, included Charles Hoag, who had suggested the name "Minnehapolis" for the new town a few years before.

In the early years the city governments of the two towns functioned in very limited capacities. Streets remained unpaved, central water systems were a thing of the future (as were most public services to which the inhabitants of cities are accustomed today), and the city offices functioned primarily as a title and deeds service. Rudimentary law enforcement was initiated early, but both St. Anthony and Minneapolis met their needs with a small number of marshals, who supplemented their incomes with other employment. Volunteer fire brigades provided protection against conflagration, and the Cataract Engine Company No. 1, the Independent Hook and Ladder Company of St. Anthony, the Minnehaha Hook and Ladder Company, and the Germania Engine Company had all been established by 1860.

The Civil War was accepted as something of a crusade by the citizens of St. Anthony and Minneapolis as it was by the rest of the citizens of the state, Minnesota having been admitted to the Union in 1858. Minnesota provided thousands of volunteers for the Union armies, and Minnesota regiments saw action in the bloodiest battles. Minnesotans performed crucial service at a critical point in the battle of Gettysburg in 1863, as they did in the siege of Vicksburg in the same year and in several other battles in the major campaigns that ended the short-lived Confederacy. Minneapolis and St. Anthony together provided some 1,400 volunteers to the Union army, even though their combined population was less than 8,000 during the war.

The citizens of Minnesota had voted for the Republicans and Abraham Lincoln by almost a two-to-one margin in 1860, and they helped reelect him in the wartime election of 1864. These two elections established the Republican party as the party that Minnesotans preferred to control the national destiny. From 1860 until 1932, in fact, Minnesotans voted for the Republican presidential candidates in numbers sufficient to give their electoral votes in all but one election. The exception was the election of 1912, when Theodore Roosevelt ran as a third-party candidate and, as a Progressive candidate, received more votes than did the Republican candidate, William H. Taft. State elections were also very much controlled by the Republicans in the same period, although frequent challenges to Republican hegemony often arose. Politics in St. Anthony and Minneapolis were also controlled by Republicans, but things were a bit more fluid at the city level, where partisan issues often became more important than party ideologies.

In the aftermath of the Civil War, the citizens of the town of Minneapolis successfully sought to upgrade the settlement to the status of city, and a charter was issued by the state legislature in 1867. The charter provided for offices of mayor, treasurer, comptroller, two justices of the peace, and twelve aldermen, three to be selected from each of the city's four wards. The office of mayor was primarily administrative, with the main powers of the office being the veto and the ability to appoint the chief of police. A police force was established in the same year, and provision was made for six regular patrolmen. In 1872 the number was extended to 10, and, for the first time, police officers were not allowed to hold other part-time or full-time jobs. Dorilus Morrison, a co-founder with Robert Smith of the Minneapolis Mill Company and an agent for some of Cadwallader Washburn's interests in the area, was elected first mayor of the city of Minneapolis.

In the course of the 1860s, the population and industry of West Bank Minneapolis approached and then surpassed that of East Bank St. Anthony. In 1865 Minneapolis had a population of 4,000, while St. Anthony had 3,500 inhabitants. By 1870, when St. Anthony had 5,013 citizens, Minneapolis had mushroomed to more than 13,000. As a result of this change in fortune, many of the civic leaders of St. Anthony desired the merger of the city with Minneapolis. The campaign for merger lasted several years and included a couple of reverses, but finally in February 1872 the state legislature passed a bill that consolidated the two cities into one. The first election was held soon after the consolidation was accomplished, and Eugene M. Wilson became the first mayor of the combined cities. The number of aldermen, of course, increased as the size of the city increased, and a peak was reached in the size of the city council in 1887, when there were 39 councilmen. The number of aldermen was cut back over the years, and by the mid-1950s there were only 13 aldermen.

As the city of Minneapolis was slowly maturing and beginning to grow to a significant size in the 1860s and 1870s, the hinterland of the city was being rippled by the first waves of agrarian discontent with the agricultural economic system that was being established. The first organized thrust of protest was the Grange movement. The National Grange of the Patrons of Industry—"grange" in old usage meaning a granary or barn—was established in the nation's capital in December 1867. One of the founders of the new movement was Oliver Hudson Kelley, a farmer who had lived and worked in Minnesota from 1849.

The Grange movement was directed at farmers and the grievances they felt, but it was not created as a political action organization. Local Granges brought farmers together to discuss

Ignatius Donnelly failed in his efforts to become a real estate magnate, but went on to a great career as a novelist and politician. A champion of workers and farmers, Donnelly was a bitter foe of William D. Washburn, the leading spokesperson for Minneapolis milling interests in the United States Senate. Donnelly was considered a crank by many, but some of his outlandish theories, such as linking the demise of the dinosaurs to comets, have taken on new life in recent scientific studies. (MPLIC)

their common problems and to seek common solutions to them. Political activity was an outgrowth of the Grange movement. The first Grange in Minnesota was created in February 1869, and the movement spread quickly. The timing was significant, for it was at this time that farmers in Minnesota and elsewhere were recognizing the grievances they felt toward railroads concerning the rates they had to pay to get their crops to market. The Granges helped the farmers articulate their protests, and in response to the agrarian outcry, the Minnesota legislature passed a law which established pricing guidelines and rate limits for the railroads operating in the state. The legislation led to long legal battles, as the railroads claimed they had been denied legal due process guaranteed to them by recent amendments to the federal constitution. For all parties involved—the farmers, the large business interests, and the state government—the attempt at regulation was but one stage in a continuing struggle.

In the late 1860s another episode occurred which was to affect politics in Minneapolis and Minnesota greatly through the rest of the 19th century. Ignatius Donnelly, a politician, writer, and entrepreneur, had migrated to Minnesota in 1856 at the age of 24. He involved himself in Republican politics, and in 1859 he was elected lieutenant governor and then reelected to the position for another term. In 1862 Donnelly was elected to Congress in the district in which Minneapolis was located and served several terms. In 1868, however, Donnelly came into conflict with Elihu Washburn, a congressman from Illinois.

Elihu was the brother of William D. Washburn and Cadwallader Washburn, the two important figures in the Minneapolis milling industry. The Washburns had spread out over the Midwest in the 1840s and 1850s and had carved economic and political niches for themselves in the various places they had chosen to settle. William in Minnesota, Cadwallader in Wisconsin, Elihu in Illinois, and others elsewhere. The conflict between Elihu Washburn and Donnelly, however, cost Donnelly his seat in Congress, as Washburn allies in Minnesota maneuvered support away from

Donnelly to another Republican candidate. As a result the Democrats gathered enough votes to win the election, and so Eugene M. Wilson, later to become the first mayor of Minneapolis after its consolidation with St. Anthony, took Donnelly's seat in Congress.

As a result of his experiences, Donnelly became somewhat embittered against the wealthy millers of Minneapolis and all privileged groups and carried on a unique vendetta against them. His vendetta was unusual because he attacked the new capitalists in literature as well as in political activities. Donnelly developed his social commentary in such books as *Caesar's Column*, which described the future destruction of civilization caused by banking interests, and *The Golden Bottle*, another assault on the evil of monopoly. Donnelly also gained fame as a writer of nonfiction for his books *Atlantis*, an exploration of the lost continent and its fabled history; *Ragnarok*, which claimed that the work attributed to glaciers was actually accomplished by comets; and *The Great Cryptogram*, which attributed authorship of William Shakespeare's plays to Francis Bacon. Regardless of his motivations or his methods, Donnelly managed to become the single most articulate voice of agrarian protest in the 19th century.

The relationship between the rural politics of protest and Minneapolis was a direct one. The farmers became dissatisfied with the railroads, the rural elevator system, the flour millers, the grain exchange, and the banks—especially the banks. In Minnesota and the rest of the Upper Midwest, Minneapolis was the center of all of this protest. The city, its business leaders, and most of its politicians were looked upon with great distrust by rural folk who had day-to-day experience in dealing with railroad agents, elevator operators, graders from the grain exchange, and banking officials.

The Republican party, however, played a major role in maintaining the political status quo in the face of such resentments. The party accomplished this in several ways, but at its root was its historic success at saving the Union during the crisis of secession and Civil War. The party of Lincoln had saved the nation for

After the Civil War, Union Army veterans formed an organization called the Grand Army of the Republic. The organization held several conventions, or "encampments," in Minneapolis over the years, and this arch, on Nicollet Avenue near its intersection with Washington Avenue, was constructed for their parade. From the E.A. Bromley Collection. (MPLIC)

particular goals, of course, and these goals, while never precisely defined in particular programs, were generally understood as being contained in the phrase "free soil, free labor, free men." The essence of the program was free economic competition for all Americans through market processes. The Republican party held that such unfettered pursuit of self-interest by individuals would lead to material prosperity and political democracy. As the economy and society became more complicated after the Civil War, however, the promise of free competition began to erode. The reasons for the erosion were many, but foremost among them was the fact that market competition led to the consolidation of economic power as some competed more successfully than others. The Republican party attempted to mollify people, like the farmers, who became increasingly disturbed by the imbalances within the economy. The sacrifices of the Civil War again came into play in this effort as Republican candidates "waved the bloody shirt." At each election they reminded the voters of the war and the GOP's role in the war, and charged that victory by the Democrats or some other party would undo the sacrifices made in that conflict. In Minnesota such appeals took on an even more strident tone because of the large immigrant population in the state, both rural and urban. Loyalty to the Republican party was often equated with loyalty to the nation by candidates seeking to win immigrant votes. And for many immigrants Civil War military service had been their first service to their adopted land, marking a crucial stage in their process of Americanization. The Civil War was thus made hallowed for different reasons and in different ways by various segments of the population.

The realities of the economic changes that swept over America in the post-Civil War period, however, began slowly but surely to erode the Republican vision for large segments of the population. Deflation, the process by which the purchasing power of money increases as the money supply decreases in size (a process unfamiliar to several recent generations of Americans), affected farmers adversely. The farmers, normally large debtors, were in the position of having borrowed during a period of inflation, when dollars were worth less, and of paying back when the dollars were worth more and were harder to come by. The financial squeeze was made more difficult by the activities of railroads that shipped the farmers' crops to market. Poorly managed and in many cases poorly planned, the railroads often developed discriminatory rate systems in their desperate efforts to meet their indebtedness and turn a profit.

The development of the elevator system of storing and grading wheat was another source of complaint for farmers. The grading of wheat had been instituted by grain exchanges in Chicago, Milwaukee, and later Minneapolis in order to reflect the real differences in the quality of grain that the farmers brought to market. The system, however, had the potential for abuse, as the graders had a vested interest in lowering the grade of the wheat and the sellers had a vested interest in seeing the grain accepted at a higher grade. The process of grading, however, was controlled by the buyers, and their lack of impartiality made the system suspect. These grievances, taken together, made the farmers suspicious of the city and the banks, railroads, and milling companies that made their headquarters in it.

The overall picture was further complicated by the rise of the organized labor movement in the United States after the Civil War. Fumbling at first and marked by halted efforts in one trade and then another, the efforts of labor to organize were viewed with disdain by proponents of the Republican view of individual economic action. The first unions in Minneapolis were organized even before the Civil War, when typographers and printers organized a union local in the city. In the post-Civil War period, the barrel makers, or coopers, attempted to cooperate in an unsuccessful strike effort in 1868. Labor, too, was affected by the changing economic conditions, which, with deflation, saw wages drop. Although prices also fell in the deflationary spiral, workers felt that they should at least maintain their wages through the period of change.

The growth of the Minneapolis work force was spectacular

Facing page: One of the first unions organized in Minneapolis was the National Typographical Union local in 1859. Labor strife has a long history in the city from the streetcar workers' and coopers' strikes of the 1880s to the Industrial Workers of the World strikes and activities during the early 20th century. Minneapolis was known as an open shop town until the violent upheavals of the 1930s marked a major turning point in labor organization. From the E.A. Bromley Collection. (MPLIC)

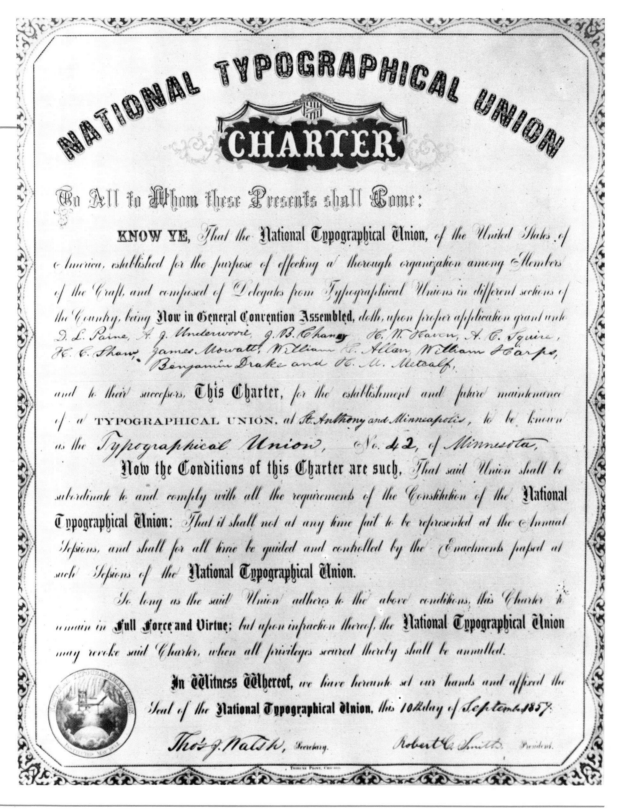

during this period. In 1850 there had been 63 manufacturing employees enumerated in the census of that year. By 1880 the number had increased to over 10,000 in Minneapolis and to more than 20,000 statewide. By 1890 there were approximately 80,000 industrial workers in Minnesota, of whom almost two thirds were concentrated in Minneapolis. This growth of the work force led to the development of labor as a major political force in the state, although the process was slow and, in Minneapolis, marked by the bitterest opposition.

The "Brass Kettle" Campaign of 1878 reflected the divisions that were beginning to wrack Minneapolis politics and state politics as well. In that campaign, Ignatius Donnelly ran for Congress against William D. Washburn. Since his defeat and imbroglio with Elihu Washburn in 1868, Donnelly had established himself as a spokesman for aggrieved farmers and workers. He had gone on lecture tours to the Grange locals around the state and made other speaking appearances in the large cities, including Minneapolis. What contributed to the vehemence of the 1878 campaign, however, was the formation two years earlier of the Minneapolis Millers' Association. This monopolistic buying pool for the Minneapolis millers, organized and operating publicly, had further upset the beleaguered farmers. The farmers and others angered by the action of the millers met in 1876 in Owatonna, Minnesota, to form the Anti-Monopoly party. The Anti-Monopolists joined the National Greenback party afterward, and the state Greenback party held a convention in Minneapolis in September 1878 and nominated Ignatius Donnelly to run for Congress against Washburn, the representative of the Minneapolis millers.

The National Greenback party represented those interests in the nation which desired an increase in the national money supply—a planned policy of inflation—through the federal government's issue of "greenback" notes as it had done during the Civil War. As a result of the National Banking Act of 1864, nationally chartered banks—that is, banks subject to federal rather than state

Facing page, top: *Ignatius Donnelly, an owner and editor of* The Emigrant Aid Journal, *was a rabid entrepreneur before he became a political firebrand and populist politician. His earliest venture was the attempt to raise his town of Nininger to prominence among Minnesota towns, above St. Anthony, St. Paul, and Minneapolis. Ironically, the quote on his masthead reads, ". . . I understand the art of raising a little village into a great city." History has shown that Donnelly really didn't. (MHS)*

Bottom: *The first Minneapolis City Hall was constructed at the junction of Hennepin and Nicollet avenues, where it shared quarters with the Board of Trade. With the construction of the Minneapolis Municipal Building, the old City Hall became superfluous and was demolished. Photo by Luxton. (MPLIC)*

supervision—were the only financial institutions allowed to issue bank notes, or money. The greenbacks issued during the Civil War were gradually taken out of circulation and redeemed with gold by the U.S. Treasury. The resulting deflation prompted the formation of the party, which attracted a great deal of support in Minnesota.

The symbolism of the Donnelly-Washburn campaign was great because of the careers of the two men. Donnelly, the unsuccessful entrepreneur who had sought riches on the frontier and who had been disappointed, contrasted sharply with the successful milling magnate, Washburn. Donnelly represented the hopes of the small producers, the farmers, in a world that was being changed by the large producers, represented by Washburn, in very dramatic ways. The device used in the process of grading wheat, a brass kettle, came to symbolize the abuses of economic concentration that the farmers held responsible for the adversities they suffered. Washburn symbolized the growing power of the milling interests, which were beginning to influence and intrude upon various government offices. In 1876, for example, John S. Pillsbury was elected governor of the state, and various members of the milling community had been elected mayors of Minneapolis over the years.

Donnelly lost the election of 1878, and the forces that had united to form the Greenback party in the state dissipated in the face of the defeat and of temporary improvements in the general economic situation. Washburn went to Congress and was reelected several times before pursuing other high offices. Although the forces of protest were turned back, they were soon to be brought back together in even greater strength.

In the same period of time, politics in the city of Minneapolis began to take on greater complexity as the city began to mushroom. In the late 1870s city administrations made improvements in police and fire protection, and in the early 1880s the paving of streets in the city began. By 1890 there were 50 miles of paved streets in Minneapolis and 80 miles of stone sidewalk, supplemented by 214 miles of wooden plank sidewalks. Development

Charles M. Loring was instrumental in the development of both the Minneapolis park system and the city's lakes and streams. As the first president of the city park board, Loring hired landscape architect H. W. S. Cleveland to plan the lakefronts and pathways which are still in use. Loring Park, formerly known as Central Park, was named in his honor. (MPLIC)

of the city's water and sewage systems began in the same period, as did the development of the city school system. In 1878 a consolidated city school board was created, finally uniting the Old St. Anthony and Minneapolis school boards. By 1880 the system boasted more than 100 instructors and more than 5,300 pupils. Central High School, the city's first, was established the same year in South Minneapolis at Third Avenue and 11th Street. The first city hospital was established a few years earlier, and gas street lighting was also introduced on a large scale. The new demands on city government increased the city payroll and the importance of the services being provided.

In 1883 a seemingly minor development in the political life of the city occurred when the state legislature authorized the creation of a park board in Minneapolis that would be independent of the city government. The park board bill had to be approved by Minneapolis voters before it could be implemented, however, and a heated contest developed over it. The issues involved stemmed from different views of what the effect of a park system would be. The proponents of the park system argued that a planned system of extensive parks would beautify the city, add to the urban quality of life, and provide entertainment areas accessible to the city's entire population. Opponents of the park board argued that the park system was primarily a tool of the wealthy and the real estate speculators to increase the value of property that was to be developed in the future. The development was to be controlled by special interests, they argued, and would not be responsive to the needs of the great mass of city inhabitants.

The Minneapolis Knights of Labor played a major role in attempting to unite opponents to the independent park board. The Knights, an organization that was an advocate for the industrial workers but which included small businessmen and white-collar workers in its ranks, passed a resolution denouncing the park board scheme as a plot to enrich the wealthy at the expense of the average citizen. Also, the city council was upset because the park board was to be beyond its control and attacked the plan as an unnecessary drain upon the city's tax coffers.

In defense of the park board plan and against criticisms that the park system would be a useless extravagance, the chief planner, H.W.S. Cleveland, responded that the park system would increase land values and, in turn, property tax revenues so that the city would get a long-term return on its investment. Cleveland cited the impact that Central Park had upon land values in New York City to give substance to his claims. The controversy raged until the issue was finally settled at the polls, and opponents of the independent park board were defeated. The issue marked the rise of labor as an active force in city politics and also demonstrated the power that the milling interests had, both directly and indirectly, upon decision-making in the city.

The election of George A. Pillsbury (father of Charles the miller and elder brother of John S. Pillsbury, who was governor from 1876 to 1881) as mayor of Minneapolis in 1884 symbolized the millers' political power. Although the mayor was primarily a figurehead, the ability of the principal millers to win office signified the respect and authority that their economic success brought them within the community. The election of George Pillsbury also had the effect of interrupting the mayoral career of Dr. Albert Alonzo Ames, one of the city's more colorful political personalities.

The son of one of Minneapolis' founding fathers, who had also been mayor of Minneapolis earlier, Ames was elected mayor of Minneapolis more times than any other individual, six times in all. Turned out of office by Pillsbury, Ames turned his attention to seeking statewide office in 1886. In that year, in the midst of economic problems and social upheaval for the entire nation, Ames was nominated for the office of governor by the Democratic party. He came close to winning the governorship because of the support he received from the Knights of Labor and the new agrarian protest organizations, the Farmers' Alliances. It was the first time in Minnesota history that a major politician from Minneapolis was able to mobilize dissident forces in the state in an effort to capture control

Above: *Theodore Wirth was responsible for the steady development and growth of the Minneapolis park system until the mid-1940s. Different parks were geared for different kinds of use, and the park system in Minneapolis now meets recreational needs ranging from athletics to quiet hiking and observation. (MPLIC)*

Facing page, top: *George A. Pillsbury, Charles Pillsbury's father and John Sargent Pillsbury's older brother, had a long and distinguished career in New England before migrating to Minneapolis at the age of 68. Enticed to come out West by his son and brother, George entered the Pillsbury Company as a partner, served in administrative capacities on the boards of other firms, and was elected mayor of Minneapolis in 1884. (MPLIC)*

Bottom: *Special lights were laid out on Nicollet Avenue for the Minneapolis Exposition Building's opening day celebration in 1886. (MPLIC)*

from the Republicans, but it was not the last.

The Farmers' Alliances had their origin in the cotton-growing South, where small cotton growers encountered problems of credit, transportation, and marketing similar to those encountered by the wheat farmers of the Midwest. The Alliances' solution was the development of farmer cooperatives for buying and selling in order to shield themselves from expensive credit, arbitrary railroad rates, and the vagaries of the market. The idea for cooperatives caught on in Minnesota and elsewhere in the Upper Midwest in the early 1880s. As was the case with the Grange when it began, the Alliances were not explicitly political at the outset. As time passed, however, political action became the order of the day. The great innovation of the Alliances was to seek out allies in the city, namely the new industrial workers, who might join with them in common political efforts. In Minnesota this joint activity led to a combined Knights of Labor and Farmers' Alliances convention in St. Paul in 1886.

Another development, however, retarded the progress of the new political movement. This was the appropriation of the inflationary issue by the national Democratic party and also by a segment of the Republican party. The advocacy of currency changes by the Democrats attracted many farmers and other elements in society who were disenchanted with the Republicans. Because the Democrats were an established party, they seemed to offer the possibility of early success. Sympathy for bimetallism, the use of silver as well as gold as the backing for America's money, also gained support among some Republicans, further diluting the move toward a third party. The Farmers' Alliances themselves felt that comprehensive social and economic policies were needed to solve the problems of the nation's farmers and looked askance at the inflation of the national money supply as a cure-all. The inflationary panacea, however, had deep roots among farmers, as they had earlier supported the Greenback party and related movements, and the silver issue always threatened the long-term prospects of the Alliances' political program.

While the farmers' and workers' movements gained momentum in the 1880s, major modifications were being made in Minnesota concerning the involvement of the state government in the workings of the economy. The main thrust of the changes involved regulations of market behavior on the part of various firms. In the administration of Governor John S. Pillsbury, who was elected to three successive terms, strict regulation of banks chartered by the state was inaugurated. Nationally-chartered banks were already subject to controls contained in the national banking legislation of 1864, but until the Pillsbury legislation, state banks in Minnesota had a relatively free hand in their operations. The supervision of the state banks reduced the competitiveness of those banks in relation to national banks, because the strict requirements placed upon them greatly reduced their profit margins and increased their capital requirements. The sum effect of the banking regulation was to increase the importance of Minneapolis banks to the state's economy. The same legislation also instituted a public examiner's office that began increased examination of the records of state banks, increasing public confidence in their operations.

Other regulatory legislation instituted in the period affected the practice of the professions. The licensing of doctors, pharmacists, and dentists began in the mid-1880s. The effect of the licensing laws was to require formal university training for people who aspired to practice those professions. The legislation gave the professional schools at the University of Minnesota a great boost, as they became the sole source of such training within the borders of the state. The state licensing of the liquor traffic was also instituted in this period. And, reflecting the growth of the state's industrial work force, a state commissioner of labor office was created to collect statistics on workers and to make reports on working conditions and wages. John Lamb was the state's first commissioner of labor; he had served previously with the Minneapolis Trades' Assembly as its statistician. Lamb reported in 1888 that more than 80 unions were active in Minnesota, with 20 located in Minneapolis.

The most important state regulatory activity of the 1880s was in the area of the wheat market and milling industry. In 1885 the state assumed responsibility for the regulation and licensing of elevator companies in Minnesota. It inaugurated a negotiable receipt system that allowed the elevators to issue commercial paper on grain received on consignment by them. This development greatly facilitated the trading of the wheat crop and enhanced the operations of the Minneapolis Grain Exchange. The control of the grading process was also placed in the hands of state inspectors to protect farmers from unscrupulous practices in grading the wheat crop. The unlawful use of trademarks was also made a criminal offense through the legislation and this ruling had an ironical twist. In the early years of the Minneapolis milling industry, the millers had often marketed their discolored and coarsely ground flour in barrels with "Made in St. Louis" stamped on them. The millers learned from experience, and while they had at times appropriated the trademarks of other millers, they were not about to let such appropriation happen to them. The new legislation also made it relatively simple to create financial trusts in Minnesota. This legislation greatly aided the development of Minneapolis as a major financial center, since it facilitated the movement and handling of large investment funds. A new probate law passed in 1889, making the transfer of large holdings through inheritance much easier, topped off the state's regulatory legislation of the period.

The Farmers' Alliances movement was not satisfied with the reform legislation passed by the legislature and developed its own program for social reform as it moved directly into the political arena. By 1892, in fact, the Farmers' Alliances of the Midwest and South had created a new national political party called the People's, or Populist party. The new party nominated James B. Weaver for the Presidency in the election of 1892, and in Minnesota he received 30,000 votes out of 255,000 actually cast. The poor showing of the Populist candidate in Minnesota was the result of wily political maneuvering on the part of the state's Republican party. First,

The Ard Godfrey House, the oldest building in St. Anthony, remains standing in the Chute Square Park. It is shown here in 1936 in front of the Minneapolis Exposition Building, the site of the 1892 Republican National Convention which has been razed and replaced by a Coca-Cola Bottling plant. Photo by A.F. Raymond. (MHS)

the leaders of the state Republicans, including William D. Washburn (who was by then a U.S. Senator) and other men of prominence in Minneapolis commerce and industry, persuaded the Republican party to hold its national nominating convention in Minneapolis. Washburn argued that the Upper Midwest, a traditional Republican stronghold, had become a "political storm center" as a result of the "hard times of the past few years." In order to stem the tide of agrarian protest, Washburn reasoned, that the Upper Midwest needed "the convention to stimulate the fresh energies of the Republican Party." George Brackett, a former Minneapolis alderman and mayor, and in 1892 president of the Minneapolis Stock Yards and Packing Company, successfully coordinated the efforts of Minneapolis civic and business leaders to capture the convention for the city of Minneapolis.

In addition to bringing the Republican convention to Minneapolis, the party leaders also made a major effort to retain the loyalties of Minnesota's major ethnic groups, primarily the Swedes and the Norwegians. In 1892 the Republicans nominated a Norwegian immigrant, Knute Nelson, for governor in order to attract the Scandinavian vote for the GOP and away from the rising Populist party and the resurgent Democratic party. The move was successful and Nelson was elected governor. The Republican Presidential candidate, Benjamin Harrison, carried the state on his coattails, but lost the national election to Grover Cleveland. Nelson's opponent in the campaign was Ignatius Donnelly, the perennial favorite of Minnesota's disaffected, who had also become a major figure in the national Populist movement and who was primarily responsible for the Minnesota Farmers' Alliances entering the political arena. Nelson went on to reelection in 1894, and in 1895 the state legislature elected him to the U.S. Senate, replacing William D. Washburn. Nelson's nomination and election stemmed the tide of the Populist party and made the top echelons of the dominant Republican party accessible to the immigrant political leaders and their descendants, a major change in the political configuration of the state.

Above: *Northern Securities Trust Company, a railroad holding company, controlled the Great Northern, Northern Pacific, and Chicago, Burlington, and Quincy railroads. Put together by St. Paul railroad magnate James J. Hill and Wall Street financier J. Pierpont Morgan, the trust was opposed by many Minnesotans who feared its potentially harmful effects upon agriculture and the Twin Cities' wholesale trade. Theodore Roosevelt, the "Trust Buster," took the merger to the Supreme Court, leading to its dissolution in 1904. From the Minneapolis Journal, February 20, 1902. (MHS)*

Facing page, top: *The Minneapolis Exposition Building was erected in the late 1880s on the site of the old Winslow House and was the location of the Republican National Convention in 1892. (MPLIC)*

Bottom: *Knute Nelson, seated in the center in civilian dress, was the first Scandinavian elected to the office of governor in Minnesota. During his second term, he was elected to the United States Senate, replacing William D. Washburn. Nelson remained in the Senate until his death in 1923. (MPLIC)*

The Populist movement did not disappear immediately, however, and it remained a viable force in state politics throughout the 1890s, helped in part by the depression of 1893. That economic catastrophe, one of the worst in the 19th century, had a powerful impact on Minneapolis as the unemployed filled the city's streets. In the course of the economic downturn, the city instituted relief measures for the first time in its history. Although relief amounted to a paltry $5,000, a small sum in relation to the degree of need, it marked the first acknowledgment by the city government of the need for public assistance to the victims of forces beyond their control.

In the midst of depression and slow recovery, the Populists developed a program that called for a decentralized banking system and massive inheritance and income taxes. The program proposed government ownership of railroads, telephone, and telegraph, and the provision for more public lands to be made available to farmers. The Populists also called for the direct election of Presidents and senators, ending the electoral process for the selection of the former and the selection of the latter by the state legislature. The Populist program attracted attention and support, and throughout the 1890s Populists continued to attempt to capture statewide offices. In 1896 they endorsed a Swedish immigrant, John Lind, for the governorship along with the Democrats and the Silver Republicans.

For the Populists 1896 was the year of "fusion" at the national level, with the process of combination with the Democrats also occurring at the state level in Minnesota. The fusion between the Democrats and Populists occurred when William Jennings Bryan was nominated by the Democrats as their Presidential candidate in 1896. Bryan was a champion of the Midwestern farmers and also one of the most vocal opponents of the national gold standard, opposition which he made famous in his "Cross of Gold" speech. Lind, a former Republican who served several terms in the U.S. House of Representatives, left the Republican party and received the endorsement of the Democrats for the gubernatorial nomination, with the Populists following suit. Lind was defeated in 1896, and the state gave its electoral votes to William McKinley, the Republican Presidential nominee. In 1898, however, Lind ran again as a fusion candidate, and this time he won. The election was memorable in that it marked the first time since the Civil War that the Republicans failed to send their candidate to the state house. Lind's election also symbolized the importance of the ethnic vote in Minnesota, as had Knute Nelson's in 1892, and the gradual opening of the political offices in the state to the immigrant population. Lind was defeated when he sought reelection, but his successor also symbolized the end of an era. Samuel R. Van Sant, who replaced Lind, was the last veteran of the Civil War to hold the office of governor.

The turn of the century had other symbols of transition. In 1901 the indefatigable Ignatius Donnelly died, as did John S. Pillsbury. Donnelly symbolized the politics of protest that became a feature of political life in Minnesota and Minneapolis as well, and Pillsbury represented the solidity and accomplishment of the state's entrepreneurs and business leaders. The differences between the two men and their supporters reflected the divisions that had developed in the state as a result of its rapid economic and social development. Pillsbury, the transplanted New Englander, reflected the virtues and standards that were hallmarks of the Minneapolis business elite that shaped Minnesota's progress for more than half a century. Donnelly, on the other hand, reflected the wave of the future—as can be seen from the security of historical hindsight—in his representation of a more democratic political and economic vision. Taken together they reflected the tensions that characterized Minnesota politics during their lifetimes and which were to come into dramatic focus after their passing from the scene.

The turn of the century also marked the movement of Minneapolis into the national spotlight as a result of a newspaper article written by the muckraking journalist Lincoln Steffens. Steffens penned a scathing expose of the graft and corruption that

Facing page: *On October 12, 1899, the city of Minneapolis welcomed the 13th Minnesota Regiment back from service in the Spanish-American War and duty in the Philippines. Here the welcoming parade is crossing Hennepin Avenue Bridge from Old St. Anthony and turning left onto Nicollet Avenue. (MPLIC)*

Facing page, clockwise from top left: *Dr. A.A. Ames was made surgeon major of the Seventh Minnesota Volunteer Regiment in 1864 at the age of 22. The son of a pioneer physician who settled in Minneapolis before the Civil War, Ames went on to a colorful career that culminated in the scandals of his mayoral administration at the turn of the century. "Doc" Ames, as he was referred to in his dingier days, made national prominence when Lincoln Steffens included his administration in the Shame of the Cities series. From the E.A. Bromley Collection. (MPLIC)*

Fred W. Ames, "Doc" Ames' brother, served with distinction as a colonel with the 13th Minnesota Regiment in the Spanish-American War. Later Minneapolis' chief of police with his brother's administration in the early 1900s, he was implicated in the wrongdoing associated with 'Doc" Ames' activities. (MPLIC)

In 1906 a sculpture entitled Mississippi—Father of Waters *was dedicated with a formal ceremony in Minneapolis City Hall. (MPLIC)*

marked the last mayoral term of Dr. Albert Alonzo Ames. Reprinted in Steffens' collection of essays, *The Shame of the Cities*, the original article found an even greater national audience.

"Doc" Ames, as he was known amiably by the time of his sixth term, was first elected mayor of Minneapolis in 1876 and then elected several more times in the 1880s. In 1900 he was elected mayor for the sixth time as a Democrat, but his administration took a different turn from his previous efforts at civic leadership. Ames began his new term by firing half the police force and installing new patrolmen who were amenable to collecting graft as well as to enforcing various ordinances on a selective basis. Ames instituted a system of protection payments made to his office by gambling houses, brothels, unlicensed saloons, and opium parlors, which were allowed to operate unmolested in the city. Ames proceeded merrily and profitably through his term until the Steffens article jolted the citizenry into action. Action came from a grand jury led by a lumber magnate and staunch Republican, Hovey C. Clarke. Clarke resisted attempts to buy him off and brushed aside threats of violence, and the grand jury finally brought indictments against the major grafters in the Ames administration.

Minneapolis was an industrial city by the first decade of the 20th century, and by 1910 its population exceeded 300,000. The growing population brought growing complexity to urban life. The rapid pace of change led to sustained effort on the part of the city to obtain a "home rule" charter from the legislature and free the city government to deal immediately and directly with city problems. Between 1898 and 1920 six major efforts were made to achieve this end by placing the proposition before the voters. The measure finally carried in the sixth referendum in 1920.

Other reform measures were also attempted in the period, some failing to win approval and others succeeding. A civil service system was instituted in 1913, and a central purchasing office for the city government was created in 1911. In 1909 a major effort was made to institute long-term planning for the future

growth and development of the city. The effort actually failed in the long run, but it was important for two reasons. First, the effort represented the last attempt by the pioneers of Minneapolis' development to shape their creation. Secondly, the planning effort was rejected by most citizens because of the restricted role given to the general public in the planning process. The episode marked the maturation of the city's essential processes.

The planning effort was carried out through the Minneapolis Civic Commission, which was formed by a group of private individuals in January 1910. Members of the commission included William H. Dunwoody, the city's foremost financier; Frederic W. Clifford, founder of the Cream of Wheat Corporation; John DeLaittre, lumberman and former mayor of the city; Lewis S. Gilette, chief executive of the American Bridge Company as well as several other construction companies; and several other prominent Minneapolis attorneys and business executives. John Walquist of the Minneapolis Trades and Labor Assembly was appointed by that body to serve on the commission as the representative of organized labor when labor was invited to send a permanent representative. The labor representative was soon withdrawn, however, when the other commission members levied a $250 fee for labor's continued participation. The Trades and Labor Assembly executive board refused to pay the money, and Walquist was directed to resign. The planning commission went on with its work and developed a grand design for the city, a design which was subsequently ignored by the city government. Eventually a city planning commission was created, but the leaders of local industry did not dominate its membership or its activities.

While the leaders of the industrial and business community were attempting to shape the city's future further, other organizations were becoming active, seeking to accomplish the same end through radically different methods. The Socialist party became active in Minneapolis after 1900, as did the Industrial Workers of the World after 1904. The Socialists advocated government ownership of industry and sought to accomplish this end

Facing page, top: *After the demolition of the old City Hall, the Gateway Center was established to provide a positive first impression for travelers arriving at the downtown railroad stations. Also, the center provided information about the city's sights, hotels, and restaurants. As times became more difficult and Minneapolis became a center for the hiring of migrant agricultural labor for the Upper Midwest, the pavilion in the rear became a meeting place for unemployed laborers waiting for work, much to the distress of city leaders. Photo by C.J. Hibbard. (MPLIC)*

Bottom: *Lakes in the city limits of Minneapolis required extensive landscaping and shoring before they achieved the pleasant and constant aspects they enjoy today. The narrow neck of land shown here once separated Lake of the Isles, to the right, from the Lake Calhoun swamp, on the left. The Minneapolis Park Board directed efforts to establish firm lakeshores and complete the landscaping. (MHS)*

John Albert Johnson was governor
of Minnesota from 1905 to 1909 and
was frequently mentioned as a
contender for the Democratic party's
1912 Presidential nomination before
his premature death in 1909. The son
of Swedish immigrants, Johnson was
the first governor of Minnesota to be
born in the state. (MPLIC)

through political processes. The Industrial Workers of the World, or IWW, sought the same end through the creation of industrial unions to organize unskilled industrial workers.

Previous labor organizations had organized workers according to their professions, such as carpenters, printers, machinists, bricklayers, and so on. These trade unions were fairly successful in the 19th century and provided the core of the American Federation of Labor, the largest labor organization in the United States until the 1930s. Because many new industries employed skilled machines instead of skilled men and employed unskilled men to operate them, many new industrial workers were not affected by the activities of the American Federation of Labor. The IWW attempted to organize these workers and made Minneapolis one of the major centers of its activities. Minneapolis was selected because it was the center of the market for agricultural labor in the Upper Midwest, and IWW wished to organize the farm workers. The IWW operated primarily along Washington Avenue and in the Bridge Square area, the area where Hennepin and Nicollet avenues moved away from the Mississippi River and proceeded through downtown Minneapolis. In this same area there were more than 40 hiring halls for agricultural workers in 1913. The IWW had moderate success in its organizational efforts, attracting the interest and enmity of the city's business community.

While the Socialist party and the IWW were making inroads in the Minneapolis political scene, a Democrat managed to get elected governor of the state. John Albert Johnson was the son of Swedish immigrants and the first governor to be born within the state of Minnesota. He was reelected twice to the governorship, despite the fact that Republican Presidential candidates carried the state in the course of the same elections. Johnson's achievements brought him the nation's interest, and he was mentioned frequently as a possible candidate for the Democratic Presidential nomination. His career was cut short by his premature death, however, in the middle of his third term as governor.

With the outbreak of World War I, Minneapolis found itself

Following pages, left: *Armistice Day brought great relief and joy to the citizens of Minneapolis. Happy throngs celebrate at Nicollet Avenue and 7th Street on November 11, 1918. (MPLIC)*

Right: *Until 1934, Minneapolis employers prided themselves on their "open shop town" and successfully thwarted attempts at union organization. Although collective bargaining was not yet a possibility, Minneapolis workers, such as these flour mill workers marching on August 5, 1904, maintained unions that provided social activities, insurance, and other services. (MHS)*

the center of hectic political activity. The city provided volunteers for the armed services as it had in previous national conflicts, but the war was also waged with great ferocity on the home front. In the heat of the war hysteria, the city and the state created Committees of Public Safety, ostensibly to protect the population from subversion and sabotage. Groups such as the Socialist party and the IWW, which were heatedly opposed to American involvement in the war, attracted a great deal of attention from the committees. Systematic repression of these groups was in fact instituted, and many of their members were arrested, tried, and sentenced to prison for lengthy prison terms for their opposition to the war. The situation was complicated by the fact that the mayor of Minneapolis, a man named Thomas Van Lear, was a Socialist and also by the fact that the activities of the Committees of Public Safety were tied to antilabor activities that predated the outbreak of war.

After suppressing strikes in the flour mills in 1902 and 1903, when the mill workers demanded an eight-hour workday to replace the standard twelve-hour day, and after breaking a machinists' strike a few years later, the employers of Minneapolis had formed a central organization to coordinate their efforts to thwart the development of labor unions and strikes. An extensive system of undercover spies and informers was the main instrument of this system, along with the blacklisting of all suspected union sympathizers. This spy system was put to extensive use by the Committees of Public Safety as they waged their campaign against home-front subversion. The war in Minneapolis against the IWW sparked a national campaign against the organization, which led to the IWW's virtual destruction by Armistice Day.

The Committees of Public Safety identified another enemy of the war effort in the latest of the agrarian protest movements which had been initiated in the Upper Midwest: the Non-Partisan League. This organization was created in North Dakota in 1915 by Arthur C. Townley, and it sought to elect individuals who supported the League's program regardless of the individual's political party. The League program centered around the perennial griev-

ances of farmers and advocated state ownership of terminal elevators and mills; state inspection and regulation of all phases of the
grain trade; and a system of rural banks. The movement was successful in North Dakota and soon spread to Minnesota, where it
began making headway just as the United States was entering
World War I.

In Minnesota the League supported the 1918 candidacy of
Charles Lindbergh (father of the famous aviator) for the Republican nomination for governor. The campaign was waged in the
midst of the war, and the Non-Partisan League was attacked as
socialistic and pro-German by the Committees of Public Safety.
One of the committees' members was Lindbergh's opponent, incumbent governor, Joseph A.A. Burnquist. The object of sustained attack during the election, League members and supporters
suffered varied sorts of vilification, and two League members—
one of them the founder, Townley—were sent to prison. Lindbergh lost the election, and Burnquist was again the Republican
nominee for governor. Burnquist's opponent in the general election, David H. Evans, was also supported by the Non-Partisan
League, as well as by the Minnesota State Federation of Labor.
Evans was the first candidate of the new Farmer-Labor party, a
third-party movement which has continued to play a role in state
politics to the present time.

The rise of the Farmer-Labor party had repercussions
throughout the state and reflected the growing uneasiness with the
status quo on the part of a large segment of the state's population.
Minneapolis was a center of Farmer-Labor activity, and in the early
1920s the party found an ideal candidate for the post of Hennepin
County attorney—Floyd Bjornstjerne Olson. After his election
Olson gained a large measure of fame when he prosecuted seven
Minneapolis aldermen for bribery and obtained convictions of five
of them. During his service as county attorney, Olson articulated
his view of government as the protector of the weak and the poor,
the agent of social and economic equality, and the forge of harmony
between competing elements in society. In 1930 he was nominated
for governor by the Farmer-Labor party and was elected.

Above: *Joseph A.A. Burnquist
served in the Minnesota state legislature from 1908 to 1912, as
lieutenant governor from 1912 to
1915, as governor from 1915 to
1921, and as attorney general from
1938 to 1952. Burnquist gained great
respect in some quarters and hatred in
others for his suppression of dissenters
during World War I. Photo by Paul
Thompson. (MPLIC)*

Facing page, top: *Minneapolis
has been the bastion of the Farmer-
Labor party since its rise in the
1920s. The party's capacity to survive
is something of an anomaly in
American politics, since third-party
movements are notorious for lasting
no longer than one election and for
not capturing any major offices. The
Farmer-Labor party, however, developed and maintained its grass roots
support over the years, captured local
and state offices, and eventually
merged with the Democratic party
while maintaining its separate identity.
(MHS)*

Below: *In 1923 Farmer-Labor party candidate Magnus Johnson challenged Governor J.A.O. Preus for the U.S. Senate seat opened up by the death of Senator Knute Nelson. To the surprise of most observers, Preus was beaten by Johnson for the last year of Nelson's term. Cartoon by John Baer. (MHS)*

The corruption that propelled Olson into the political limelight was the result, in part, of Prohibition and the continuation, in part, of past corrupt practices that had first surfaced in sordid detail during the "Doc" Ames administration. Prohibition made the production and sale of alcoholic beverages in the United States illegal, and almost immediately the law ran into trouble. In Minneapolis and elsewhere demand for liquor increased rather than disappeared, and the bootlegging of liquor and the development of liquor parlors, or speakeasies, to sell the contraband began to increase rapidly.

Minneapolis, as the center of wholesale and retail trade in the Upper Midwest, was in a key position to serve as a terminus in the international and domestic trafficking in liquor. The development of the truck had revolutionized the carrying trade and made the protection of the Canadian border, with its many roads, impossible to cover by limited numbers of Prohibition enforcement agents. Minneapolis, along with St. Paul, was a trucking center, and both cities had hundreds of blocks of warehouses that served as both storage and distribution points for alcohol and secret still locations. Before Prohibition the Minneapolis underworld was limited to purveying gambling and prostitution to the vice-seeking members of the public, but Prohibition provided an opportunity the underworld could not pass up. The dollars involved in bootlegging were mind-boggling and the vast sums that the local crime bosses could employ gave a great boost to their efforts to find friends in city hall and in the police department.

The openness of city and police officials to bribery was not simply a question of money but also the result of cynical reasoning. The law against liquor, for example, was hard to comprehend in light of mass interest in continued consumption. An air of unreality cloaked the entire Prohibition experiment in Minneapolis, as most law enforcement officials as well as cops on the beat were skeptical about efforts to control the vices of the populace. The fact that drinking, gambling, and prostitution didn't hurt anyone directly, in the view of the period, made it possible for

Facing page: *During World War I great patriotic fervor developed in Minnesota as well as extreme distrust of reform movements. The Non-Partisan League, a farmers' organization that had some political success in the Dakotas and Minnesota, attracted especially violent attention from voluntary and official organizations hostile to both labor organizers and farm politicians. (MHS)*

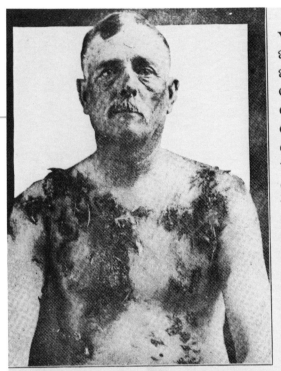

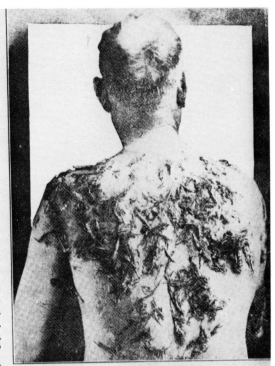

"I can never accept any man as a champion of liberty either for ourselves or for the world who does not reverence and obey the laws of our own beloved land, whose laws we ourselves have made. He has adopted the standards of the enemies of this country, whom he affects to despise."
Woodrow Wilson.

John Meints, Luverne, Minn.; present address Sioux Falls, S. D. Deported by a mob into Iowa June 18, 1918. Tarred and feathered August 19, 1918. At the time of the assault he was shocking grain. His only crime was a desire to express his thoughts for political and industrial democracy.

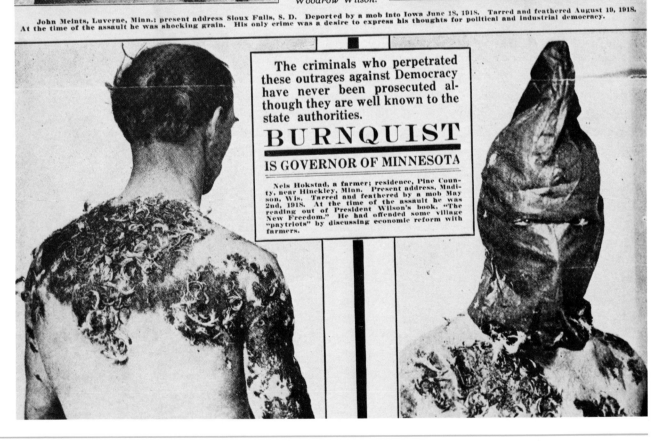

The criminals who perpetrated these outrages against Democracy have never been prosecuted although they are well known to the state authorities.

BURNQUIST

IS GOVERNOR OF MINNESOTA

Nels Hokstad, a farmer; residence, Pine County, near Hinckley, Minn. Present address, Madison, Wis. Tarred and feathered by a mob May 2nd, 1918. At the time of the assault he was reading out of President Wilson's book, "The New Freedom." He had offended some village "paytriots" by discussing economic reform with farmers.

police and aldermen to desire to get a "piece of the action" in return for nonenforcement of nonenforceable laws.

The international aspects of the liquor trade through Minneapolis made the dollars involved even greater, as much of the Canadian hooch destined for Kansas City, Chicago, St. Louis, and other points south and east passed through Minneapolis, usually in Minneapolis-based trucks. This volume of cash made certain that no local effort of any serious proportions would be made to contain the trade. Money, of course, sometimes failed to buy out recalcitrant individuals, and there were fallings-out among thieves over the profits from the illicit trade, and so violence too often came into play. Underworld killings, thug killing thug, became commonplace as the citizenry occasionally had to dive for cover from hails of bullets. More often than not, however, such activity was carried on by the criminal element in the privacy of its own garages.

The violence, though, was especially directed at individuals who were active on the fringes of the Minneapolis newspaper world. From the early 1920s various weekly scandal sheets had developed in various Minnesota towns, scandal sheets which were filled with gossip, personal defamations, and lurid tales of the exposure of the elite's vices, tales that titillated the reading public. To discourage such yellow-press activities, the Minnesota state legislature passed a Public Nuisance Law in 1925, permitting a judge to suppress any newspaper forever if he found it "obscene . . . or malicious, scandalous and defamatory." In the wide-open atmosphere of Minneapolis, such scandal sheets developed and played a role that transcended their immediate, grasping ends.

As it turned out, it was the scandal sheets that proved to be the only voice that attacked the graft and corruption that plagued Minneapolis during Prohibition and afterward. This was an accident, however, as the editors of such sheets dug up dirt on prominent officials and citizens and then offered not to publish in return for payment. Such attempts at extortion failed as often as not, and so the weeklies were filled with interesting tidbits that outlined generally the trail of graft that wound its way through city hall.

The introduction of evolution studies in American educational institutions was debated in the 1920s. As this editorial cartoon from the March 8, 1927, Minnesota Daily indicates, the student editors of the University of Minnesota newspaper were worried about the effects of an anti-evolution studies bill considered by the state legislature in the late 1920s. (MHS)

The *Saturday Press*, founded by Jay M. Near and Howard A. Guilford, was one of the most turgid and lurid scandal sheets to operate in the Minneapolis-St. Paul area. The editors were unprincipled fellows who followed the worst traditions in American journalism and were, in addition, racial and ethnic bigots. Rabidly anti-Semitic, the *Saturday Press* managed to offend about every member of the community of Minneapolis, both law-abiding and not. Within a few weeks of beginning publication, an attempt was made on Guilford's life as he drove his automobile into town from Robbinsdale. Matters came to a head in 1927, when the *Saturday Press* accused Mayor George Leach, Charles G. Davis, and County Attorney Floyd Olson of being either party to or blind to the gambling syndicate in Minneapolis.

Utilizing the 1925 Public Nuisance Law, Olson attempted to suppress the *Saturday Press*. The resulting court case went all the way to the Supreme Court, with the result being the Minnesota law's being declared unconstitutional in 1931. Olson by that time was governor of Minnesota, but Minneapolis was still a wide-open town, and Guilford and Near continued their earlier depredations. The whole drama came to a climax in September 1934, in the aftermath of the tumult surrounding the truckers' strike in Minneapolis, when another attempt on Guilford's life was successful. Near died of natural causes the following year. In December 1935 another editor, Walter W. Liggett, was also killed by gunfire after publicly stating that the same elements which had killed Guilford were also pursuing him. Despite these and other unseemly occurrences, no massive effort at cleanup and reform was made until the closing days of World War II.

The Great Depression paved the way for Olson's election to the governorship, but the Farmer-Labor party had earlier elected a candidate to the United States Senate. In 1922 Henrik Shipstead, the Farmer-Labor candidate, defeated the incumbent Republican, Frank B. Kellogg, who later went on to fame as Secretary of State in the Coolidge administration and as the coauthor of the Kellogg-Briand Pact, or the Pact of Paris. The election of Olson, then, in 1930 was no fluke but represented the culmina-

tion of a long effort on the part of the third party.

The Great Depression struck a major blow against the Republican party because it had long been the party of big business and the financial community. Business leaders had long promised continued prosperity if business was allowed to run its own affairs. The calamitous economic downturn of 1929 which continued in 1930 shook the faith of the electorate in the business and market-oriented programs of the GOP and gave the criticisms from the third-party opponents a new viability. It was this disillusionment which propelled Floyd Olson to the governorship.

The Depression affected Minneapolis in much the same way that it affected other major American cities of similar size. Unemployment was high and business did well to stagnate without going under entirely. Massive problems of relief arose, with the city and state feebly equipped to handle them. Hunger stalked the city's streets along with the large numbers of jobless workers. As the economic disaster dragged on through 1930 and 1931, it became apparent that the city was unable to contend with problems caused by the downturn, and city and state leaders began to look to the federal government for assistance.

By 1932 the electorate sought a change in the national government and a more energetic and imaginative approach to the crisis. It was in this mood that the voters of Minnesota voted for Franklin D. Roosevelt in 1932 by a margin of two to one. Roosevelt was the first Democratic candidate for President to receive the state's electoral votes since Minnesota became a state in 1858. Minnesota had been a Republican bastion for nearly three quarters of a century as a result of its rapid economic development and relative prosperity, but four years of the Depression created a large number of defectors.

The programs of the New Deal, which began to be developed in great profusion within 100 days of Roosevelt's inauguration, greatly affected Minneapolis and the rest of the state as well. One of the most far-reaching bits of legislation concerned orga-

Facing page: *Farmers suffered a loss of income as prices and demand for their products dropped drastically during the Great Depression, a situation which was aggravated by their dependence on loans for survival between harvests. As a center of a productive agricultural hinterland, Minneapolis was constantly reminded of agrarian unrest as farmers carried their protests into the city. From Acme News, Chicago, Illinois. (MHS)*

Following pages, left: *During the Great Depression, the unemployed found it difficult to acquire sufficient food. Efforts were made to enable them to grow food in gardens with implements provided by public authorities. From the Graphic Arts Studio Collection. (MPLIC)*

Right: *Emergency Gardens were organized during the Depression to provide food and work for the unemployed. Such desperate local efforts were eventually supplemented by federal aid. From the Graphic Arts Studio Collection. (MPLIC)*

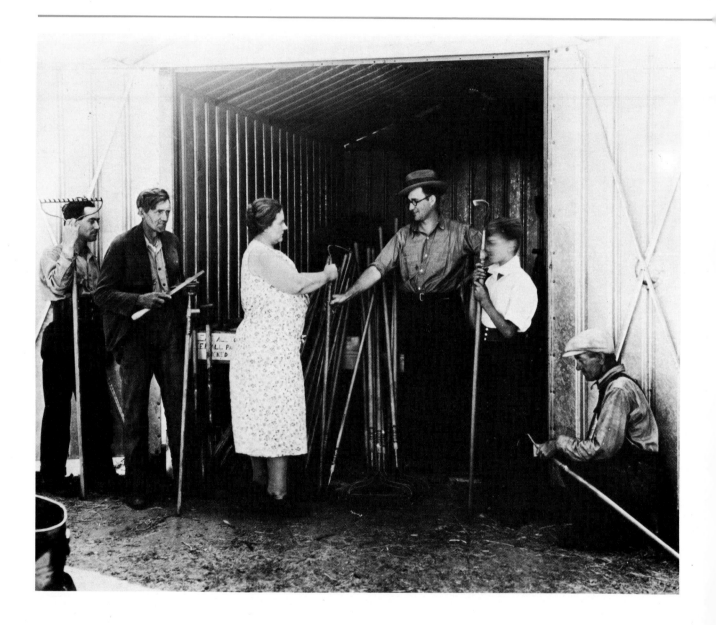

Labor strife in Minneapolis often became violent during the major conflicts of the 1930s. Members of the Drivers' Union, Local 574, pay last respects to their slain local president, *William Brown, outside Drivers' Hall on Plymouth Avenue in 1937. From the Minneapolis Star and Tribune Company. (MPLIC)*

Citizens Alliance Bulletin

Vol. 8   Minneapolis, Minn., July-August, 1924   No. 7-8

Main Office, 212 Builders Exchange.   Employment Office, 707-9 3rd Ave. So.

"Hired Men" In Industry

THE idea is altogether too prevalent that the leaders of our great industries are not workers themselves and do not attempt to work in co-operation with their employes.

This is a very much mistaken idea. As a matter of fact, the executive officers of ninety per cent. of all the successful industries of the country achieve their greatest results by working and co-operating with their employes, both being workers, although in different classifications.

From the highest officer to the humblest laborer, they are all "hired men," taking orders and directions from those higher up; the workman from his foreman, the foreman from his superintendent, the superintendent from the executive officers, and these officers from the stockholders.

Nearly all of the successful men at the head of affairs today rose from the ranks, and each worker, no matter how lowly his present position, has the same opportunity if he possesses the ability and will take advantage of it.

O. P. BRIGGS,
President,
Citizens Alliance of Minneapolis.

Above: *The Great Depression affected Minneapolis as it did other American cities and caused widespread unemployment and related social dislocation. Local resources for dealing with those out of work, often in need of shelter and clothing, were severely tested. Some of the more fortunate found temporary assistance at the Union City Mission in the dark days of the fall of 1932, before the beginning of the New Deal. (MPLIC)*

Top: *As this masthead of the* Citizens Alliance Bulletin *indicates, the labor-management conflict that erupted in 1934 had simmered in the minds and hearts of both workers and managers for a long time. (MHS)*

nized labor. Section 7 (a) of the National Industrial Recovery Act of 1933 permitted workers to form unions and to bargain collectively as part of the general program of industrial recovery. Workers all over the United States took advantage of this legislation to attempt to form unions.

In Minneapolis the truck drivers, or teamsters, took the lead in attempting to form their unions, to achieve employer recognition, and to bargain collectively. In the late winter of 1934, the teamsters of Minneapolis went on strike in the coal yards of the city and won. Flushed with this success, they decided to attempt to organize all the teamsters in the city. The organizing effort was spearheaded by Local 574 of the national Teamsters Union, led by Karl Skoglund, the Dunne brothers—Miles, Grant and Victor— and William "Bill" Brown. The leadership of Local 574 was avowedly Socialist, ideologically the adherents of Leon Trotsky's interpretation of Marxism, but throughout the strike they maintained that they were primarily interested in the unionization effort and not ultimate political goals.

The truck drivers were faced by the employers' organization, known as the Citizens' Alliance of Minneapolis. This organization represented more than 800 city businesses and had a permanent staff as well as a network of paid informers. The Citizens' Alliance had a long and successful record of combating unions, and it geared up for a showdown with the Minneapolis truck drivers.

The leaders of the union effort made their preparations throughout the spring of 1934, and a high point in the organizational drive was a mass meeting held in April. Governor Olson attended and urged the workers to "organize and fight for their demands." With the support of the governor, the workers felt assured that the state would not intervene and break the strike, as had happened on occasion in previous labor difficulties. With preparations complete, the union attempted to enter into collective bargaining with the employers. The employers refused to negotiate and on May 12 the union members voted to strike.

The strike garnered considerable support from the general public, and within three days the union received $15,000 in contributions, including a $500 donation from Governor Olson. Well organized and amply funded, the union proceeded about its task of halting truck traffic in Minneapolis. The strike proceeded under relatively peaceful conditions for several days, but on Saturday, May 19, a group of pickets was attacked and beaten. The pickets then began to arm themselves with boards and clubs, and on Monday, May 21, a clash occurred between union members and police in the city market area, with the workers achieving a victory in what came to be called the "Battle of Deputies Run." The next day, Tuesday, May 22, another clash occurred in the market area, this time between members of the Citizens' Alliance and the members of the union. During this encounter, which was covered by radio broadcasters on the spot, several members of the Citizens' Alliance were killed as they battled the strikers with clubs and nightsticks. The escalation in violence shocked the city, and on the following Saturday an agreement was reached between the striking Teamsters and the employers. The agreement, was, however, subject only to voluntary compliance on the part of the employers.

Although it seemed the labor difficulties were over, it became clear that the employers were not going to honor the agreement. On July 16, 1934, the leaders of Local 574 called a new strike to compel the employers to abide by the May agreement. The strike again began peacefully, but on July 20 a truck filled with 50 heavily-armed police ambushed a group of strikers, killing 2 of them and wounding 67. Because this marked the first use of firearms in the labor troubles, and, fearing open warfare in the streets of Minneapolis, Governor Olson declared martial law in the city on July 26.

During the strike the governor instituted a permit system to allow some trucks to move through the picket lines to make emergency deliveries of food and medical supplies. It soon became apparent that the Employers' Association and the Citizens' Al-

Facing page: *Two men were killed in the Minneapolis City Market area, both special deputies with the Citizens' Alliance, during the May 22, 1934, clash with striking truckers. Here, C. Arthur Lyman, vice-president of the American Ball Company and attorney for Citizens' Alliance, receives a fatal blow. The fighting in the market and the failure of police to maintain order without resorting to the use of firearms and massive bloodshed led directly to Governor Floyd B. Olson's decision to mobilize the National Guard. Photo by Dave Silverman, Minneapolis Star and Tribune Company. (MHS)*

Following pages, left: *National Guardsmen enter the Central Labor Union headquarters at 612 First Avenue North in an attempt to prevent further organized activities by the city's labor unions during the 1934 truckers' strike. (MHS)*

Right: *National Guardsmen raided and took charge of the truckers' strike headquarters as 215 South 8th Street on August 3, 1934, and arrested the strike leaders, suppressing the striking truckers' center of resistance. (MHS)*

liance were subverting the permit system in order to move other goods, and on August 5 Governor Olson revoked the permits in order to apply further pressure on the employers. In the same period the Employers' Association attempted to revoke the martial law order through the courts but failed. The employers remained intransigent, however great their losses of income, and it appeared as though the strike and martial law would continue indefinitely.

At that time President Roosevelt traveled to Minnesota to participate in ceremonies honoring the Mayo brothers, William and Charles, both physicians, at their clinic in Rochester. Governor Olson took advantage of this opportunity to meet with Roosevelt and pleaded with him to intervene in the strike. Roosevelt declined to intervene publicly, but he sent word to the Minneapolis Employers' Association that unless it recognized the truck drivers' union, he would order all funds being made available to firms in Minneapolis through the Reconstruction Finance Corporation to be withheld. The Minneapolis banking community would have been severely affected by this action. The banks, which were the center of employers' resistance to the union, gave way to the pressure that Roosevelt had applied to them, and employer resistance crumbled. Two weeks after Roosevelt took his action, the employers recognized the union and agreed to enter into collectively-bargained agreements with their workers.

The strike of 1934 in Minneapolis dealt another serious blow to the Republican party in Minnesota. Already discredited by the length and severity of the Depression, the party's primary supporters were now made to appear greedy and selfish. The demise of the party in Minnesota politics seemed assured. Floyd Olson was easily reelected governor in the fall of 1934, and Franklin D. Roosevelt carried the state by a greater margin in 1936 than he had in 1932. Floyd Olson, however, died of cancer in the summer of 1936, and the Farmer-Labor party began to experience major internal difficulties. Also, a group of rising younger Republicans began to reassess the positions of the party and, led by

Above: *Hubert H. Humphrey's first elected office was mayor of Minneapolis. Humphrey was one of the architects of Minnesota's Democratic-Farmer-Labor party in 1944 and went on to a distinguished career in the United States Senate. After becoming Vice-President in 1964, Humphrey made a close bid for the Presidency in 1968, was defeated, and finished his career in the Senate. (MPLIC)*

Facing page: *After less than 48 hours of confinement in an open stockade, truck drivers' strike leader Grant Dunne, at left, meets strike leaders captured by the National Guard, William Brown, Miles Dunne, Victor R. Dunne, and on the right, their attorney, Albert Goldman of the Communist League. (MHS)*

Harold Stassen, began to call for a new party perspective on social issues. "Enlightened capitalism," Stassen maintained, was the appropriate ideology for a rejuvenated Republican party in Minnesota.

Stassen argued that the gains made in the New Deal period in the areas of social justice and humanitarian concern were compatible with the competitive ideals of capitalist ideology and that earlier rigidity in such matters should be abandoned. Stassen's efforts bore fruit and in 1939 he was elected governor of Minnesota, sweeping the Republicans back into office. The Republicans continued to hold the governorship until the mid-1950s, and primarily because of Stassen's tireless efforts, the party once again became a major factor in the politics of the state.

In the early 1940s, in the midst of World War II, a new political personality who was to help create dramatic changes in the state's political configurations came on the scene. Hubert H. Humphrey ran for mayor of Minneapolis in 1943 and was defeated as the Democratic nominee. In 1944 he managed Franklin D. Roosevelt's campaign in Minnesota and helped bring about the consolidation of the Farmer-Labor party with the Democratic party in Minnesota. In 1945 Humphrey again ran for the office of mayor of Minneapolis.

Humphrey campaigned for the office of mayor as a reform candidate who was determined to end graft and corruption in city hall and to restore pride, dignity, and trust to the police department. The campaign was made more exciting when Arthur Kasherman, publisher of the *Public Press* and a convicted extortionist, admitted publicly to having seen money pass between Mose Barnett, a reputed gambling figure, and Police Chief Brunskill in 1927. A few days later Kasherman was killed in gangland style, and the election between Humphrey and incumbent Marvin L. Kline became heated. Humphrey's associates and friends included several members of the Minneapolis Jewish community, including Arthur Naftalin, who himself would be a four-term mayor of Minneapolis between 1961 and 1969, and anti-Semitic attacks also marred the conduct of the campaign. Despite the negative issues pursued by

Youthful Arthur Naftalin, shown here in 1948, began his career as an aid to Hubert H. Humphrey, when the latter was mayor of Minneapolis. Naftalin went on to become the mayor of Minneapolis in the 1960s and also made a successful career as a university professor and raconteur. (MPLIC)

various parties in the campaign and those just observing from the side, Humphrey managed to win a hard-fought election.

Humphrey was reelected mayor two years later, and with a remarkable group of aspiring politicians that included Eugene McCarthy, Orville Freeman, and Arthur E. Naftalin, he helped sustain the Democratic-Farmer-Labor (or DFL) coalition through divisive controversy in 1948. In that year Humphrey was himself elected to the United States Senate and was subsequently re-elected to two more terms, leaving the Senate in 1964 to run for the Vice-Presidency on a ticket with Lyndon B. Johnson.

In 1968 Humphrey became the first Minnesotan ever to receive the nomination of a major party for the office of President of the United States. Defeated by Richard Nixon in the election, Humphrey returned to the Senate in 1970 and remained there until his death in 1977. Eugene McCarthy served several terms in the House of Representatives before going on to serve in the Senate, and Arthur Naftalin served in the administration of Governor Orville Freeman and later was elected mayor of Minneapolis.

Hubert Humphrey was the apotheosis of the aspirations and successes of a century of Minneapolis politics. He represented the compassion and yearning for social justice that were the hallmarks of several generations of agrarian and labor protest that centered in Minneapolis and the Upper Midwest. Humphrey, however, also embodied the virtues and qualities that characterized the entrepreneurial pioneers and financiers who created the industries of Minneapolis, for he believed that industry and hard work were patterns of activity worthy of pursuit by an energetic people.

Humphrey also symbolized the links between Minneapolis and its hinterland, for he was himself a migrant to the city. Born and raised in the middle of South Dakota farm country, Humphrey had a strong grasp of the attitudes and views that had been shaped by generations of agrarian political activity, from the Greenbackers and the Grange to the Farmers' Alliances and the Non-Partisan League. He also reflected the ethnic mix of the city and the region surrounding it. His mother was Scandinavian and Humphrey was always sensitive to the source of his roots. He was the son of a small businessman who struggled through prosperous times as well as the Depression. Humphrey also witnessed and experienced deeply the selling of the family home to pay off mounting debts. These traditions and experiences made him sensitive to the inadequacies of the system as well as its great potential. Humphrey expressed his political philosophy in his "politics of joy," which stressed equality of opportunity for all Americans and which rejected the programs of the extreme left and the right. His philosophy and his energetic pursuit of his goals carried him from city hall in Minneapolis to the national political arena.

The resurgence of the Republican party under the guidance of Harold Stassen and his concept of "enlightened capitalism," along with the formation of the Democratic-Farmer-Labor party coalition under Hubert Humphrey and others, marked a new era in the politics of both Minneapolis and the state of Minnesota. The electorate of the city and the rest of the state began to approach elections with a growing sophistication that transcended party allegiance or rigidity of mind. This sophistication was also reinforced by continued high faith in the voting process as a worthwhile political activity. Since 1900 Minnesota voters have gone to the polls in consistently higher proportions than have voters in most other areas of the country. This high degree of involvement and growing voter sophistication has prevented the domination of government at city and state levels by one party.

The city government of Minneapolis has also entered a new age of sophistication in recent years. In the mid-1960s, recognizing the growing complexity of problems facing the city and also recognizing that these problems were common to the suburbs and other communities in the vicinity, the city of Minneapolis actively supported the creation of the Metropolitan Council. The council sets guidelines for such matters as sewage, pollution, highways, and open-space preservation in a seven-county area that includes Min-

Facing page: *Prominent visitors to Minneapolis who arrive in the fall are often taken duck hunting by local officials. Here the lucky visitor is Adlai E. Stevenson, a Presidential candidate in the 1956 election, who is after the mallards along the Mississippi below the Twin Cities in the company of State Director of Conservation Leonard Schwartz. Stevenson got the duck but lost the election. (MHS)*

neapolis and Hennepin County. The council also coordinates other planning activities with 321 political units in the metropolitan area. While Minneapolis is actively involved in the work of the council, it still retains control and responsibility for law enforcement, education, zoning, and taxation. In the early 1970s the Metropolitan Council's responsibilities were expanded to include planning for regional parks, housing, health services, and public transportation. While the council has had its critics and mistakes have been made in certain operations, the experiment has been an overall success and has greatly contributed to the high quality of life in Minneapolis and the rest of the region, impressing outside observers informed about life in contemporary urban America.

In the 1960s the city of Minneapolis was guided by the liberal administration of Arthur Naftalin, which was in harmony with the New Frontier and Great Society programs of John F. Kennedy and Lyndon B. Johnson at the national level. For Minneapolis it was a time of urban renewal, as federal funds became available to establish housing for the elderly (making Minneapolis a leader in this regard among the nation's cities of similar size) and to eliminate the areas of blight that had developed in the area around Washington Avenue, the Gateway area where Nicollet and Hennepin avenues are joined, and various other areas in the city. The modern redevelopment of downtown Minneapolis with the initial creation of the Nicollet Mall, the construction of new office buildings in areas of blight, and the beginnings of the city's skyway system occurred in this period.

The 1960s were also a time of major social upheaval for Minneapolis as the city was affected by the turmoil surrounding the national debates over the civil rights movement and the Vietnam war. The location of the University of Minnesota in Minneapolis made the city a center of active discussion about the war as doves and hawks encountered each other in a variety of forums. The tensions that developed around the civil rights movement concerned controversies in employment and housing and the problem of equal access and opportunity. Minneapolis, under Hubert H.

Anoka County members of the Democratic-Farmer-Labor party express their support for Lieutenant Governor Sandy Keith's challenge to incumbent Governor Karl Rölvaag. Neither of them, however, won the election—Republican Harold LeVander became the next governor of Minnesota. (MHS)

Humphrey in 1946, had created the first urban Fair Employment Practices Commission in any American city, so Minneapolis had a 20-year history of concern in this area by the late 1960s. This background eased some of the tensions that affected other cities in more dramatic ways, from the events in Watts in Los Angeles in 1965 to the major urban riots in the North and East in 1967 and 1968. The assassination of the Reverend Martin Luther King, Jr., in April 1968 shocked and saddened the Minneapolis black community and led to spontaneous demonstrations of sorrow among both the black and white communities.

By the time of the 1969 mayoral election, however, a spirit of reaction had set in among Minneapolis voters, a spirit primarily directed at the anti-war movement and the perceived loosening of morals and attacks on traditional values seen within the university community. At that moment, Charles Stenvig of the Minneapolis police department entered the race for the mayor's office on a "law and order" platform. As an independent candidate (even though party designations were not used on ballots in city elections until the mid-1970s), Stenvig articulated middle-class worries about the excesses of the anti-war movement and the challenge to traditional values (represented by patriotism, family, and business values) that the student counterculture represented. After a campaign that was watched by national observers because of the trend it possibly could set for urban politics generally, Stenvig was swept into office. It was a remarkable turnaround from the campaign of 1945, when Hubert Humphrey had been brought into the mayor's office at least partially as a result of his promise to clean up the police department.

In 1973 Albert J. Hofstede of the Democratic-Farmer-Labor party successfully challenged Stenvig in the election of that year. With the American involvement in the war officially ended, quietude settled upon the city as the main issues became economic ones and new developments occurred in the area of civil rights. The large Indian community in Minneapolis began to cohere politically as the American Indian Movement, or AIM, and other organizational bodies attempted to rejuvenate the urban Indian populations' sense of esteem and internal powers of organization for economic and political ends. These and other questions challenged the ability of the city government to be innovative and effective and, while no permanent solutions were found, major strides were made in coping with such major and lingering issues.

Hofstede and Stenvig traded terms again, with the latter serving from 1976 to the end of 1977 and Hofstede serving from 1978 to the end of 1979. In 1979 Donald M. Fraser entered the mayoral race as the DFL candidate and was elected to a two-year term, the last two-year term in the city's history. In 1981 Fraser was reelected, this time to a four-year term, the first in the political history of the city. Fraser was fortunate to be in office during a period of great economic activity in downtown Minneapolis as a major building boom peaked. His administration has also faced major challenges as the city has been faced with financial problems caused by federal policy shifts in regard to the cities in 1981 and by an economy experiencing a recession. Fraser and the other political leaders of the city are optimistic about the future because of Minneapolis' diversified economy, private-sector commitments to the well-being of the city, and to an interested and active electorate.

The political history of Minneapolis, then, spans a period which began with community meetings in John H. Stevens' solitary home on the West Bank and extends to the meetings of the Metropolitan Council, which often involve demographers, economists, and statisticians and include lengthy discussions of regression coefficients and trend lines. The development reflects the growing complexity of urban life as it has evolved in Minneapolis as elsewhere. The city's political history also reflects the progression of issues and changes in values which have characterized American development. The unbridled development of the 19th century and the laissez-faire philosophy eventually gave way to more orderly development of natural resources and more humane interaction between the peoples who were competing to use them. Government by elites

Facing page: *In April 1968 the assassination of Martin Luther King, Jr., shook Minneapolis, especially the black community. Almost 2,000 people participated in a spontaneous march the day after King's murder. Beginning at North 7th Street and Lyndale, the solemn procession of mourners proceeded down Plymouth Avenue North to Theodore Wirth Park. Photo by Powell Krieger. (MHS)*

that were distinguished primarily by their commercial successes gave way to more democratic forms of government that took notice of the aspirations of laborers as well as those of financiers. It was this process of democratization that eventually enabled Minneapolis to develop the city government that provided for the common good as the citizenry defined it.

The process of change was one of conflict, in the sense that competing groups advocated their own view and wished to have that view shared by others. The remarkable aspect of the process of conflict in the history of Minneapolis is the orderliness that accompanied it. Legal processes were the channels of protest, and elections were the main battlegrounds, although there were notable exceptions in the hysteria of World War I and the labor struggles of the 1930s. The exceptions are even notable, however, when one remembers the degree of change that was being wrought. In light of the enormity of social change caused in the course of these events and upheavals, one marvels that more violence and chaos were not the result. From the organization of the claim protection associations in pioneer Minneapolis through the tensions of industrialization and the corruption of the "Doc" Ames administration, Minneapolitans retained their faith in the legal process and democracy. Though severely tested in World War I and the Depression when the state became repressive, this faith was maintained. It is this tradition which makes the citizens of Minneapolis look to the future with confidence rather than apprehension.   •   •   •

Political passions die hard in Minnesota as is evidenced by this tombstone erected in a St. Paul cemetery by the Hallenbecks. Depression and New Deal experiences, the latter personified by Franklin D. Roosevelt and Harry Truman, challenged strongly held beliefs nurtured by several generations of citizens. From the St. Paul Dispatch/Pioneer Press. (MHS)

Paper mementos of Minneapolis' past have been saved and treasured over the years. Trade cards with decorative designs were used by early retailers and manufacturers to publicize their products. Merchandise, from corsets to twine binders, was advertised on engraved and lithographed cards, which often bore addresses of the businesses. Some Minneapolis firms, such as J.F. Peterson and Company, printed the reverse side of their cards in Scandinavian languages. Other printed memorabilia have been preserved at the University of Minnesota Archives. Colorful yearbooks, football programs, posters, and sketches of the campus provide a glimpse of early college life. Those who value the past will appreciate these attractive tokens of bygone years. Illustrations courtesy of University of Minnesota Archives and the Minneapolis History Collection (MPLIC).

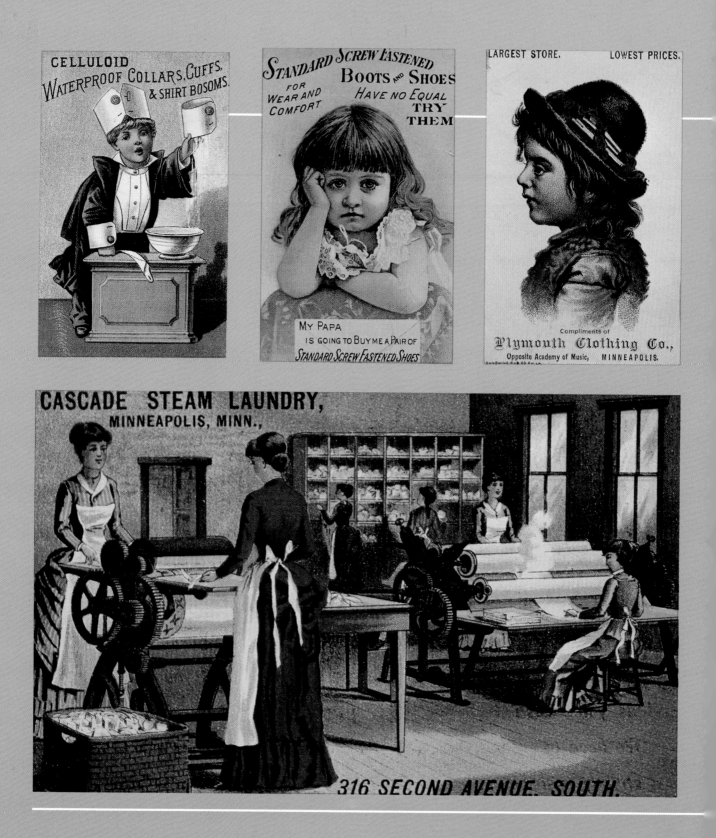

CHAPTER IV
YANKEES AND IMMIGRANTS:
THE MAKING OF A COMMUNITY

Above: *During the 1920s businesses and corporations began the tradition of sponsoring athletic teams composed of their employees as part of a general social movement known as "industrial paternalism." This hockey team was one of the thousands of teams that competed in sports of all seasons in Minneapolis. From the Minneapolis Journal. (MHS)*

Facing page: *On the other side of their advertising card, Willis and Dunham boast "The very latest spring styles, the very largest stock, and the very cheapest ever shown at retail. Trimmed and untrimmed goods. An elegant line of laces, satin, ribbons, etc. An opportunity never before offered to the ladies of Minneapolis. Call early to avoid the great rush." From the Minneapolis History Collection. (MPLIC)*

A city may experience rapid economic growth and even achieve a degree of political stability fairly early in its existence, but the creation of community is accomplished only over a long period of time. The development of common interests and the recognition of common problems requiring joint efforts for their solution take time in the growth of any city, and Minneapolis was no exception. The process was complicated in Minneapolis, as elsewhere, by the arrival in the city of disparate groups of migrants and immigrants from overseas, peoples whose backgrounds were diverse in a multitude of ways. Different religions, different family structures, different languages, and differing attitudes toward work and recreation were among the cultural and social characteristics that divided the newcomers. These barriers and others had to be overcome in order for true community to come into being in Minneapolis.

The first settlers to come to Minneapolis were primarily old stock New Englanders from Maine, New Hampshire, and Massachusetts. These Yankee pioneers were part of a general exodus from New England that occurred at varying levels of intensity throughout the first half of the 19th century. The exodus was caused partly by the reduction of commercial and agricultural opportunities in the New England area and stimulated at the same time by the attractions of opportunities in the developing frontier regions of the Midwest. The lumbering industry attracted a large number of New Englanders because of their long familiarity with the complexities of the industry and because the early lumber operatives, such as Ard Godfrey, Franklin Steele's millwright, were recruited directly from Maine to the Falls of St. Anthony. This recruitment led to a chain reaction as other Maine natives responded to the opportunities that had drawn the first settlers.

The movement of the New Englanders to Minneapolis took several different forms that are worth examining briefly. One group of such migrants came with clear-cut intentions and even prearranged business connections that enabled them to move right into the fledgling community and begin to carve out their

Above: *Pence Opera House was among the first of many theatrical and entertainment facilities developed by the citizens of Minneapolis. It opened in 1867 at Hennepin and Washington avenues. From the E.A. Bromley Collection. (MPLIC)*

Facing page: *Children participate in an ice pageant at Logan Park in Minneapolis in 1925. Ice festivals and carnivals have been a traditional way for Minneapolitans and Minnesotans to combat "cabin fever" brought on by inactive and sedentary winter behavior. From the Minneapolis Journal. (MHS)*

niches in the developing lumber industry. Ard Godfrey, Caleb Dorr, and others are representative of this group. Other New Englanders arrived, however, without local connections and even without capital and became the work force of the new industries. Some members of this group, as a result of hard work and occasionally sheer luck, also became wealthy from lumbering. Among this group were the professional men of the early community, including doctors, lawyers, and men with other skills, who hoped to find a place to sell their services in the community. Dr. Alfred Elisha Ames, the first physician in Minneapolis and father of Dr. Albert Alonzo Ames, himself later to achieve notoriety as head of a scandalous city administration, was among this group. The third group of New England migrants was a cut above their fellow migrants. Firmly established in their native towns and region, this group represented the wealth, power, and education of the New England elite. William D. Washburn, from Worcester, Massachusetts, his brother Cadwallader, and the various members of the Pillsbury family—especially John S. Pillsbury, who arrived in the 1850s—are most representative of this group.

The New England migrants made a strong impact upon the general course of development of Minneapolis. They established the local lumber industry, a project in which they were greatly aided by their accumulated experience in the lumbering areas of Maine. They also built the first waterpowered mills on the Falls of St. Anthony, another skill they had acquired in the process of harnessing the power of the rivers and falls of New England. It is interesting to note that many of the early settlers were in favor of naming the new town "Lowell" after the Massachusetts mill town. The Yankees also made their presence felt in the development of early political institutions. The claim protection associations, for example, bear striking resemblance in their organization and operation to the town-meeting form of self-governance, which was long a hallmark of New England civic politics. The New Englanders were, however, loath to give up their control of the political development of the city. In later years, when they were outnumbered by other groups,

they attempted to retain their control by manipulating intrusions into the city's affairs through the state legislature. It was through this stratagem that the New England elite was later able, in the 1880s, to establish a city park board independent of the city government.

This longer-term aspect of the settlement of the migrants from New England in Minneapolis requires some explanation in order to avoid misinterpretation. As descendants of the earliest settlers in America and as progeny of the cradle of the American Revolution, these people had a sure sense of what the American republic represented and which values that system should promulgate and support. This sense of assuredness was greatly reinforced by the Civil War experience. The triumph of the Union, led by New England and the Republican party in the course of the Civil War, greatly strengthened the sense of leadership of this group in political, commercial, and cultural matters. Initially, this fact was of minor importance, but as the numbers of non-English-speaking immigrants to Minneapolis increased, it complicated social relations in the city.

The New Englanders brought their religious traditions with them as well as their political and cultural ones. In 1849 the Oak Grove Presbyterian Church was established, with the Reverend Gideon H. Pond, of Indian missionary fame, as pastor. The services were held in John H. Stevens' house on the Mississippi River bank. The First Presbyterian Church grew out of this effort by 1853. In 1849 the First Methodist church was established, with Reverend Enos Stevens leading the congregation. By 1851 the First Congregational Church was also established under the tutelage of the Reverend Charles Secombe, and the Holy Trinity Episcopal Church was created the following year. The First Baptist Church began services in 1850 in St. Anthony, and the following year the First Free Baptist Church was organized on the west side of the river. In 1859 the Church of the Redeemer, a Universalist church, was established and was noteworthy, as William D. Washburn was from the beginning a prominent member of the congregation. These and

Above: *St. Mark's Episcopal Cathedral is shown here from across the Armory Gardens at the Parade Ground in 1913. (MPLIC)*

Facing page: *First Baptist Church in Minneapolis was erected in 1868 at the corner of 5th Street and Hennepin. It has since been replaced by commercial buildings as the central business district grew around the site. From the E.A. Bromley Collection. (MPLIC)*

Above: *Lake Minnetonka, west of the city of Minneapolis, attracted the city's residents from the 1870s onward. The Minnetonka Yacht Club was organized by sailing enthusiasts whose facility was constructed on Light House Island near Deephaven. The building burned down in August of 1943. From Northwestern Architect, 1891. (MPLIC)*

Facing page, clockwise from top left: *All lakes in Minneapolis have been utilized for recreational purposes to some degree or another. Lake Harriet Pavilion was used for concerts and dances or as a starting point for a canoe ride around the lake in warm weather. Canoeing and sailing have always been favorite summer pastimes on the lakes. Photo by Sweet. (MPLIC)*

Minikahda Club, located on the western shore of Lake Calhoun, was one of the most exclusive private clubs in Minneapolis' early history. Here members could dine, bask on the Lake Calhoun shore in summer, golf, and ice skate in winter. From the E.A. Bromley Collection. (MPLIC)

Nonswimming men wearing starched white shirts, ties, and suits and women wearing ground-length dresses watch men and women in ample coverings at Lake Calhoun in the 1890s. Minneapolis lakes have served as refuges during the city's brief but intense summer. (MPLIC)

other churches formed the religious base of the New England community in Minneapolis, and together they reflected the major interpretations of Christianity associated with mainstream American culture.

The church and the meeting hall formed two supports for the Yankee community, and another, the selective association, formed a third. Freemasonry had deep roots among the New Englanders and they established their first lodge in 1851. Organized by Dr. Alfred Elisha Ames, the Cataract Lodge was the first Masonic lodge in the city and included John H. Stevens and Ard Godfrey in its membership. By the late 1880s Masonry was flourishing, and a $300,000 Masonic temple was built in the downtown area of the city.

Other voluntary associations also developed in the city as lodges of the Odd Fellows, Good Templars, Knights of Pythias, and, after the Civil War, the Grand Army of the Republic veterans' organization were established and affiliated with national organizations. The Young Men's Christian Association, or YMCA, was organized in 1866 and the Young Women's Christian Association, or YWCA, in 1891. The YWCA, within a few years of its founding, was the second largest such organization in the United States. It had its roots in a Ladies' Aid Society that had been established in 1866. As Minneapolis entered its early periods of abundance and prosperity, the New England elite developed new voluntary associations that were much more exclusive and selective in their membership. The prestigious Minneapolis Club was organized in 1886, and the Minikahda Club, with its golf course on the western shore of Lake Calhoun, was founded in 1898. The exclusive Lafayette Club and the Minnetonka Yacht Club were also organized in the same period.

The host of voluntary associations served several purposes. They provided, of course, a framework for social intercourse among the city's social elite. They also formed a sophisticated information network that provided, through informal means, a backup to the formal channels of business and political inter-

Facing page, clockwise from top left: *Two women tackle a Minnesota winter with a sense of humor as they play a round of golf at the Columbia Golf Course in 1925. From the* Minneapolis Journal. *(MHS)*

the Columbia Golf Course in 1925. (MHS)

An impressive foursome watches theater entrepreneur S.L. "Roxy" Rothafel demonstrate his putting prowess at Minneapolis' exclusive Minikahda Club. From left to right are Sumner T. McKnight, of newspaper fame; Eugene Ormandy, former director of the Minneapolis Symphony; Jimmy Johnston; and William Hamm, Jr., of the brewing family of St. Paul. Rothafel owned some theaters in Minneapolis but is best remembered for his Roxy theaters in New York City. From the Minneapolis Star and Tribune Company. *(MPLIC)*

Five-globe electric lamps decorated the corner of Second Avenue South and 7th Street until 1925. These lights, made by the Flour City Ornamental Iron Lamp Company, replaced ornate gas lamps. (MPLIC)

change. It was through these and associated institutions of the churches and politics that the city leaders established consensus on a variety of social and political issues. That consensus provided the framework for the creation of the city park board, gave important support for candidates to the state legislature and the United States Senate, and helped provide an impetus for special projects such as an effort to bring the Republican National Convention to the city in 1892 and a host of other functions. Later it also served as the background for projects in civic philanthropy that led to the creation of the Minneapolis Institute of Art and other similar institutions.

Another aspect of social involvement on the part of the New England settlers was in the development of social welfare agencies in the city. This activity took many guises, but the salient areas of effort were in the organization of orphanages, civic charities, and settlement houses. The Washburn Memorial Orphan Asylum was founded in 1886 under a bequest from Cadwallader C. Washburn, and the building was erected upon land donated by his brother William. In the same period the Associated Charities of Minneapolis was organized with the strong support and leadership of George A. Brackett, a prominent businessman and politician. This organization sought to inculcate those who took advantage of its services with the values of thrift and independence that the founders prized so highly. In 1895 such activity was organized on a grander scale with the establishment of the Union City Mission. Nondenominational in character, the mission provided inexpensive lodging, public baths, and an employment service for those seeking work in the Washington Avenue South area.

Three primary settlement houses were established in the city in the late 19th and early 20th centuries. The Pillsbury House was sponsored by the Plymouth Congregational Church and was housed in a building donated by Charles S. and John S. Pillsbury as a memorial to their parents, Mr. and Mrs. Charles A. Pillsbury, in South Minneapolis. The Unity Settlement House was established in North Minneapolis and was sponsored by the Church of

*The Metropolitan Opera House
entered this ingeniously festooned
automobile in the annual Civic
Celebration parade, circa 1910.
(MHS)*

In 1870 the roof was raised over the auditorium of the Minneapolis Academy of Music building on the southwest corner of the intersection of Washington and Hennepin avenues.

The academy opened to the public in January 1872 and had a successful career until Christmas Day 1884, when it burned to the ground. From the E.A. Bromley Collection. (MPLIC)

the Redeemer. At one time Miss Caroline M. Crosby, of the flour-milling Crosby family, directed the activities of the settlement. The third settlement house was also located in North Minneapolis and was sponsored by St. Mark's Episcopal Church. These settlement houses provided social services to the working-class, immigrant population that was struggling to adapt to the economic and cultural realities of American urban life. Their goal was to help ease immediate hardships caused by a variety of dislocations and to help facilitate the long-term adaptation of the immigrants to American society.

Viewed separately and collectively the religious, social, cultural, and political associations and institutions of the New England settlers reflected their primacy in the city's affairs. This primacy was based upon their early arrival and their success at building the city's foremost industries. It also reflected their interest in shaping the city that they had made their home. Their influence was out of all proportion to their numbers. At their peak in 1890 they numbered only 10,000, a small fraction of the city's total population, but their wealth and prestige and deep roots in the American past combined to maintain their position of civic leadership. As a result they greatly shaped the evolution of the city in innumerable ways. Their stamp was left on almost every major civic institution, either because they created it and controlled it for decades or because their values served to guide it for countless more. The aura of the New England town, in fact, stays with Minneapolis to the present day and stands in rather sharp contrast to the atmosphere of other cities in Minnesota. The contrast has its roots in the New England heritage that was transplanted so effectively and so thoroughly by a remarkable group of pioneers.

While the New England connection is paramount in the cultural atmosphere of the city and its institutions, other cultural groups also flourished in the city. One of the oldest non-English-speaking groups was the French-Canadian. The French were among the first Europeans to explore the interior of North America and were the first to travel extensively in Minnesota. But

Above: *As Minneapolis grew as an urban center, it experienced periodic mass unemployment and related social dislocation. Minneapolis was also a major staging area for migrant agricultural labor, and these two factors combined to place heavy demands on private charities. Union City Mission on Washington Avenue near Third Avenue North was one of many charitable organizations that ministered to the working poor. From the E.A. Bromley Collection. (MPLIC)*

Facing page, clockwise from top left: *Row houses, such as this structure on Vine Place at 14th Street, were popular in Minneapolis in the late 19th century. (MPLIC)*

A carriage ride through the parkways around Lake Calhoun made a pleasant Sunday outing in the 1890s. (MHS)

Loring Park and Loring Pond are shown in the center of this circa 1940 photo of the Hennepin-Lyndale "bottleneck" area. The Walker Art Center is in the immediate foreground, and the Guthrie Theater has since been built to the left of it. (MHS)

while Father Louis Hennepin visited the present site of Minneapolis in 1680, about a century and a half passed before a sizeable French-speaking colony developed in the area.

The origins of the colony were tied to the activities of Pierre Bottineau, who settled in the vicinity of the Falls of St. Anthony in 1846. Bottineau was of mixed descent, his father a descendant of French Protestant immigrants, or Huguenots, and his mother an Ojibwe Indian. Bottineau was the local agent for the American Fur Company and engaged in real estate speculation in the area of St. Anthony. In fact he owned considerable areas of land in what is now Northeast Minneapolis. In 1849 Bottineau donated a tract of land in St. Anthony for use as a site of a Catholic church at the instigation of Father Ravoux, the local cleric. A small wooden church was built in 1851 and was named the Church of St. Anthony of Padua, after the same saint for whom the Falls of St. Anthony and the town of St. Anthony were named. The church was dedicated by the French-speaking Bishop Joseph Cretin of St. Paul. The small church was soon outgrown by the congregation, and an effort was mounted to erect a new church for the almost 1,000 people who resided in the parish. A new stone church was built, again on land donated by Pierre Bottineau, and was completed in 1861. In succeeding years, however, large numbers of non-French-speaking Catholics began to join the parish, and the French-Canadians soon found themselves seeking to create a new and separate parish for themselves.

In 1877, to satisfy their need for a new church building for the French-speaking Catholics in Northeast Minneapolis, the parishioners purchased the old First Universalist Church building, constructed in 1858, which was located in Southeast Minneapolis. The new French-speaking parish was named Our Lady of Lourdes, the first to be so named in the United States, and continues to function to the present time. Interestingly, the old church, originally built in 1851, went through a series of dramatic changes through this period and afterward. At first used as a parochial school, it was sold to Polish Catholics in 1866 and was used

Pierre Bottineau, one of the early French-Canadian settlers in the St. Anthony area, worked as a fur-trading agent for the American Fur Company in the 1840s and donated land for the early Catholic churches erected in St. Anthony. Bottineau was also instrumental in the founding of the town of Osseo, now in the northwest suburbs of Minneapolis. (MPLIC)

The Native American contingent in this circus troupe parade leads the way down Hennepin Avenue, circa 1908. Ironically, a land and immigration office stands in the background, suggesting the opportunities available for settlers on the Indians' former lands. (MHS)

as a church by them until 1881. At that time it was transferred to the Ruthenian church of St. John, which was a parish composed of Catholic, or, more precisely, Uniate Slavic immigrants from Central Europe. The Ruthenians used the church as a hall rather than as a church until the structure was demolished in 1937. The second Church of St. Anthony of Padua, vacated by the French-speaking element in 1877, continues to function as the local English-speaking church in the area.

The French-Canadian population served as a sharp contrast to the New England group of settlers. Although they arrived at about the same time, the French-speaking population had very limited influence on the development of the city as a whole. Despite their long experience in lumbering in Maine and other parts of Canada, they served primarily as wage-earners in the lumber mills and logging camps in and around the city. Aside from Pierre Bottineau, who went on to found the settlement at Osseo in northern Hennepin County, none of the early settlers could legitimately claim entry to the inner circle of the city's founders. The French-speaking community, like many others that were to come later, struggled to maintain its sense of community in the face of rather severe pressures. Its language and religion were the bonds that held families together within the community they created. Inward-looking and restrained, it maintained itself in the midst of hectic change.

In addition to the settlers from New England, other native Americans made their way to Minneapolis and to the surrounding countryside in these years. The majority of these Americans came from other parts of the Midwest, especially Illinois, Indiana, and Ohio, and from the Middle Atlantic states—especially Pennsylvania. These settlers were, for the most part, farmers who followed the frontier as it expanded to the west. Settling on the new land, they would clear it, erect farm buildings, plant crops, and wait for the value of the land to increase. As settlement became denser and the market value of the land increased from its base of $1.25 an acre—the price at which the federal government sold

public lands to settlers for many decades—the farmers would sell their holdings and move on to develop another farmstead. Along the way, some of these frontierspeople would settle permanently, and others would be absorbed by the cities that were springing up and offering new opportunities in the Midwestern agricultural regions. This migration helped spread the cultivation of wheat in the region, the crop that was so instrumental in the rise of Minneapolis industry. Wheat was frequently the choice crop because its cultivation was relatively simple and required few skills and little investment to be made profitable. Wheat also traveled well, an important consideration in agricultural areas where transportation away from rivers was frequently expensive or even nonexistent.

This group of highly mobile Americans left few tangible traces of their social activities, although much of them are embodied in the folklore of the agrarian regions in the Midwest. In the city they became even more invisible, and their experience in Minneapolis was not different in this respect from what it was elsewhere. Lacking a high profile as a group, these settlers contributed much to the stability and stolidity of community in Minneapolis and numerous other cities and villages in the Midwest.

As the frontier was being opened by lumbermen and wheat farmers in the 1850s and the 1860s, another source of settlers opened and flooded the plains and the prairies. The new source of settlers was Scandinavia—the nations of Sweden, Norway, and Denmark today. Major changes were occurring in these countries in Northern Europe, especially in Sweden and Norway. Most basic was the massive increase in population that began in the mid-1700s and that continued unabated throughout the 19th century. The growth of population had roots in several causes, but the decline of the death rate, improved diets, and an increase in the birth rate all played major roles. As the population increased new strains were placed upon the economies of these regions.

The problem was compounded by the emphasis placed upon agriculture for livelihood in Scandinavia. Despite efforts at bringing

Before airplanes and automobiles, and even before the railroad arrived, Minneapolis depended on the horse and stagecoach for overland transportation. This 1857 poster marks the inauguration of a new line between some early Minnesota towns, including Minneapolis. From the E.A. Bromley Collection. (MPLIC)

new lands into cultivation and working existing farmlands more intensively, the agrarian economies could not provide the land to satisfy the growing population that was dependent upon it. As the population grew the cities of Norway and Sweden did not grow enough to absorb significant numbers of the new citizens. Even after rapid demographic growth, the cities of Norway contained only one out of seven inhabitants, while in Sweden the cities provided space for less than one out of 10 citizens. The industries of the country, which aside from agriculture were primarily lumbering and fishing, did not expand enough to create sufficient new jobs to draw the rural people away from the land. It was in the context of these changes that opportunities to settle new land in distant America were made known to the peoples of these countries.

Scandinavians began to arrive in the United States in the mid-1820s in small numbers. Small groups made their way across the Atlantic in sailing vessels and into the interior of the country by railroad, steamboat, and by horse and wagon—and, on occasion, even on foot. The numbers were insignificant, however, when compared to the numbers that could have emigrated and to the opportunities that were available. The stimulus for major emigration from the Scandinavian area came about from a group of disparate sources, some of the most important of which were foreign in origin. In the 1840s and 1850s, for example, Scandinavia was made the object of intense missionary activity by the American-based Church of Jesus Christ of Latter-day Saints. The Mormons, as they were referred to colloquially, eventually removed to Utah in the West, and in the process attracted thousands of Norwegians and Swedes with them. While this process was going on, other Scandinavians began to migrate independently, seeking opportunities on their own accord. The outward movement reached a pre-Civil War peak in the 1850s, when Swedish immigration to the United States was averaging around 1,700 people a year and Norwegian immigration was running at about the same level. Most of these settlers found their way to farmlands in the Upper Midwest.

Swedes were to be found around Pine Lake and Lake Kosh-konong in Wisconsin in the early 1840s, and slowly their numbers in the area grew. The early settlers not only busied themselves in their struggle with raw frontier conditions but also made constant efforts to remain in communication with their native lands. As a result of these efforts, primarily carried out through the mails, conditions in America were made more generally known throughout Scandinavia. In their letters the immigrants not only told of the abundant land but also related the political and social freedom which they found in their adopted home. For many of the land-hungry Swedish immigrants, America became *framtidslandet*, or "the land of the future." In the wilds of Wisconsin and Minnesota Territory, the Scandinavians also faced rugged climactic conditions that offered them no respite from the conditions to which they had been accustomed in Europe. As one young immigrant wrote home, "We Swedes carry the winter with us."

While economic conditions in Norway and Sweden were the primary catalysts for emigration from the two countries, there were other significant factors that also played major roles. One of the most important was religious in nature. In all of the Scandinavian countries, there was an established state church, denominationally Lutheran, which controlled the religious life in each nation. This fact in itself presented no problem, but over the years the clergy and hierarchy of the churches became estranged from large segments of the population. The university-educated clergy, for example, became more rationalistic in its interpretation of theology and development of canonical matters during the period of massive economic transformation, while many elements in the population at large were becoming more evangelical and experiential. Religious dissent to the national churches, then, provided much of the early impetus to the emigration. The Mormon missionaries had tapped this resentment in the 1850s, and further erosion occurred as economic changes made emigration a solution to a larger number of grievances felt by the population.

It was the 1860s that saw the major initial influx of Scan-

Facing page: *A broomball game gets into full swing with the action approaching the net in a contest at Nicollet Field in the late 1930s. Winter has always offered a challenge to outdoor enthusiasts in Minnesota who have learned to meet it head on. (MHS)*

dinavians into Minnesota. Handfuls of settlers had arrived earlier. Minneapolis itself had a small population early on that had followed in the footsteps of the first Scandinavian settlers in the city. Nils Nyberg, a Norwegian shoemaker, had arrived in 1851, followed in 1854 by a countryman, Andrew Matteson, blacksmith. A well-educated Swede by the name of Claes Axal Widstrand arrived in 1854, and in the following year a Danish watchmaker, known only as B. Thompson, also arrived in the city. From this beginning the Scandinavian population in the city and the surrounding country-side grew. Famine in Sweden and the end of the Civil War in America combined in the mid-1860s to cause Scandinavian immi-gration to the United States and to Minnesota to increase rapidly.

This migration was greatly facilitated by the activities and writings of two Scandinavians who had early become familiar with Minneapolis. One was Frederika Bremer, who visited the city in 1850 and wrote rather glowing accounts of St. Anthony and the conditions of life to her countrymen. Bremer School in North Minneapolis was later named after her to honor the public rela-tions effort which she mounted so early in the city's history to such great effect. While Bremer reached a primarily Swedish audi-ence, another early visitor, Ole Bull, a concert violinist, reached a Norwegian one. Bull toured Minneapolis in the mid-1850s and was well connected with most of the Norwegian settlements that then existed in the United States. He was closely involved in a variety of Norwegian-American activities and was successful in propagandizing the beneficial aspects of Norwegian immigration into the United States.

Another source of information about Minnesota for pro-spective immigrants in Scandinavia was provided by railroads. The railroads that built the first lines across the state were capitalized primarily through grants of land made by the federal government and, to a lesser extent, by state governments. Proceeds from the sale of these lands were to help finance the cost of the railroad construc-tion and the acquisition of initial operating equipment. Naturally the railroads sought to find buyers for the land they were attempting

Above: *Swedes and other immigrants in Minneapolis placed a high premium on the value of education, and their dedication led to the creation of the fine educational system that Minnesota today enjoys at local as well as state levels. This Swedish-language handbill advertises the Swedish-American Business School at the corner of Washington and Nicollet avenues. The school, founded and maintained by Alfred Soderstrom, offered classes in double Italian bookkeeping, penmanship, arithmetic, English, and German. (MHS)*

Facing page: *Number 637 of the Burlington Line, behind the locomotive, was a refashioned boxcar. Second from the left in this 1892 photo is the "Zulu," the immigrant car that contrasts sharply with the combination sleeping and coach car directly behind it. (MHS)*

to sell. In their sales efforts many of the railroads dispatched agents to Europe to inform prospective immigrants about the lands that were available for purchase, their location and cost, and the conditions of sale. A Swede by the name of Hans Mattson served for many years in Sweden as one of these agents for the railroads and, as one of his many activities, helped to establish the settlements at Red Wing and Vasa, Minnesota.

By 1870 the population of Minnesota had climbed to 439,706, and the population of Minneapolis with St. Anthony's was hovering around 17,000. About 58,000 of the state population were Scandinavian, as were about 2,000 of the city's inhabitants. From these figures it can be seen that the majority of the immigrants were attracted to the land. They had been disappointed in their efforts to get land in the old country and were able to acquire it in America. The major influx of Norwegians, Swedes, and Danes into Minneapolis and Minnesota generally came later, however, in the late 1870s and in the 1880s.

The early years of Scandinavian immigration and settlement were important ones, though the numbers were small, for the future development of the immigrant colonies. First, the early immigrants made important linkages with American culture and political traditions, linkages that established patterns of behavior in their communities for succeeding decades. Allegiance to the Republican party was one of these early important connections.

The Republican party had its roots, partly, in the dissenting religious tradition that was the essence of the American Protestantism. Republican ideology also stressed virtues of temperance, thrift, and piety that were in harmony with America's developing democracy as well as with its free-market economic system. The Protestant religions that emanated from New England and that were transplanted to Minneapolis by the New England migrants who settled there, as well as to other places where they moved in the country, had these same virtues at the core of their beliefs. American religions such as Methodism, Presbyterianism, Congregationalism, and a host of others found in the ideology of the Republican party a secular expression of their religious beliefs. The dissenting Lutherans who formed the great bulk of the Norwegian and Swedish migrations found their values in harmony with those of American Protestantism and the ideology of the Republicans.

The attractiveness of Republicanism was greatly enhanced by the moral symbolism of the Civil War. Slavery was opposed on moral grounds by the devout Scandinavian immigrants, but it was also opposed because it triggered emotions which had come to play in their original decisions to emigrate. The absence of farmland in Norway and Sweden had forced many of the immigrants into the status of agricultural laborers, a condition which they looked upon as being akin to slavery because of the importance of landholding in their cultural and social systems. Opposition to slavery thus came naturally to these immigrants in a personal way. The promise of the free-market economic system espoused by the Republican party was also attractive to the Scandinavian immigrants because they had rather immediate evidence that it in fact functioned. They had chanced the hardships of immigration to America in search of land and had been rewarded by acquiring it. In addition, as they worked the land they prospered to degrees that would have been only dreamed of at home.

The obvious rewards of personal industriousness were symbolized by the career of the leading Republican political figure, Abraham Lincoln. As one Swedish immigrant wrote, the royalty of the European governments paled "in comparison with this man, Lincoln, who began life as a simple working man and is now head of the world's largest and most powerful republic." Lincoln, a product of a religious, agrarian social and economic system, represented the openness and opportunity available in the American system for simple, God-fearing people. The historical experience of Scandinavians prior to emigration and the process of immigration to America itself combined to predispose them to acceptance of and support for the main currents of social and cultural development in Minneapolis and the rest of the state.

This harmony between the native founders of Minneapolis and the later-arriving Scandinavian immigrants in social values, religious outlook, and political allegiance greatly facilitated the development of community in the city. Common interests were established by the very process of settlement. This is a remarkable occurrence in immigration history, because conflict is normally generated by the meeting of dissimilar cultural groups. In the case of the Yankee New Englanders and Scandinavians, language was one of the few barriers that separated them. And the Scandinavians went to great lengths from the beginning to eliminate that barrier as rapidly as possible.

This is not to say that the Scandinavian immigrants denied their cultures or their heritages. The ties with the homeland were to be treasured. Just as New Englanders continued to send their offspring to college in the East, preferably Harvard or Yale, and continue to do so to the present out of respect for their old roots, so too did the Scandinavians transmit awareness of their cultural past to their progeny. As early as 1869 the Norwegian community in Minneapolis began to celebrate the 17th of May, the national Norwegian holiday, and within a few years the Swedes were celebrating their *Svenskarnas Dag,* or Swedes' Day. Consciousness of the homeland never conflicted, however, with passionate devotion to the new land.

In the 1860s and early 1870s, two major developments occurred in the Swedish, Norwegian, and Danish immigrant communities which gave them a greater cohesion, at least in various localities. The first development was the creation of voluntary associations among the immigrants along ethnic lines. In Minneapolis a Scandinavian Society was organized in 1869 primarily through the efforts of the violinist Ole Bull, and the Society "Norden" was formed a short time later. In the early days in the city, when the numbers of each Scandinavian group were relatively small, the different nationalities banded together in composite organizations. As time passed and the numbers of each immigrant group mushroomed, they began to separate along more

Facing page: Svenskarnas Dag *festivities are an important part of each summer for the Minneapolis Swedish community and many other citizens. On June 24, 1946, the Count and Countess Bernadotte attended the celebration as official representatives of the Swedish government. Count Bernadotte was later killed in Palestine while attempting to mediate between Arabs and Jews. From the Minneapolis Times. (MPLIC)*

restricted ethnic lines. Society "Norden," for example, became exclusively a Swedish society by the end of the 1870s, when the Danes and Norwegians had withdrawn to form their own organizations.

The Swedish, Norwegian, and Danish immigrant press in Minneapolis also began to develop in this period. The first Norwegian-Danish paper in Minneapolis was the *Nordish Folkeblad.* The paper was established originally in 1868 in Rochester, Minnesota, by the publishers of the *Rochester Post,* Leonard and Booth. The paper was purchased the following year and moved to Minneapolis by Christensen and Soren Listae. From this halting beginning Minneapolis became one of the primary centers of the Scandinavian press in the United States, matched only by Chicago. By the early 1900s a dozen major dailies and weeklies were being published in the city for Scandinavian immigrants and their descendants around the country. Among these were the *Minneapolis Tidende,* a Norwegian daily and weekly; the *Vikingen-Minneapolis,* a Danish-Norwegian publication; and the *Svenska Amerikanska Posten,* a Swedish weekly.

The last-named paper was owned by Swan J. Turnblad of Minneapolis, who literally made a fortune as a result of his activities in immigrant press publication. He built a mansion in Minneapolis in 1907 at a cost of $1.5 million dollars. The mansion was so large that members of his family could not acclimate themselves to it and so moved into an apartment across the street. Turnblad, who was born Sven Manson, donated the building to the American Swedish Institute in 1929. Located at 26th Street and Park Avenue in South Minneapolis, the building continues to function as the home of the institute to the present.

Another accomplishment of the early Scandinavian immigrant arrivals was the establishment of their community churches as well as the national umbrella organizations, or synods, which bound like-thinking congregations together despite great geographical distances between them. The Evangelical Lutheran Augustana Church was organized in Minneapolis in April 1866 by five Swedish

Swan Turnblad, a Swedish immigrant who made a fortune publishing newspapers in the Swedish language for his fellow immigrants in the United States, built a luxurious mansion at 2600 Park Avenue. After a few weeks of residence, the family moved into an apartment in a building across the street because they couldn't adjust to the size and opulence of the mansion. Today the building serves as the Swedish Museum. Photo by Joseph Zalusky. (MHS)

Margaret Towson, Minnesota Historical Society tour guide, displays some of the "America" chests used by Swedish immigrants to carry their personal belongings to the United States. Artifacts from the Swedish migrations to Minnesota have been preserved for future generations. (MHS)

and three Norwegian families. Following the pattern of the voluntary associations, the Norwegians and later-arriving Danes split off from this congregation to form the Norwegian Danish Trinity Church in 1868.

Splits occurred between the three Scandinavian groups and within them as well. Because the ranks of the immigrants were filled with dissenters who had earlier rebelled against the established churches at home in favor of more democratic organization and theology, it came as no shock to observers that splits occurred among the immigrants after they arrived in this country. The religious history of the Scandinavians in America would fill several volumes in all its intricacies and developments. Such religious involvement and discussion and activity affected all Scandinavian communities to a degree and occupied a great deal of time and energy on the part of the immigrants. Suffice it to say that these activities were also paramount among the Scandinavian communities in Minneapolis as well.

Dissent against rigid orthodoxy had another long-term implication for the development of the Scandinavian immigrant community in Minneapolis and Minnesota generally. Simply put, it served as the base from which sprang many of the protests that characterized the agrarian political movements of Minnesota from the 1870s into the middle of the 20th century. The Grange, the Anti-Monopoly party, the Greenback movement, the Farmers' Alliances, and the Populist movement were all fueled, in part, by the tradition of dissent in the Scandinavian heritage. Within the urban environment of Minneapolis, the dissenting tradition found expression in various workingmen's movements which influenced political life in the city. The Knights of Labor attracted Scandinavian adherents in the 1870s and 1880s, and in 1876 the Scandinavian Workingmen's Society was organized.

While the first waves of Swedish, Norwegian, and Danish immigrants accomplished a great deal in their efforts to develop their communities in harmony with the indigenous community of Minneapolis, their numbers remained relatively small until the late 1870s. At that time emigration from Scandinavia to America began to accelerate rapidly. Between 1861 and 1870 approximately 125,000 Scandinavians had arrived in the United States. Between 1871 and 1880 more than 240,000 Scandinavians arrived. In the 1880s the numbers skyrocketed to more than 650,000, with more and more of the new immigrants coming to Minneapolis and Minnesota. According to the 1870 census there were around 35,000 Norwegians, 20,000 Swedes, and 2,000 Danes residing in Minnesota, mostly in rural areas. By 1890 the number of Norwegians in Minnesota had increased to more than 100,000, the number of Swedes to nearly 100,000, and the Danes to more than 14,000. By 1910 the Norwegian population remained just above 100,000, the Swedes numbered about 120,000 and the Danish numbers hovered around 16,000. The 1880s, then, represented the peak period of Scandinavian immigration to the United States and to Minnesota in particular.

The 1880s, of course, were a decade of phenomenal growth for the city of Minneapolis, and the arriving Nordic immigrants took advantage of the opportunities in the booming metropolis. The skilled immigrants found good wages and fairly good working conditions in the city's flour and lumber mills as well as in the railroad facilities and woodworks that had sprung up around town. Unskilled workers found employment in the same industries as well as in construction and general manufacturing. There also developed opportunities for enterprising businessmen who attempted to cater to the needs of the rapidly-growing immigrant community.

The new immigrants settled in two primary areas upon arrival. South Minneapolis had attracted many of the earlier Scandinavian immigrants, and the later arrivals also clustered in that area of the city. They congregated in an area from Washington Avenue, along the industrial area near the river, south to Franklin Avenue and from the edge of the commercial district to the east running into the river again. At the eastern edge of this area, where Riverside Avenue, Cedar Avenue, and Washington Avenue converged, there developed the "Snoose Boulevard"

Facing page: Svenskarnas Dag, an annual Swedish holiday, has been celebrated by the Swedish immigrants and their descendants since they arrived in Minneapolis. Here a Swedish men's chorus performs at the 1939 Svenskarnas Dag beneath the coat of arms of the Swedish royal family. From the Minneapolis Journal. (MHS)

community, primarily Swedish in composition. Following Cedar Avenue towards the south, there were to be found the main clusters of Norwegians in the city. Scandinavian settlements also were located in North Minneapolis, where immigrants had moved to find employment in the sawmills on the river's edge. Swedes coming along later also were attracted to the area. The main congregations of immigrants remained in the eastern half of South Minneapolis in the last years of the 19th century, however.

Although the number of Norwegians in North Minneapolis was small, the community there boasted a singular achievement in the development of the Norwegian-American community. For there, in January 1895, a group of immigrants founded the Sons of Norway, a fraternal insurance organization that helped organize cultural and philanthropic activities among the immigrants and their descendants throughout the country. The organization also channeled communications between the immigrant community and the cultural institutions of the old country. Such activities included coordinating the visits of famous Norwegians, including the polar explorers Roald Amundsen and Fridtjof Nansen. The Sons of Norway helped organize the massive 17th of May celebration of 1914, the most extravagant in the history of the city of Minneapolis, which celebrated the centennial of Norwegian independence. In 1925 the organization also helped mark the centennial of the arrival of the sloop *Restaurationen*, which brought one of the first boatloads of Norwegian immigrants to the United States in 1825. The Sons of Norway continues its operations to the present, and its organizational headquarters remains in Minneapolis. Lutheran Brotherhood, also a fraternal insurance society, with headquarters in Minneapolis, also has its roots in the period of development of cooperative institutions among the Scandinavian immigrants.

While the Scandinavians had their areas of concentrated settlement in the early years, they soon dispersed over the city as they became acclimated to the new environment. By 1930 the dispersion of the foreign-born Scandinavian immigrants around

Above: *A massive rally and musical celebration topped off the 1925 Norse-American Centennial. Participants literally jammed the bandstands at the Minnesota State Fairgrounds. (MHS)*

Facing page: *During the Norse-American Centennial in 1925, a pageant was organized which recreated the highlights of Norwegian history and mythology, including the early development of Viking culture, the conversion of the Scandinavians to Christianity, and the development of the modern Norwegian nation. Here, the recreated Leif Erickson asks for divine guidance in the course of his voyages, with two monks in attendance. (MHS)*

the city was complete, with interesting results. Of the city's 13 wards, foreign-born Swedes outnumbered other foreign-born groups in 11 of them. The Norwegians were the second-largest group of foreign-born citizens in these same 11 wards. The bulk of the Swedes and Norwegians were concentrated, however, in the eastern half of South Minneapolis, even though they outnumbered the other foreign-born groups in most of the rest of the city.

As their numbers increased the Swedes and Norwegians began to make their presence felt in the political and economic activities of the city and of the state. Drawn to the Republican party from the beginning, the Scandinavians began developing potential candidates for office early on. George H. Johnson, an early arrival who served in the Civil War, became a police officer in Minneapolis in 1869 and in the following year was elected sheriff of Hennepin County. He was reelected twice and went on to serve in the state legislature and, later, was a deputy sheriff in the county. Knute Nelson, a Norwegian, was the first Scandinavian to be elected to the U.S. House of Representatives in Minnesota. A Swede, A.H. Edsten, was elected to the Minneapolis city council in 1874, and two Norwegians were elected to that body four years later. In succeeding years Swedes and Norwegians and their descendants were elected to all the major political offices in the state. Most governors of the state since 1900, in fact, have been of Scandinavian descent. The judiciary also was served by the Scandinavians, and one of the most prominent immigrant jurists was Andreas Ueland, who came to Minneapolis in 1871 and went to work as a construction laborer. Ueland went to law school at night and was admitted to the bar in 1877. In 1883 he was made a judge in the probate court system. The Scandinavians made the transition to the American political system with relative ease in Minnesota.

The Scandinavian immigrants in Minneapolis arrived after the city's primary industries were established and in operation, but they found, nonetheless, substantial opportunities to absorb their productive energies. Small businesses, financial service activities, construction and building, and the professions were the main

Facing page: *Minneapolis was one of the major centers of Swedish immigrants in the Midwest. The establishment of the Swedish-American National Bank as well as a great many cultural and social institutions reflect the vitality of Swedish-American community life in Minneapolis, circa 1904. From the E.A. Bromley Collection. (MPLIC)*

areas of their efforts. They even created their own banking institution, the Scandinavian American National Bank, which was originally designed to meet the needs of the immigrant entrepreneurs and community members. The bank's first president was Nils Werner, and John Lind (later governor of the state), Andreas Ueland, Aaron Carlson, and Eugene Tetzlaff served on the board of directors. Over the years the bank evolved into the Midland National Bank.

The Scandinavians also greatly contributed to the development of culture and the arts in Minneapolis. Highly supportive of efforts to develop indigenous art forms, the Swedes and Norwegians also made substantial efforts to develop their own. Musical and choral groups sprang up in such profusion that a great festival, or *Sangerfest*, was held in Minneapolis in 1891. Swedish, Norwegian, and Danish groups came from all over the United States to take part in the event. Norwegian sculptor Jacob Fjelde arrived in Minneapolis in 1887 and was commissioned to execute a great many works which commemorated parts of the city's past. Fjelde made the statue of John H. Stevens which stands today in Minnehaha Park, a statue of Ole Bull which was placed in Loring Park, a bust of the Norwegian dramatist Henrik Ibsen which was placed in Como Park, and the statues of Hiawatha and Minnehaha which were deposited in the park around Minnehaha Falls.

In partial response to the influx of Scandinavians in the state, a chair in Scandinavian languages was created at the University of Minnesota in Minneapolis in 1884. The descendants of the first immigrants were drawn to the university in great numbers from the beginning, and members of the second generation made substantial contributions to its development. Swedish historian George Stephenson and Norwegian scholar Theodore C. Blegen stand out in this regard. Both men also made impressive contributions to the development of the Minnesota Historical Society as well. Their work was carried on by other scholars such as Professor Carlton Qualey, who helped to establish general immigration studies throughout the United States. The Scandinavians par-

Facing page: *Minnehaha Falls changes from season to season, from a light flow in late summer and fall, to heavy volume in spring, to a solid state in winter during weeks of subfreezing temperatures. (MPLIC)*

Above: *Longfellow's "The Song of Hiawatha" captured the imaginations of the early generations in Minneapolis. This statue of Hiawatha and Minnehaha, executed by Norwegian-born sculptor Jacob Fjelde, was placed in Minnehaha Park just above the falls. (MPLIC)*

Facing page: *Jacob Fjelde's statue of violinist Ole Bull in Loring Park was the site of a choral presentation on the Norwegian Syttendi Mai national holiday in 1929. Norwegian singers under the direction of S. Watten sang "Ja Vi Elsker," the Norwegian national anthem. Ole Bull made numerous tours to Minneapolis and was active in various phases of Norwegian immigrant community life in the United States. From the Minneapolis Star and Tribune Company. (MPLIC)*

ticipated in existing educational institutions and also created their own. In Minneapolis Augsburg College represents the pinnacle of their efforts. Originally a seminary, it was moved to Minneapolis from Wisconsin in 1871, and over the years it evolved into a four-year liberal arts college, although it retained its basic religious orientation.

While the Scandinavians constituted the major foreign group to come to Minneapolis, other groups also carved out niches in the city. German immigration to Minnesota was significant in the last quarter of the 19th century, and many of the immigrants made their way to Minneapolis. Unlike the majority of Germans who migrated to America, the greater part of the German immigrants in Minneapolis were Catholic rather than Lutheran. These immigrants settled primarily in Southeast and Northeast Minneapolis, although there were substantial numbers in North Minneapolis as well. A German-language Catholic parish was organized in Old St. Anthony in 1858, and by the mid-1870s parochial schools were operating in conjunction with the parishes of St. Boniface and St. Joseph. By 1930 there were approximately 7,500 German immigrants living in Minneapolis. Unlike other groups who came to the city, however, the German community in Minneapolis was subjected to intense scrutiny and even repression as a result of the political developments in the state during World War I. German books were banned selectively, German language instruction was restricted, teaching in German in parochial schools was limited, and German organizations were prevented from meeting. The hostility against the German community was intense and muted the cultural vitality that it once possessed.

Another major immigrant community to develop in Minneapolis in the late 19th century was that composed of German and Eastern European Jews. The three main elements in the Jewish community in Minneapolis were the German Jews, who arrived earliest; the Russian, Polish, and Lithuanian Jews, who arrived from those areas later; and the Rumanian Jews, who arrived subsequent to them. By 1900 there were approximately

Emil Oberhoffer was the first in a distinguished line of conductors of the Minneapolis Symphony Orchestra, later the Minnesota Orchestra. Oberhoffer overcame problems of finance and performance location and managed to get the orchestra performing on a regular basis. He also initiated the orchestra's touring programs. Photo by A. DuPont. (MPLIC)

8,000 Jews living in Minneapolis, and by 1918 their numbers had increased to about 15,000. While the German Jews were dispersed somewhat around the city, the Jews from Russia, Poland, and Lithuania clustered in the near north side of the city, while the Rumanian Jews congregated on the south side of Franklin Avenue near 15th Street. The synagogue was the center of Jewish community life in Minneapolis as elsewhere, and the major synagogue in Minneapolis was the one founded by the German Jews. Originally called Shaarai Tov, or "Gates of Goodness," this synagogue became a focal point of activity in the Minneapolis Jewish community. The synagogue later became Temple Israel and was initially located at 10th Street and Fifth Avenue South. The synagogue is located presently at 24th Street and Hennepin Avenue.

The various subelements within the Jewish community were sources of division rather than unity. German Jews often looked with disdain at their brethren from Eastern Europe, and language divided them all. They were also divided by varying degrees of religious orthodoxy, as well as by differences in political outlook. A remarkable individual helped overcome these divisions and transform the divided Jewish community into a unified one. The man was Samuel N. Deinard, who came to Minneapolis to become rabbi of Shaarai Tov in 1901.

Deinard was born in Raseinai, Lithuania, in 1873, and as a youth he migrated with his family to Palestine, then part of the Ottoman Empire and today the independent state of Israel. Deinard was thus exposed early to the political program of Zionism and was to support this program for the rest of his life. He was a gifted scholar and was educated in Berlin and Cologne before immigrating to the United States in 1892. Once in this country Deinard continued his studies at the University of Pennsylvania in Philadelphia, and in 1897 he received his A.B. degree from DePauw University. In 1900 Deinard received his M.A. degree from the University of Chicago, and he came to Minneapolis in 1901. In 1901 he was awarded the Ph.D. by the University of Minnesota.

Archbishop John G. Murray, left, is welcomed by Rabbi Albert G. Minda at Temple Israel in Minneapolis in 1939. Minneapolis has diverse religious groups active in the community, and cooperation has marked many of their social and cultural activities over the years. From the Minneapolis Star and Tribune Company. (MPLIC)

As rabbi of the major synagogue in Minneapolis, Deinard worked assiduously to overcome the ethnic and linguistic diversities that divided the community. Fluent in several languages, he was able to approach each element on its own terms, in ways that were acceptable to each, and in ways that they could easily understand. Deinard also made great use of the Zionist philosophy to weld the Jewish community together with common purpose and vision. By 1909 he was national vice-president of the Federation of American Zionists. In 1915 he organized the publication *American Jewish World*, which systematically treated a variety of issues in politics and culture facing the American Jewish community.

While Deinard was devoted to serving the interests and needs of the Minneapolis Jewish community, he also stressed the importance of the struggle for general social justice. He was active in the National Association for the Advancement of Colored People and served as first president of the local chapter of that organization. Deinard argued that the rights of all citizens were jeopardized when the rights of any minority were threatened. Mindful of Jewish history in Europe and elsewhere, he pressed for the involvement of the Jewish community in issues that transcended their immediate needs and interests. By the time of his death in late 1921, Deinard had welded the Jewish community of Minneapolis into a coherent body with established patterns of cooperation and social involvement. Although numerically a small group the Jewish community of Minneapolis maintained such activity over the succeeding decades and in the 1950s saw one of their number, Arthur Naftalin, elected mayor of the city.

Along with the Jews, people from other groups in Eastern Europe made their way to Minneapolis in the 30 years prior to the outbreak of World War I. Poles, Ukrainians, Czechs, and Slovaks were among them. By 1930 about 15,000 of these immigrants resided in the city. The Poles were the largest single Slavic group in the city, and they began arriving in the 1860s. The great majority of Poles who migrated to the United States came seeking industrial employment, and many later returned to their native country. In

Facing page: *Pupils from Adams School are shown here planting an elm tree on Arbor Day in 1916. Sixty years later the large elm population in Minneapolis was ravaged by Dutch elm disease, which caused the loss of a large part of the city's finest tree stock. Massive planting in Minneapolis of new trees along more diversified lines has been effected in order to avoid repeating this disaster. (MHS)*

Minnesota, however, a significant number of Polish immigrants became farmers. Some of these people eventually ended up in the city, where a separate Polish community of workers developed. The Poles in Minneapolis settled primarily in the Northeast section of the city in the residential areas closest to the Mississippi River. In the area of the First Ward, the Poles were the largest foreign-born group in 1930, when they numbered about 2,000. Another 1,000 lived in the adjacent ward that comprised the rest of Northeast Minneapolis.

The Poles who came to the city were predominantly Roman Catholic, and the religion served as the primary organizing force in their community. Primarily industrial workers, the Poles structured their community around church and home. The church was a source of strength in the community, but it also proved to be a source of dissension. The problem developed from conflicts between the Polish immigrants and their Polish clergy as well as from struggles with a Catholic hierarchy that was predominantly Irish. Anticipating the ecumenical movement of the last 20 years by more than half a century, the Poles desired to use the church to maintain their language and culture through the use of the Polish language in the church and parochial schools as well as the use of the parish as a base for diverse types of organizations that the Poles desired to develop for political and economic as well as purely religious ends. The Irish hierarchy within the diocesan structure opposed these activities, however, and stressed the importance of Americanization for the immigrants and strict subordination to the leadership of the church in temporal matters. This conflict reached such dimensions that a schism developed, and dissenting Poles created a separate church in the United States, the Polish National Catholic Church, in 1896. The majority of Poles in Minneapolis and other centers of Polish settlement such as Chicago and Buffalo remained loyal to the Roman Catholic church, but the conflict affected the entire community.

The Polish community in Minneapolis, unlike the native American elements and the Scandinavians, was also preoccupied with events in the homeland. Denied national independence from the 18th century, the Polish people sought to use every means to regain it, and the Poles in America supported these efforts. Except for the Irish people in the United States, few European immigrant communities in America were so continually rocked by political events in the old country. The outbreak of World War I and the creation of an independent Poland at the end of the war was, thus, a signal event in the Polish community in Minneapolis. The high hopes of this period were dashed subsequently with the outbreak of World War II and the political settlements that concluded that conflict. The Polish community in Minneapolis remains interested in the events in the mother country to the present day and remains loyal to Catholicism, a loyalty that was rewarded with the election of a Polish prelate to the Roman Papacy a few years ago.

Other groups from Eastern Europe also immigrated to Minneapolis in the last part of the 19th century, although they came in smaller numbers than did either the Poles or the Jews. Among them were Ukrainians, Czechs, Ruthenians, and Slovaks. The Ukrainians began to arrive after 1900 and settled primarily in Northeast Minneapolis, where they sought work as laborers in the industries located in the area. The Ukrainians were primarily Orthodox Christians in religious faith; that is, members of the Christian church that had refused to accept the supremacy of the Roman popes in the 10th century. The Orthodox Ukrainians celebrated the liturgy in their native tongues, and the interiors of their churches reflected the ornamentation of the Eastern regions, with icons and the iconostasis serving as a barrier between the altar and the congregation.

Part of the Ukrainian immigrant community, however, was Uniate in its religious orientation. The Uniate church represented those Orthodox Christians who accepted the supremacy of the Roman popes but who were allowed to retain their Orthodox liturgies and practices in return. Similar divisions marked the Ruthenian community, which developed in Minneapolis at the same time that the Ukrainians also were arriving. Today these two commu-

Facing page: *In 1936 St. Mary's Church in Northeast Minneapolis was visited by the head of the Russian Orthodox churches in the United States. Northeast Minneapolis had the largest Slavic population in the city, made up of a large number of Catholic Poles and Czechoslovaks and Orthodox Ukrainians, Rusins, and Russians. The area retains a large degree of this historical ethnic flavor to the present. From the Minneapolis Star and Tribune Company. (MHS)*

Facing page: *Minneapolis welcomed several groups of refugees in the years after World War II. Private and public groups in the city have been instrumental in resettling Ukrainians, Poles, and Jews in the city as well as, in more recent times, the Cambodians, Vietnamese, and Hmong people fleeing from Southeast Asia. Pictured are three Ukrainian women, with a bountiful supply of pisanka, decorated Ukrainian Easter eggs, which were sold to raise funds for the Ukrainian Refugee Relief Fund in the late 1940s. From the Minneapolis Star and Tribune Company. (MPLIC)*

Following pages, left: *Logs were often swept over the dam and apron at the Falls of St. Anthony during heavy rains or spring snow melts. The inhabitants of the Bohemian Flats would take advantage of these fortuitous incidents to replenish their stocks of firewood and all-purpose lumber. Women from the Flats engage in such a salvage operation, circa 1910. From the E.A. Bromley Collection. (MPLIC)*

Right: *In the background of this 1903 photo, imperiously perched on the Mississippi River bluffs, stand the buildings which compose the University of Minnesota. Across the river is the immigrant settlement of Bohemian Flats, inhabited by poor citizens. Photo by Sweet. (MPLIC)*

nities are thriving in Northeast Minneapolis as well as in other parts of the metropolitan area as a result of the early efforts of the original immigrants and also as a result of a fresh influx of immigrants in the period immediately following World War II. In the Old St. Anthony district, where Southern gentlemen and belles strolled around Winslow House at the end of the "Grand Tour" to the falls, there now echo the accents of Eastern Europe amid the shops, delicatessens, and restaurants that specialize in Slavic meats and pastries.

While the Poles and Ukrainians settled primarily on the East Bank of the Mississippi River, other Slavic immigrants, the Czechs and Slovaks especially, tended to settle on the West Bank. A particularly famous area of settlement to which they were attracted has become part of the folklore of the city. Below the Falls of St. Anthony, the riverbanks rise high over the river, and as the river bends to the south, a large flat area develops on the West Bank. Today the area is used for coal storage and is also the site of several large petroleum storage tanks. Above the wall of the gorge is the West Bank campus of the University of Minnesota, and across the river is the main campus of the school. Until the 1930s, however, the river flat on the West Bank was the site of a bustling immigrant community.

The "Bohemian Flats," as the area was called, was originally known as the "Danish Flats," because Danes had originally settled on the shore. After 1880, however, Slovak immigrants began to arrive in the flats area along with a few Poles, some French Canadians, and a handful of German and Irish families. The Slovakian immigrants were from the northern area of Hungary and differed from most of their countrymen in that they were Protestant rather than Roman Catholic. The Lutheran Slovaks left their European area of settlement to escape religious persecution and the attempts of the Hungarians to absorb them into the Magyar culture. They came to work in the flour mills that were concentrated along the edge of the river upstream toward the falls. In order to reach their places of employment, the Slovak workmen had to climb to the top of the embankment overlooking their settlement and then make

their way back to the river where the mills were situated. This climb was necessary because there was no way to go upriver from the flats themselves. A series of steps made of wood were constructed by the settlers to enable them to make their way to the top of the gorge. Each morning there would be a procession up the stairs, in winter and summer, as the workers made their way to their jobs, and in the evening the procession would be reversed as they returned to their homes.

The Bohemian Flats was divided into two separate areas, one closer to the river than the other. At its peak the area boasted some 500 inhabitants and contained some 120 rude homes. Three streets, (or, more appropriately, three lanes) wound their way through the area. The highest street, Mill Street, was the Park Avenue of the Flats. Above an upper levee and somewhat better protected against periodic spring flooding, rents averaged about $25 a year on Mill Street. Below Mill was Cooper Street where rents averaged about $18 a year, and the lowest street, Wood Street, next to the river's edge, had rents averaging $15 a year. For these reasonable prices the immigrants received housing that provided minimal shelter against the icy blasts of winter and that had no running water or water closets. Wells were the source of water, and the community pump was a center of social activity in the Flats, much as in the old-country villages of the immigrants. While the housing was inferior it was the equal of much of the working-class housing in the rest of the city. The spirit of the community was its primary resource, and the tightly knit social relations in the Flats helped the people to overcome several disasters. One such disaster occurred in the spring of 1920 when the Coon Rapids dam burst, resulting in the total immersion of the lower levee area.

The inhabitants of Bohemian Flats recovered from this and other floods, but final disaster was visited upon the community not by the river but by city hall. The city was looking for a site for new municipal coal docks and found it on the river flats. The residents attempted to ward off the action but were unsuccessful. In February

1931 eviction notices were sent out to some 50 residents, and by the end of March the inhabitants were busy dismantling their houses in efforts to salvage as much as they possibly could. The coal docks were constructed after the residents were gone and remain at the site to the present day. The Bohemian Flats flourished for some 50 years and reflected the marginal material existence that characterized much of the initial immigrant experience but at the same time reflected the strength the immigrants found in cooperation as they struggled to adapt to their new environment.

In addition to native white American migrants and immigrants from Europe, Minneapolis also attracted small numbers of other groups prior to World War II. There was a small black population in Minneapolis from the mid-19th century, and that population grew after 1880, as did the black populations of many cities in the Midwest. In 1880 there were 362 blacks in Minneapolis, and by 1930 their numbers had increased to 4,176. The blacks who came to the city were attracted by employment opportunities in the service sector of the city's economy, especially with the railroads. Minneapolis was a good distance from the major areas of black population in this period, and this fact explains in part why that community did not increase as rapidly as in other cities such as Chicago. Also, employment opportunities in Minneapolis for unskilled workers were the objects of intense competition on the part of many migrants from rural areas who came to the city from short distances. Domestic service, which often served as a primary employment field for blacks in many other cities, was dominated in Minneapolis by Swedish and Irish immigrants.

Racial discrimination played a major role in the lack of opportunities for blacks in the cities, but general economic conditions and the peculiarities of the Minneapolis economy explain why their numbers did not grow more rapidly. The blacks who did settle in the city collected in two areas of residence, one on the near north side of the city on the periphery of the central business district, and the other in South Minneapolis near Fourth Avenue South and

Facing page: *In the era before
television and radio, local sports
played an important role in
Minneapolis and the rest of the
country. Professional players from the
smallest towns vied for titles at the
county and state levels. Minnesota's
1901 state champions were the
Waseca Eago Flour players. In a
period of systematic segregation in
Minneapolis and the rest of the
nation, it is interesting to note that
semi-professional baseball was
integrated, at least among the players.
(MHS)*

38th Street. Other clusters of blacks were to be found west of the Seven Corners area and near the Milwaukee Road railroad tracks between Tenth Avenue South and Franklin Avenue.

Attempts by individual blacks to venture into predominantly white areas of residence were met with hostility by the white population and led to some ugly incidents in the city's history. In July 1931, for example, a white mob numbering in the hundreds intimidated and abused a black family that had bought a residence in a white neighborhood in South Minneapolis. Conditions for black residents have changed for the better since the 1930s, but the problems of blacks in Minneapolis parallel those that blacks continue to encounter in urban America generally. Since Hubert Humphrey's tenure as mayor in the mid-1940s, Minneapolis city government has taken many steps to eliminate discrimination, and while the record is not unblemished and the present is not perfect, progress has been substantial. Blacks are closely involved in the political and economic life of the city and have developed a variety of cooperative organizations to maintain and enhance their community.

Before the post-Vietnam War period, few nonwhite immigrants made their way to Minneapolis. In 1930 there were some 220 Chinese residing in the city, about 150 Mexicans, and 38 Japanese. Minneapolis did not serve as a powerful magnet for these groups and others that arrived about the same time. The reasons are explained by the pattern of development of the city. Minneapolis received the majority of its immigrants before the end of the 19th century, when the city experienced its greatest period of economic growth. The immigrants who were arriving in the United States were primarily Scandinavians and Germans, and so, not surprisingly, these groups were dominant in the ethnic mix of the city. Also, the agricultural region or hinterland of the city of Minneapolis developed at the same time, so the great majority of rural immigrants were also members of these groups. More Scandinavians and Germans became farmers in America as immigrants than any other foreign-born people, and they established many farmsteads in Minnesota,

Cambodians, have been resettled in the city and surrounding counties in efforts to provide these displaced persons an opportunity to build new lives for themselves in this country. The shock of immersion in an alien culture, sophisticated economy, and subarctic climate have tested the refugees severely, but results to date have been promising.

The development of community in Minneapolis has proceeded over the decades despite diversity among the people who settled in the city. Accidents of timing were of assistance in making the transition relatively smooth, but major obstacles were encountered along the way. Minneapolis was, for example, once identified as one of the most anti-Semitic cities in the nation. The charge arose from a study conducted in the post-World War II period by an eminent sociologist, Carey McWilliams. In the years after the charge was made, Minneapolis elected a mayor of Jewish descent and also provided a haven for a number of Jewish refugees from Eastern Europe. Blacks have also encountered difficulties in the city, similar to those they have encountered elsewhere. Yet Minneapolis has pioneered in the development of affirmative action programs at the city level, and it was a mayor of the city, Hubert Humphrey, who injected the issue of civil rights into the agenda of the national Democratic party.

The development of community in Minneapolis, then, represents a long process of struggle which has not ended. It also reflects the foibles and passions that have characterized American history and which make the pursuit of true community a goal worth striving for. There have been setbacks and disappointments in Minneapolis as elsewhere, but the tradition of effort is well-established at the grass roots. Fragile as it sometimes has proven to be, the sense of community in Minneapolis is remarkable in light of the diversity in the origins of its inhabitants and the adversities that it has encountered. In meeting these trials as often as not, it should be stressed, it has come away a winner.

◆   ◆   ◆

Minneapolis baseball fans cheer the Millers at Nicollet Park, circa 1925. The team has since moved its games to Metropolitan Stadium in Bloomington and then to the domed stadium named for Hubert Humphrey. (MHS)

Facing page: *The confluence of the Mississippi and Minnesota rivers is clearly visible in this landsat photograph of the Minneapolis area. Courtesy, EROS Data Center, U.S. Department of the Interior.*

Top right: *Josephine Lutz Rollins painted* Old St. Anthony District *in 1949. (MHS)*

Bottom right: Minneapolis Farmers' Market *was painted by Edward Nooleen in 1938. (MHS)*

Facing page: *Elof Wedin, a Swedish immigrant, painted* Mills at Minneapolis *in 1934–1935. Wedin depicted the Pillsbury mills and the Stone Arch Bridge in strong colors outlined in black. (MHS)*

Below: *An historic celebration was organized for the Riverplace redevelopment project on Main Street in Old St. Anthony.*

Facing page, clockwise from top left: *The Como-Harriet Streetcar Line, which runs between Lake Harriet and Lake Calhoun, was reopened in 1971 after being closed since 1954. Streetcar Number 1,300, built in April 1908 at TCRT Snelling Shops in St. Paul, has been restored, and the 46-foot streetcar now carries visitors between the two lakes. Other restored streetcars can be viewed at the Minnesota Transportation Museum, one of the organizations responsible for the restoration of this streetcar and line.*

Svenskarnas Dag is the annual

Swedish celebration that attracts the largest gathering of Swedes in the United States. Swedes form one of the largest ethnic groups in Minneapolis. Courtesy, Minnesota Tourism Division, Dept. of E.P.D.

During the summer months, visitors to Fort Snelling can experience life as it was during the early days of settlement in Minneapolis, when the safety of the fort, situated near the confluence of the Minnesota and Mississippi rivers, was central to the stability of daily life. Courtesy, Minnesota Tourism Division, Dept. of E.P.D.

Visitors to the annual Renaissance Fair witness various reenactments of aspects of daily pioneer life in early Minneapolis. A woman spins thread on a treadle-operated wheel at the 1974 fair. Courtesy, Minnesota Tourism Division, Dept. of E.P.D.

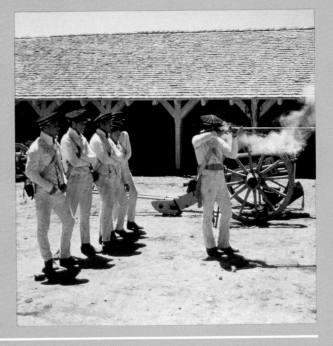

Top right: An aerial shot of St. Anthony Falls shows the Third Avenue Bridge (right) and the stone arch railway bridge (left). The Pillsbury A Mill and grain elevators are located in the foreground. Courtesy, Minnesota Tourism Division, Dept. of E.P.D.

Bottom right: This stone arch railway bridge is the only structure of its type to span the Mississippi River.

Facing page: Locks are vital to safe navigation of the upper Mississippi through Minneapolis by coal and grain barges as well as private pleasure craft. Courtesy, Minnesota Tourism Division, Dept. of E.P.D.

Facing page: *Downtown Minneapolis' east side and points beyond can be seen in this view from the IDS tower.*

Below: *Lights glitter along the Minneapolis skyline. Local artist Joseph Panone reflected a spotlight off the IDS tower on May 20, 1977, for his piece entitled* The IDS Project—A Surface Reflection. *(Private Collection)*

Top right: *Wintertime fishermen left their mark on the ice of Lake Calhoun. (Private Collection)*

Bottom right: *Moist air and cold March nights create ice sculpture out of ordinary trees, a sight to be viewed by early risers, as the morning sun melts the ice by noon. Courtesy, Minnesota Tourism Division, Dept. of E.P.D.*

Facing page: *Minneapolis' skyline, with the distinguished IDS building standing tall, was photographed in the winter of 1979 from the new wing of the Minneapolis Institute of Arts. (Private Collection)*

Top: *Minnehaha Falls spills over amidst lush greenery in the summer of 1976. Courtesy, Minnesota Tourism Division, Dept. of E.P.D.*

Bottom: *Sailboats lie moored for the evening on Lake Calhoun in 1974. Minneapolis' recreational lakes were dredged and lanscaped between the late 1880s and the mid-1920s. Courtesy, Minnesota Tourism Division, Dept. of E.P.D.*

Facing page: *Minneapolis residents enjoy an evening walk in late autumn along Powderhorn Lake. (Private Collection)*

CHAPTER V
PARTNERS IN PROGRESS
by Dick Schaaf

They started in garages and basements and back rooms, many of them. On shoestrings, many of them. With borrowed money and borrowed furniture and original ideas, many of them.

In the beginning they were family businesses—both in the boss' office and out in the shop (and often that was one and the same place) several generations worked for the company. The sense of community in the plant fostered a sense of community between businesses and their city. They sent down roots, becoming much more than simply a name imprinted on a paycheck or hot-stamped on a product.

And they grew. They grew because the people who ran them and worked for them and cared for them worked hard. Some grew very large and succeeded. Some grew more modestly, but succeeded too. Their growth and success they shared with the city, so it grew and succeeded as well.

As they grew and succeeded they stayed in the hometown that had historically been so good for them: some by conscious decision made in spite of the lure of other places, others because there was never any good reason to consider moving. They are here still, still deeply involved in the lives of the community and its people.

Minneapolis, the business heart and soul of the Upper Midwest and part of a uniquely dynamic tandem with sister city St. Paul, shows the evidence of its family of businesses. The number of major corporations headquartered in the Twin Cities is out of all proportion to population or regional clout. Entrepreneurs continue to find the area a hospitable climate in which to bring new ideas into reality. Downtown Minneapolis bustles with people and shops and development as few American cities still do, sustained and renewed by its business community.

It is an international town, seeing the comings and goings of people bound for the far corners of an ever-smaller commercial world. It is a cosmopolitan town, celebrating its confidence and achievement through the arts and sports and recreation, both indoors and out.

And yet it is somehow still a small town, where people get to know other people because those people will be around for a while, where an uncommon form of peer pressure makes things happen that would only be dreamed of elsewhere. These are the stories of some of the businesses which shaped—and continue to shape—the history of Minneapolis.

ALEXANDER & ALEXANDER INC.

In 1969, when Alexander & Alexander went public, the insurance brokerage firm had about 300 employees in fewer than 20 offices around the country. Today it is the second largest insurance broker in the world with 11,000 employees in nearly 90 U.S. cities and 44 countries—and the Minneapolis office, opened in 1970, is larger than the entire company was when Alexander & Alexander came to the Twin Cities.

The foundation for the firm's success in Minneapolis was actually laid in 1884 when Charles W. Sexton opened his own insurance office—in a onetime saloon—at No. 9 Washington Avenue

Charles W. Sexton Company became one of the largest and most successful insurance brokerage firms in the Midwest before forming the cornerstone of Alexander & Alexander's Twin Cities operations. This photo shows the office about 1910.

• • •

North. That was almost 10 years before Charles B. and William F. Alexander set up shop in a two-room storefront in Clarksburg, West Virginia. Sexton had come west from New York as a field representative for Fireman's Fund in Wisconsin and southern Minnesota, specializing in those industries impor-

tant to the growth of the region's economy: grains, milling, and lumber. After nearly a century of successful service, especially under the direction of Waldo Hardell, Charles W. Sexton Company was acquired on January 1, 1970, to be the cornerstone of Alexander & Alexander's Minnesota operations.

Just 10 months later the new Minneapolis office took a second major step with the addition of Wirt Wilson & Company. Founded in 1913 by Wilson and Ed Force, the company was a fixture in the Minneapolis Builders Exchange for half a century, first under Wilson, later with Glenn Wyer at the helm. The president of Alexander & Alexander's Minnesota office, William D. Baker, began his insurance career with the Wilson firm.

Other additions in Alexander & Alexander's early years in the Twin Cities included the acquisitions of Harold Gottlieb Company and Paul Burke & Associates in 1972 and Traff & Associates in 1974. Both the Gottlieb and Traff firms trace their roots back to the 1930s.

From its new headquarters in the Alexander & Alexander Building on Theodore Wirth Parkway, the local office's more than 300 employees today serve a cross section of Upper Midwest businesses. They range from better than three-quarters of the top 20 major companies on the Corporate Report 100 down to smaller enterprises such as gift shops and restaurants. More than simply advising on the purchase of insurance, Alexander & Alexander serves as an important source of information and expertise on risk management and loss forecasting (often involving complex computer modeling), management consulting and human resources planning, and benefit consulting.

ARTHUR ANDERSEN & CO.

Arthur Andersen & Co., founded in Chicago in 1913, opened its Minneapolis office in 1940 when Wallace E. Lunden came from Chicago to be the first resident manager. In its first year the office provided auditing and tax services to several area utilities and manufacturing companies, generating $5,500 in fees with a staff of seven to handle the growth prospects before it.

The major growth of the office took place in the 1960s under the guiding hands of A.R. Nelson and Fred L. Moore, Jr., as local companies that had previously been privately held moved into public ownership and many new businesses emerged. In 1974 the firm opened an office in Saint Paul. Today the Twin Cities offices have nearly 300 professional men and women providing accounting and auditing, tax, and management information consulting services to businesses both large and small throughout the Ninth Federal Reserve District. Annual billings are in excess of $15 million, putting Minneapolis well up in the firm's top 20 offices among some 130 worldwide.

Early in its history, the firm reacted to the growth of specialized industry segments, each with their own specific problems, by establishing a policy of industry specialization for its personnel. Clients served by the Minneapolis office cover a very broad spectrum—the more significant industries include manufacturing, oil and gas exploration and development, health care, banking, utilities, food and beverage, advertising, high technology, printing, and professional sports. Early on, the firm also recognized the needs of closely held businesses, and since 1944 the small business division has offered accounting, tax, systems, and business consulting specifically designed for entrepreneurs in all industries.

Founded by a college professor, Arthur Andersen & Co. has always placed a very high priority on professional training and development of its personnel. The office is particularly proud of its many personnel who have gone on to become leaders in other offices of the firm, as well as those who have become chief executives or top financial officers in industry.

The present managing partner and chief executive officer of the worldwide firm of Arthur Andersen & Co. is Duane R. Kullberg, a 1954 University of Minnesota graduate, who headed the Minneapolis office from 1970 to 1974 before moving to Chicago. While in Minneapolis, Duane was involved in many civic activities. The present partners, led by Jay H. Wein, managing partner since 1974, continue that tradition of community leadership and service by being involved in numerous civic and charitable activities in the greater Minneapolis area.

• • •

The Minneapolis office of Arthur Andersen & Co. reflects the international nature of its clientele.

AMERICAN LINEN SUPPLY COMPANY

Delivery wagons similar to this one were used by American Linen until 1927. Shown here is "Konkora," Grand Champion Percheron at the 1926 State Fair.

• • •

to the point where he could take his brother into the business as an equal partner. From the original green and white pushcart they were also able to move up to a horse-drawn delivery wagon. Nearly a century later American Linen Supply Company is one of the largest suppliers of the towels, uniforms, and other linens used every day by heavy industry, retail stores, restaurants, hospitals, hotels, and other businesses in the United States, Canada, and Europe.

When the Steiner brothers were getting started, Minneapolis and Salt Lake City were the boom towns of the day. In 1895 George Steiner went west to open the company's first branch, in Salt Lake; a year later Frank arrived in Minneapolis after a laundry machine salesman told him the city had no towel service. It did, so the Steiners contracted with the company, the S&H Laundry, to wash its towels too. The owner, being cautious, continually demanded cash-on-delivery payments, but that put such a strain on the fledgling business that the Steiners made their first "big move"—with a loan of $400, they bought the competing laundry.

Early towel service consisted of a single loop of cloth hung on a roller in washrooms. It was clean for the first person who happened to use it, but after that it tended to deteriorate rapidly. Recognizing how unsanitary the practice was, the Steiners responded by developing their own continuous towel dispensing units, the first of several patents they would register for their busi-

Times were hard for the Steiner family of Lincoln, Nebraska, back in the 1880s. To augment their father's income as a traveling salesman, George and Frank Steiner took a variety of odd jobs. They peddled papers, worked in shoe stores, and delivered messages for Western Union before George landed a more substantial position earning three dollars a week delivering towels. His employer,

a Mr. Johnson, had started a new business based on providing each customer with a clean towel every day for one dollar a month.

In 1889, at the seasoned age of 15, George Steiner purchased the business for $50.80—$25 in cash and the balance from assuming Mr. Johnson's bill at a local drug store. His Lincoln Towel and Apron Supply Company soon grew

nesses. They later formed the Steiner Sales Company of Chicago to manufacture and sell their growing line of towel cabinets.

In Minneapolis, a shuttle wagon carried linens over to St. Paul, a 20-mile round trip that took all day. As a result, a separate St. Paul plant was added in 1914. In the 1920s, while on a Canadian vacation, Frank Steiner was so impressed by the beauty and opportunity to be found north of the border that he immediately made plans to start a Canadian plant. Canadian Linen Supply was born in Vancouver, British Columbia, on June 1, 1925; today its branches can be found in virtually every major Canadian city.

For many years deliveries were made via horse-drawn wagons designed specifically for laundries. The wagon's sloping roof kept moisture from running off over work areas, while an automatic brake system—a weight hung under the floor in front of the driver and attached to the reins—would stop and hold the horse when lowered.

The Minneapolis operation took a good deal of pride in its livestock. "Koncora" was judged Grand Champion Percheron at the 1926 Minnesota State Fair. "Daisy" delighted children along delivery routes by drinking soda pop, opening her own water spigots, and pausing now and then to lean against telephone poles for a short rest. The last horse-drawn vehicles were retired by 1927.

American Linen has been headquartered in the Steiner Building at Ninth and LaSalle (the latter once a cobble-stoned street known as Mary Place) since its construction in 1926. In the '30s, with growing operations on both sides of the border, the Steiners realized they could best ensure the quality of

The Minneapolis Delivery Department posed along Mary Place (now LaSalle), a dirt road in the downtown. Evidence of the coming demise of the horse-drawn era—the fleet's first two Hupmobile trucks at right.

•   •   •

the linens they handled by going into the textile manufacturing business. That led to the founding of American Uniform Company in 1932; the Canadian Uniform division serves the firm's Canadian plants, while manufacturing units in Italy and Tunisia supply European customers.

The business begun by two brothers from Nebraska continues today under the direction of George R. Steiner, Frank's son. American Linen (and its counterparts, Canadian Linen and Euroblan) rents work clothing and related items to virtually every type of business and industry, from small enterprises to major operations. To meet the varying needs of its customers, the business has developed into a highly automated service firm. Coded programs are used to regulate the amounts of chemicals, hot water, and laundry time for washloads of 800 pounds and more. Special drying and ironing machinery developed

by American Linen handles large lots of sheets and towels quickly and efficiently.

Starting with a single pushcart in Lincoln, Nebraska, the Steiner family has developed a multi-branch organization with over 5,000 employees operating more than 50 plants in the United States, Canada, and Europe, and serving more than 600,000 customers each week. From simple hand towels to sophisticated industrial garments, hotel and restaurant linens to professional uniforms, American Linen has made a profitable business of keeping business clean.

APACHE CORPORATION

On December 6, 1954, a new business venture was officially incorporated in Minneapolis—Apache Oil Corporation.

One of its founders was Raymond Plank, a former tax accountant who had operated an oil investment firm which provided Minnesotans with an opportunity to invest in drilling oil wells.

Prior to Apache's formation, individuals had only been able to invest in one well at a time. Plank and his associates formulated the concept of a drilling "program," whereby the customers would only have to sign up once to participate in a number of wells and increase their chances of striking oil and generating a return.

To implement this new idea, however, a different corporate structure was required—hence the formation of Apache Oil, a pioneer in the oil program investment industry. Within two years the firm had 25 employees and was drilling wells in Texas, Oklahoma, Louisiana, Kansas, and the Denver Basin.

Apache had produced its one-millionth barrel of oil by 1957 and was selling its investment programs in several states outside Minnesota. The company passed the million-dollar revenue mark two years later, and expanded its exploration activities into Canada.

But almost from the beginning, Plank was among those in the oil business who warned of the long-term consequences of federal price controls on natural gas to keep it artificially inexpensive and encourage large-scale consumption. That policy, as many predicted, drastically altered the already risky economics of exploration and brought about an industry-wide decline in domestic drilling activities. To

Raymond Plank, who founded Apache in 1954, is presently chairman of the board and chief executive officer.

♦   ♦   ♦

stay in business, Apache made the decision to diversify into more rewarding industries while biding its time until oil and gas exploration again would be profitable. To reflect the changing nature of the company's business, Apache Oil became Apache Corporation.

Apache had entered the real estate business in 1959 when it acquired Minneapolis' then-most distinctive landmark, the Foshay Tower, the tallest building in the metropolitan area. At one time thought was given to changing the name of the Foshay Tower to "Apache Tower," but in deference to the landmark's place in the city heritage stretching back to the 1920s, the change was never made. From 1967 to 1973, when the IDS Center displaced the Foshay Tower as the city's tallest building, Apache operated a museum and observation deck on the 30th floor. The firm also built, and later sold, Apache Plaza, one of the first enclosed suburban shop-

ping malls in the Twin Cities.

The '60s and early '70s saw an aggressive diversification program as Apache entered a variety of industrial markets by acquiring relatively small businesses with growth potential. This strategy enabled Apache to maintain its growth and build the financial strength to accelerate its oil and gas operations in the mid-'70s.

As the economics of exploration began to change in the early 1970s, Apache streamlined its operations in anticipation of once again concentrating on the business it knew best: oil and gas exploration. All real estate and most of its industrial operations, which had kept the organization growing during the preceding decade, were sold, and the proceeds reinvested in its drilling operations.

Since then, Apache's strategy has been to concentrate on promising but relatively undrilled areas where large enough blocks of acreage could be leased to sustain drilling activities for a number of years. Major exploration areas include the Anadarko Basin in western Oklahoma and the Texas Panhandle, the Williston Basin in North Dakota and Montana, and the Rockies.

Apache had established itself as one of the most experienced deep-drilling companies in the United States by 1978. This yielded substantial dividends with the decontrol of natural gas discovered below 15,000 feet—in 1980 approximately half of Apache's natural gas reserves were below 15,000 feet. And 25 years after the company proudly reported oil and gas sales of $315,000 in its first year of operation, 1981 oil and gas sales reached $65 million, and total revenues for the company exceeded $150 million.

By the end of 1981, the firm had organized and managed 58 consecutive drilling partnerships on behalf of some 14,000 individuals investing over $525 million. Program sales had increased from $1.7 million in the first year to $70 million in 1981. Apache programs, directly and in partnership with major oil companies and other independent oil companies, have drilled more than 2,500 wells in the United States.

Recognized as one of the leading independent oil companies in America, Apache is participating with Amoco Production Company in a joint venture to explore and develop 2.5 million acres of leases in the Williston Basin of North Dakota and Montana. And in 1981 the company began offshore drilling in the Gulf of Mexico in partnership with Shell Oil Company.

◆　　◆　　◆

Apache wells in western Oklahoma are drilling three to five miles below ground in search of natural gas.

BENSON OPTICAL COMPANY

Nils Peter Benson, founder of Benson Optical Company.

When Nils Peter Benson got off the boat from Sweden in 1890 New York City, he was 16 years old, spoke not a word of English, and knew nothing about the human eye or the making of prescription lenses to help it see better. Today the company that bears his name is one of the acknowledged leaders in the production of prescription lenses and eyewear: Benson Optical.

Benson's first jobs in America included working on a small farm in Connecticut, apprenticeship as a carriage painter, and clerking in grocery and meat markets. Later he became a traveling salesman for a wholesale jeweler out of Massachusetts. The jeweler had a one-man optical department, and when that one man left and created an opening for an optician who could speak Swedish, the company's young Swedish-born salesman asked for the chance. Optical school (all six months of it) followed, and a foundation for the future was laid.

By 1906 Benson was a top salesman for New York's E.B. Meyrowitz and was sent west to run the company's store in Minneapolis. Over the next few years, a number of local doctors urged him to launch his own business. In 1913 Benson rented a small space on the second floor of the old Syndicate Building at 519 Nicollet. His first five employees included a $7-a-week office boy, Will R. Anderson, who would later become company president. The N.P. Benson Optical Company, financed in part by a mortgage on the founder's home, was on its way. Its modern descendant now employs more than 1,300 people in 190 retail outlets and 19 wholesale laboratories in 25 states, primarily in the Midwest and West.

Through the years Benson Optical has made significant contributions to the progress of eyewear. It pioneered the fitting of corneal plastic contact lenses in the 1930s. Early innovations included improved cosmetic edging for rimless eyewear (Cosmet Edge) and frame coloring and trimming with sterling silver plating. Recent developments include BlendEdge, Fashion Blend, and Color Line, which enhance the beauty and function of eyewear. Benson continues to lead the industry in functional and beautiful glasses.

Acquired by Connecticut-based Frigitronics in 1970, Benson Optical has since tripled its size and quadrupled its annual sales, yet still preserves the best traditions of its founder, who died in 1964 at the age of 90. Perhaps they said it best in his native village of Halland, Sweden: "Vi kan göra det bättre"—We can make it better.

• • •

Nicollet and Fifth as it looked in 1913, when the N.P. Benson Optical Company began.

BOKER'S INC.

Vitus Boker (center, with hat) in his early plant, where belt-driven lathes were powered by pulleys mounted to the ceiling. Working in foreground are sons John and William.

•   •   •

V itus Boker brought his wife and two young children to America from Denmark in 1901. He eventually settled in Minneapolis, where he went to work for a small manufacturing company. There he displayed the two traits he had in abundance: willingness to work and attention to detail. He was quickly made shop superintendent, and when son John was 16 his father hired him as an apprentice metalworker. A few years later, in 1919, Vitus Boker started his own company.

The year 1919 was a lean one for the new Boker Manufacturing Company. To save money, Vitus Boker and his son operated out of the basement of their home. The firm's first products were an envelope folding machine and a small hand check protector, which they sold to Twin City enterprises. Business was steady but slow, and to earn extra money the venture began manufacturing inventor's prototypes and a few special parts for automated machinery.

Word soon spread that a small company in southeast Minneapolis did high-quality short-run work, and businesses began sending orders for stamped parts. Outgrowing the basement workshop, the Bokers moved to a building on Erie Street, and in 1932 to a larger building on Washington Avenue near Seven Corners.

Envelope folders and check protectors were soon replaced by orders for precision parts and prototypes. Boker's parts found their way into the new fields of aviation and electronics, and at one point the firm patented a tractor design that was later sold to General Motors.

In 1939 Boker's moved to its present home on Snelling Avenue South. With the help and guidance of Vitus' four children, John, William, Richard, and Marie, the company grew through the war years, supplying parts for aircraft, electronics, and guided missiles, then readjusted to a consumer economy when peace returned. By 1964 the Snelling Avenue plant had been enlarged four times.

Four years later the firm was purchased from the Boker family by four employees: William Tedlund, Joseph Basara, Chester Engquist, and Joseph Kantorowicz. Today Boker's is still guided by Tedlund and Basara—and by Vitus Boker's principles of hard work and attention to detail. The company employs more than 150 and maintains over 2,000 different raw materials in inventory. As a major supplier of high-precision stampings to industry and government, Boker's counts some of the largest companies in America among its steady customers. Quite a record for a "basement business" started by a Danish immigrant 63 years ago.

BOR-SON CONSTRUCTION COMPANIES

The Centré Village construction in downtown Minneapolis consists of a parking ramp, hotel, office space, and condominiums. (Photo courtesy of Lea Babcock.)

From an idea in 1955 to the formation of the company in 1957, Bor-Son Construction, Inc., has emerged as one of the largest builders in the Upper Midwest. Founded by R.C. Nelson, president, a masonry contractor, and Jack E. Boran, a home builder (who retired in 1974), the firm achieved a major milestone in 1980 of having signed over $100 million in new construction contracts for the year.

Bor-Son today is recognized as a leader in high-rise construction and an expert in structural concrete systems. The many landmarks visible while driving the freeway system and in downtown Minneapolis are testimony to this experience in such projects as the Honeywell corporate office building, the Hyatt Regency Hotel, and the Bor-Son Towers, just off I-94. This expertise is also visible in large commercial, governmental, and corporate offices throughout Minnesota, Wisconsin, Iowa, and the Dakotas.

Bor-Son's industrial projects have grown increasingly larger and more complex over the years, including a new processing plant for the George A. Hormel Company in Austin, Minnesota, which—with 30 acres under one roof—is the largest facility of its kind in the United States, and a $30-million wastewater treatment plant for the city of Albert Lea, Minnesota.

Bor-Son is Minnesota's largest multi-unit housing contractor. Since its inception in 1957, the company has completed more than 100 private and public housing facilities totaling nearly 20,000 units. Included in this extensive list are the first new condominiums built in downtown Minneapolis and six other projects in the Loring Park area, the Cedar Riverside Development, and numerous facilities designed to meet the special needs of the handicapped, the elderly, and lower income households. In the '60s and early '70s, during the era of large-scale federal projects, Bor-Son built public housing throughout the United States.

The Bor-Son headquarters is located in a prestigious office complex on Killebrew Drive in Bloomington, which the firm developed and built. The first building containing approximately 130,000 square feet was built in two phases, each requiring only five months from construction start to tenant move in. This proves once again that the commitment of Bor-Son management to invest in their people and develop a professional staff of long tenure has been a wise decision. The Bor-Son Construction Companies, celebrating their 25th anniversary this year, specialize in general contracting, construction management, investment properties, and development.

◆　　◆　　◆

Among the many landmarks of Bor-Son Construction Companies is the Hyatt Regency Hotel, Minneapolis. (Photo courtesy of Roy Stevens.)

BURGESS-BECKWITH DIVISION OF BURGESS PUBLISHING COMPANY

P ostcards were just a penny when 27-year-old Merrill C. Burgess borrowed a small grubstake to start his own letter-shop in downtown Minneapolis in 1918. Gilbert I. Beckwith joined him in the business a few years later. With two employees and a few pieces of second-hand duplicating equipment, Burgess started to build a small custom printing business based on hard work and personal service. Some 60 years later his fledgling venture has grown into a diversified printing service whose skills include photo offset, printing, composition, addressing, and mailing.

By 1925 Burgess-Beckwith had outgrown its original space in the McKnight Building at Second Avenue South and Fifth Street and moved to better facilities across the street. About the same time Burgess Publishing Company's first college textbook was coming off the presses. For the next 50 years the two operations would form a mirror image of each other, an image

From its former location (pictured) in the printer's district on the southeast edge of downtown Minneapolis, Burgess-Beckwith and Burgess Publishing moved to its present home in suburban Edina in 1973.

• • •

whose shape would markedly alter in that time. While Burgess Publishing struggled through the '20s and Depression years, the postwar baby boom brought boom times for textbook publishers. Today Burgess Publishing, which serves a national and international market, dwarfs its more locally focused Burgess-Beckwith Division.

Both continue to have much in common. Both grew through the '20s, managed to survive the Depression and war years, and rejuvenated themselves in the 1940s. The publishing company became a separate corporation in 1948 until re-merging with Burgess-Beckwith in 1974.

Through the years Burgess-Beckwith

has been characterized by the long-term loyalty of its employees and its reciprocal commitment to them. The company has long had a policy not to lay people off due to lack of work, even in the worst of the Depression. In return it has known many employees who have spent virtually their entire professional lives with the firm, including current officers H.G. McFarlane and Elaine Johnson, both of whom joined Burgess-Beckwith in the 1940s. Other officers are Bernard J. Brey, Richard Wik, and Gerhard Brahms.

For its part, Burgess Publishing now markets hundreds of titles of primarily college-level textbooks, with special strengths in physical sciences (such as geology and biology), anthropology, agriculture, home economics, and physical education.

• • •

Merrill C. Burgess, founder of Burgess-Beckwith and Burgess Publishing Company.

CPT CORPORATION

In 1969 Dean Scheff and Jim Wienhold, his service manager, took apart an IBM Selectric typewriter and developed a word processor that stored information on magnetic tape. It took them two years to put it back together modified the way they wanted it, but by June 1972 the first batch of CPT 4200s was ready for delivery (CPT from Cassette-Powered Typewriter, 4200 from the new venture's address on Bloomington Avenue). Dick Eichhorn, who had once recruited Scheff for a job at Honeywell, joined him as a partner; Wienhold was chief engineer. And CPT Corporation

The CPT 8000, introduced in 1977, boosted company sales in one year by 70 percent.

•   •   •

was on its way.

The company turned a profit after just one year, went public in 1972 as well, grew at a compounded rate of 50 percent annually for 10 years, and broke the $100-million mark in sales in 1981—a phenomenal success story, even in an industry known for such tales.

The original CPT 4200 used cassette tapes to record typewritten text. When

the microprocessor revolutionized the infant word processing field, CPT began to develop software-based systems. While major firms like IBM and Wang worked the corridors of power in the major markets, Scheff set out to develop markets too small for larger competitors. And while the industry was structured around rentals, Scheff from the beginning concentrated on selling CPT systems. Both tactics helped the young organization put down roots and begin to grow. Today CPT ranks among the top six word processing companies in the nation.

That ranking stems in large part from the CPT 8000, CPT's first software-based system, introduced in 1977. In one year it boosted sales by 70 percent. Unlike conventional systems, which confront operators with green or white characters on dark backgrounds, the CPT 8000's high-resolution screen looks just like the finished text: black characters on white. Validating its renowned "user friendliness," Datapro Research's authoritative user popularity poll in 1980 ranked the CPT 8000 best stand-alone word processing system in the business.

CPT software is now available in 17 languages, including Arabic, and each system can telecommunicate material to any other CPT word processor around the world. The CPT 8100 and 6100 were introduced in 1981, more powerful versions of the CPT 8000 and 6000. CPT's worldwide distribution system now reaches more than 60 countries and international sales account for about one-third of the company's total. Domestically, research and development, manufacturing, and headquarters functions are centered in facilities in Eden Prairie and the southwestern suburbs of Minneapolis.

CAMPBELL-MITHUN

In the world of advertising, New York's Madison Avenue is a potent lure to the profession's top talent. But not to Ralph Campbell. When the New York agency of Batten, Barton, Durstine & Osborn wanted to ship him east from its Minneapolis branch office, he left the firm to open his own agency, taking with him a young University of Minnesota graduate, Ray Mithun. That was April 1933. Campbell-Mithun has been part of Minneapolis ever since, the largest advertising agency in the Twin Cities and among the top 30 agencies in the country.

Campbell was 47 when he turned down the move to New York; Mithun was just 23. With three employees, $1,500 of borrowed capital, and borrowed office furniture, they opened an office in the Northwestern Bank Building on April 1, 1933—the day President Franklin Roosevelt declared a "Bank Holiday."

But despite the inauspicious times, and a first year's bank account that never got above $5,000 (and once dropped to $3), Campbell and Mithun and the business they built caused a stir in the industry by gradually bringing Minnesota advertising dollars back from New York. They successfully convinced clients that the same quality of talent and services was available closer to home. Today the agency has 400 employees locally, a Chicago office, and a client list that runs up the scale from small, emerging businesses to the likes of General Mills, Honeywell, Land O'Lakes, and 3M.

Advertising agencies often become known for their creations, and Campbell-Mithun is no exception. It gave birth to the famous Hamm's Bear and the "God's Country" campaign for Heileman Brewing Company, helping both brews attain national stature. It developed the "Incredible Edible Egg" campaign for the American Egg Board. It gave Northwest Airlines its "Orient," red tails, and distinctive gong. And as media have changed through the coming of age of television, and now cable, the agency's skills have evolved accordingly.

For Campbell-Mithun, there have been two major growth periods. From 1952 through 1967, under the guidance of Mithun, Al Whitman, and Cleo Hovel, billings jumped from $10 million to $75 million. And since 1973, guided by an executive committee which includes Mithun, Stan Blunt, George Gruenwald, Dave Seibel, Ray Sachs, and Bill Stein, the agency has gone from billings of $80 million to more than $225 million.

Campbell-Mithun has been very active in the development of public television (Gruenwald serves on both KCTA-TV's and national public television's boards), and is one of Minnesota's renowned Two Percenters. The agency became a subsidiary of Ted Bates & Company of New York in 1979, but retains its own autonomy, continuing to justify Ralph Campbell's belief that there is more to advertising than Madison Avenue.

• • •

Officers of Campbell-Mithun, Inc., are Raymond O. Mithun, founder-chairman (seated); George H. Gruenwald, chief executive officer; Stanhope E. Blunt, chairman, executive committee; David R. Seibel, chairman of the board, chief operations officer; and Raymond L. Sachs, vice-chairman of the board (left to right).

CARLSON COMPANIES, INC.

Curtis LeRoy Carlson, chairman of the board of Carlson Companies, Inc.

When Curtis LeRoy Carlson quit an $110-a-month job selling soap for Procter & Gamble in 1939, no one expected him to build one of the nation's largest privately held corporations. Few, in fact, held out any hope that he could persuade small grocers to give away his Gold Bond Stamps to boost sales, since up to then the practice was common only to department stores. But Carlson nursed the business along, especially through the World War II years (when merchants, confronted with widespread shortages, saw little reason to offer stamps). In 1952 Super Valu became the first supermarket chain to offer his stamps—and its sales skyrocketed. The ensuing rush to stamps made Carlson a millionaire a quarter of a century after he

had begun carrying around personal goals—like earning $100 a week—on little pieces of paper tucked in his wallet. Carlson Companies have been growing ever since.

That growth has been accomplished largely through acquisitions that have taken the son of Swedish immigrants far from his grocery store roots. The first step was taken in 1960 when Carlson bought into the stately Radisson Hotel in downtown Minneapolis. The "Radisson Collection" now includes more than 24 hotels, inns, and resorts in the United States and one in Cairo, Egypt.

From hotels, food logically follows. In addition to Radisson restaurants, there are more than 300 Country Kitchens in the Carlson collection as well as over 50 distinctive TGI Fridays. Additional restaurant expansion is under way around the nation. Carlson Properties, the company's real estate arm, owns or manages more than $200 million of holdings, including the 1,000-acre Minneapolis Industrial Park (MIP) in the western suburb of Plymouth where many of the Carlson Companies are now headquartered.

In addition, the Carlson umbrella covers catalog showrooms; marketing and leisure products; manufacturing operations in gold and silver products, hardboard, and residential housing; travel agencies; design, leasing, and financial services; and acquisitions groups and supporting services. Carlson Companies also includes the largest incentive and motivation organization in the world—E.F. MacDonald of Dayton, Ohio.

Through it all, Carlson Companies (the name was officially adopted in 1972) has grown at a phenomenal 33 percent annual compound rate since

1938, when Curt Carlson asked his landlord to defer a month's rent so he could put $55 more operating capital into his stamp business. The billion-dollar annual sales volume was surpassed in 1978; the $2-billion level will be reached in 1982. "As long as current goals remain signposts to future accomplishments and not destinations in themselves," Curt Carlson has said, "Carlson Companies will continue to grow and prosper."

• • •

"Sandy Saver," symbol of Gold Bond Stamps, was a familiar sight at the company headquarters at 1629 Hennepin Avenue before Carlson Companies moved to suburban Plymouth in 1962.

RADISSON HOTELS

Between 1900 and 1910 the population of Minneapolis exploded by 100,000 to top the 300,000 mark. The center of downtown had traditionally been along the Mississippi, but interesting things were happening around Seventh and Nicollet. George Draper Dayton's dry goods store was thriving and two vaudeville houses were packing them in. What was needed to solidify this "new" downtown was a first-class hotel.

In the middle of the decade, Miss Edna Dickerson of Chicago inherited a large amount of property and money, much of it in downtown Minneapolis. When she came to town to collect the inheritance, local businessmen convinced her to invest $1.5 million in a hotel next to Dayton's store. Named for the great 17th-century French explorer, Pierre Esprit Radisson, then believed to have been the first white man to explore Minnesota, the Radisson was considered the finest hotel between Chicago and the West Coast when it opened on December 15, 1909.

Each room offered cold water pumped from an artesian well 975 feet below the hotel. The $1.50 rooms didn't have baths, but for $2.50 to $5 finer accommodations were available. There were two restaurants, including the Viking Cafe, which featured a silver model of a long ship that has remained the centerpiece of succeeding Viking rooms.

More than 1,000 guests thronged the ballroom opening night to hear the Radisson Orchestra play composer Franz Dicks' specially written "Radisson March" and feast on a lavish banquet—at an elegant cost of $5 per person.

During the '30s Dickerson and her husband, Simon Kruse, lost the hotel to its major creditor, the Philadelphia Fidelity Trust Company (a not-uncom-

Radisson Hotel Corporation board chairman Curtis L. Carlson is pictured with the "Golden Strings" violin show, which he introduced in the Flame Room on Valentine's Day, 1963, and which played until the hotel's closing in 1981.

• • •

mon fate for major hotels during the Depression). But the Radisson re-emerged under local control in 1943 when Coca-Cola franchiser Tom Moore (a desk clerk at the hotel shortly after it opened) and hotelier Byron Calhoun combined forces to acquire it and start it on the comeback trail. Numerous renovation projects followed and the new Flame Room—patterned after small New York City nightclubs—began its rise to prominence, bringing some of the biggest names in entertainment to Min-

neapolis.

In 1960, to underwrite a major expansion that also put the distinctive rust-and-white facade on the Seventh Street front of the hotel, prominent Minnesota businessman Curtis Carlson and several other local investors acquired a half-interest. By 1962 Carlson had become sole owner. Since then the Radisson name has been extended to more than 24 hotels, inns, and resorts across the country and to the pyramids near Cairo, Egypt.

The original Radisson Hotel closed in 1981 and a new, more elegant flagship Radisson will rise on the site of the original by 1985 with 650 rooms topped by some 70 condominiums in a modern 37-story hotel. It will provide the same things—convention and business services plus first-class hotel accommodations—that Minneapolis businessmen were seeking back in 1909.

• • •

Gas and electric lights lined Seventh Street as the new Radisson Hotel prepared to open in 1909. Dayton's is down the block toward Nicollet; across the street is the Miles, a thriving vaudeville house in early Minneapolis.

CENTURY MANUFACTURING COMPANY

When Century Manufacturing began in 1937 (under the name Twentieth Century Manufacturing), an automobile cost about $700 and the firm's newly introduced Dial Welder $300. Today ordinary cars command prices in the $7,000 range—and Century makes welders that sell for $249. That as much as anything helps explain how, in an industry that once numbered more than 180 manufacturing companies, Century has survived to become the biggest and the best of the seven who remain, one of the leading producers of battery charger boosters and maintenance-type welders.

The first years were anything but smooth. From a small shop at 719 Third Street, the firm's few employees would assemble three or four welders, then hit the road to demonstrate them

to farmers, service station owners, and welding shops. When one was sold, another could be built. What made the Dial Welder unique was the patented dial, which allowed an operator to select any amperage desired. Beginners found setting requirements and rod sizes for various jobs right on the dial. Since the Dial Welder was easier to use than anything anybody else made, the little Minneapolis company was able to hold its own against bigger and better-financed rivals.

During World War II, however, Century was forced to shut down briefly due to materials shortages, labor problems, and management changes. In 1948 the organization was revived by two brothers, Clem and Clark Peterson. A short time later, Clem Peterson took in a

boarder, a young farm boy from Spring Grove, Minnesota, who was studying at the University of Minnesota. Lee Sundet not only proved a good tenant, he also became such a good salesman that he worked his way up to sales manager by 1953. In 1973 he became both owner and president; later he became chairman of the board. In 1981 Sundet was named Minnesota Small Business Person of the Year in recognition of his business and community activities, including involvement with the executive committees of the Courage Center and the state's Muscular Dystrophy campaign.

Century's turning point came in 1956. A new welder was developed that could cut faster and weld with more types of electrodes, and the basic welder technology was used to produce the first compact charger that could start vehicles with dead or weak batteries. In the '60s Century patented a low-cost welder with a duty cycle approaching 100 percent (competitive models allowed a 20 percent cycle, meaning 8 minutes out of 10 had to be set aside to let the equipment cool). Since 1965 sales have multiplied 40 times over.

Century sells battery chargers through parts stores, garages, and repair shops, and welders to hardware stores and agricultural cooperatives. A division builds welders sold under more than 50 private labels while another, due to the key patents Century holds, actually builds welders for the competition. In 1967 Century moved to a new production facility in Bloomington that can produce a welder every 26 seconds and a battery charger every 30 seconds.

•   •   •

Century Manufacturing's Lee Sundet with the modern descendant of the Dial Welder the company pioneered.

DELOITTE HASKINS & SELLS

In 1921 Minneapolis was a thriving city of 380,000 just entering the Roaring '20s when the New York-based public accounting firm of Charles Waldo Haskins and Elijah Watt Sells opened an office downtown to better serve the branch operations of a number of its clients, primarily in manufacturing. Today the local office of Deloitte Haskins & Sells ranks among the largest public accounting firms in the Twin Cities. After a working relationship spanning 80 years, Haskins & Sells and Deloitte & Co., a British firm, in 1978 adopted the current name to be used worldwide.

The first office began with just one accountant, but a year later the practice was augmented through acquisition of the established firm of Archibald F. Wagner. Wagner and his three young associates contributed greatly to the growth of the firm's business in the Twin Cities, as well as the professionalism of the accounting community in the state during the 1920s. The onset of the Depression put a drastic end to the vitality of all manner of businesses, not the least of them accounting firms. During the first few years following the stock market crash in 1929, the Minneapolis office was reduced to a manager, one staff member, and a secretary. The problems of the office disappeared and the size of the staff grew rapidly with the recovery of the economy and the expansion of regulatory requirements. General Arthur Carter, one of its managing partners, was the principal advocate in congressional testimony for audits being the responsibility of public rather than government accountants.

The growth in services rendered was explosive in the '70s, culminating in the merger with the Burnsville-based firm of Robert G. Engelhart & Co. in 1981. Engelhart's practice, established as a one-man agency in 1945, had grown to more than 100 professionals and better than 300 clients before the merger, resulting in a near doubling of Deloitte Haskins & Sells' Twin Cities operations.

Today the firm is particularly strong in the areas of health care, manufacturing, utilities, transportation, construction, and high technology. It was a driving force in the creation of the masters program in business taxation at the University of Minnesota and donated the university's tax library.

The first American public accounting firm to open offices abroad, Deloitte Haskins & Sells is a worldwide organization of more than 300 offices in 65 countries. The Twin Cities operation—with offices in Minneapolis, St. Paul, and Burnsville—ranks in the firm's top 10 percent and has contributed five past presidents of the Minnesota Society of Certified Public Accountants, including Wagner and current partner-in-charge Frederick W. Bassinger.

• • •

Robert G. Engelhart, founder of Robert G. Engelhart & Co., joined Deloitte Haskins & Sells in 1981.

• • •

Archibald F. Wagner joined the Deloitte Haskins & Sells firm in the 1920s.

CONTINENTAL MACHINES

Julius C. Wilkie (1870–1932), founder of Continental Machines.

Continental Machines is the modern descendant of the Wilkie Machine Works, which was founded in 1912 at Winona, Minnesota, and specialized in the repair and rebuilding of early motor cars. Founder Julius C. Wilkie also manufactured and sold auto repair tools of his own design throughout the country. Today Continental Machines ranks as one of the nation's leading machine tool builders and is the largest manufacturer of metal-cutting band machines. It also manufactures special machine tools and hydraulic equipment.

Julius Wilkie, son of an immigrant German brickmaker and his Swiss wife, came west to settle at Alma, Wisconsin, along the upper Mississippi. Wilkie spent his spare time working in the family brickyard, where he early on demonstrated his mechanical aptitude by building a miniature patent model of a steam tractor designed to traverse steep hills without quenching the fire under the boiler. Later he designed and built marine engines. These were installed in boat hulls called launches. They were the first speedboats on the upper Mississippi. A river steamboat named for him will grace the new Winona Steamboat Museum on the Mississippi river-front at Winona. Growing up in this atmosphere, it was small wonder that his sons—Leighton, Robert, and James—developed their own knack for mechanical engineering.

The automobile was a natural focus for their attention. In the early days of the "horseless carriage" as many as 2,500 different makes and models could be found on the mostly dirt roads of the nation. At the Wilkie Garage and Machine Shop, Wilkie invented a number of tools for use in the rebuilding of automobile engines. Among these was a device to check the alignment and facilitate the straightening of connecting rods and the alignment of the pistons. These tools were sold throughout the country.

By 1926 the Wilkies had developed a unique die-stamping method which became known as the Continental Process. To take best advantage of this breakthrough they moved the family business to Minneapolis and renamed it Continental Machine Specialties. Besides tool and die work, the firm made models and performed job shop work. The first plant was located in a former fire station, furniture store, and morgue at 1301 Washington Avenue in what was called Seven Corners (it is now the roadbed for I-35W).

Automobile work continued to be important through the '20s and '30s with the Wilkie name being added to machine tool accessories and other repair

◆ ◆ ◆

The three sons of Julius Wilkie (from left)—James, Leighton, and Robert—have prepared and sponsored numerous educational programs, such as "The Dawn of This Age" display, to advance knowledge of American technology.

items. As quality control in the automobile industry improved, the reliability of automobile engines improved as well and the cost of engines decreased significantly. Because of these factors, the need for engine repair declined substantially. Continental turned to its stamping business in response, and that shortly led to the introduction of the first metal-cutting bandsaw, built from parts of a woodworking saw and an old Chevrolet transmission, and christened the DoALL bandsaw. In 1935 the first off the line was sold to Woodward Governor in Wisconsin for $495, less than one-tenth of what its more sophisticated modern descendants command today. That same year the company was renamed Continental Machines to reflect the changing nature of its activities.

From 20 employees in one plant in the late '30s, Continental Machines began to grow in the next decade, spreading out to a total of five downtown plants (including an old Hamm's brewery) for its several hundred World War II-era employees by 1943. As the firm's operations became increasingly scattered, the Wilkie brothers began looking for a place to consolidate manufacturing and office functions. Born with a love of water, they naturally looked for river-front property, settling for 27 acres just south of the Minnesota River in Savage, which was "way out of town" in those days. In 1942 they moved a new division to the site, naming it Savage Tool; six years later all operations were reunited south of the river as Continental Machines.

It was a daring move in many ways. Transportation was far from developed —a wooden swivel bridge spanned the river at Lyndale Avenue to provide primary access. There was concern that some employees would find the com-

The first DoALL bandsaw (model ABW), produced•in Minneapolis in 1935, and number 100,000, circa 1980, provide graphic evidence of the advance of band-machining technology.

◆　　◆　　◆

mute too much to handle, disrupting the close-knit family feeling the company cherished, but daily they came from as far away as North Minneapolis, Anoka, and even Wisconsin.

Today Continental Machines makes more than 70 models of the original bandsaw sold under the DoALL label, in addition to DoALL surface grinders, precision slicing machines, lapping machines, and gauging equipment. It can point with pride to a record of technological achievement which includes most major improvements in band machining, recognized in 1967 by the National Machine Tool Builders Association as one of the seven basic machining methods.

In addition to its general product line, Continental Machines also makes one-of-a-kind custom machines for major in-

During World War II, Continental Machines' downtown headquarters on Washington Avenue was the hub of activity for five downtown plants producing metal-cutting machines for defense contractors from coast to coast.

◆　　◆　　◆

dustrial and manufacturing customers, some costing upwards of half a million dollars and requiring more than a year for design and manufacture. A subsidiary, Continental Hydraulics, was established in 1961 to ensure the quality of the hydraulic pumps and valves used in the company's equipment; it also sells variable-volume vane pumps, directional control valves, flow control and check valves, and complete packaged power units to the industry at large through mill supply houses and more than 100 direct distributors.

Over 100,000 DoALL band machines have been built and sold since the first one was dispatched to Wisconsin in 1935. To commemorate that achievement Continental Machines tracked down and bought back the original machine to display alongside of number 100,000.

Headquartered in Savage, Continental Machines has subsidiary operations and licensing agreements in a growing number of companies around the world. It is the largest of the more than 70 corporations associated in the DoALL network.

DAYTON'S

I n 1895 the Westminster Presbyterian Church at the corner of Nicollet Avenue and Seventh Street was destroyed in a fire. Several years later the city fathers, worried about the future of the property "on the wrong side of the street" beyond Seventh the border between the city's commercial and residential districts— persuaded George Draper Dayton, a Worthington, Minnesota, banker who wanted to move his operations to Minneapolis, to buy the land for $165,000. Dayton put up a six-story building on the corner and moved in a dry goods company he had purchased in 1902. There may not be a more valuable piece of property in the history of downtown Minneapolis than that on which rests Dayton's department store.

It wasn't completely by chance that Dayton settled on that particular cor-

ner, anxious city fathers notwithstanding. He had first made a point of standing on various street corners around town, counting and comparing the traffic patterns and evaluating future prospects. The count confirmed his feeling that the downtown's growth would go right past his door, making Nicollet Avenue one of the most promising commercial thoroughfares in the Midwest.

At first Dayton was a silent partner in Goodfellow's, the business he moved down the block from Third and Nicollet. A year after the move, however, he bought out his partners and changed the name to "Dayton's Daylight Store," later the Dayton Dry Goods Company. He built his business on principles of customer satisfaction, service, and liberal credit and return policies—and probably

Dayton's, 14 years after George Draper Dayton built the dry goods company on the corner of Seventh Street and Nicollet Avenue.

♦ ♦ ♦

no other retail establishment holds quite the dominant niche in local shopping and fashion habits as the one Dayton's has occupied through the years.

Located in the heart of the downtown, Dayton's flagship store eventually grew to occupy 12 floors with numerous fashion and home decorating specialty shops. But the Dayton's name became known for more than simply merchandising. Year-round, its 12,000-square-foot auditorium hosts a variety of public events, from fashion and art shows (including an annual benefit for the Minneapolis Institute of Arts), to the spring flower show which has become a tradition in the Upper Midwest, to the animated Christmas events, which attract more than a quarter of a million visitors each year.

But in the 1950s the five sons of George Nelson Dayton (who had suc-

♦ ♦ ♦

Dayton's major events include an annual spring flower show presented jointly with Bachman's. The 1981 flower show, "Gardens of the Midnight Sun," featured an actual-size replica of a Viking ship.

ceeded his father in 1923), concluded that the future of small family businesses was anything but bright. In fact, the consensus reached by Donald, Kenneth, Bruce, Wallace, and Douglas Dayton was that their one-store operation might be obsolete in as little as 10 years. Neither the prospect of coasting into graceful eclipse nor that of selling the business was attractive. Instead they determined to build a national company.

The first step was taken in 1954 with a new Dayton's store in downtown Rochester, Minnesota. Two years later, a 500-acre cornfield southwest of the downtown became the nation's first enclosed shopping mall: Southdale, with Dayton's as the anchor store. Built at a cost of $20 million (by comparison, Walt Disney spent a little less than that in 1955 to build something called Disneyland), Southdale was initially "in the sticks." But it was also in the path of suburban growth on the side of the city where many of the firm's customers lived. And, as the Viennese architect Victor Gruen remarked (admittedly exaggerating the facts a little), between the state's chilling winters and sweltering summers, there really wasn't one decent shopping day all year long. The Dayton family introduced the country to 365 days of good shopping weather every year.

While the Dayton name grew to be synonymous with progressive retailing, expansion of Dayton's department stores continued at an aggressive pace. As of 1982, Dayton's regional chain of department stores has expanded to 13 in a four-state market (seven in the Twin Cities metro area, plus Rochester and St. Cloud, Minnesota; Fargo and Grand Forks, North Dakota; Sioux Falls, South Dakota; and La Crosse, Wisconsin), with an additional three home furnish-

When the Dayton brothers opened Southdale, the nation's first enclosed shopping mall, the festivities included modeling of the latest fashions of 1956.

• • •

ings stores in the Twin Cities.

(Within the expansion years, the Dayton brothers began to diversify their retailing interests, opening the first Target discount store in 1962 and the first B. Dalton bookstore in 1966. In 1969, realizing the need for a stronger department store base, the Dayton Corporation merged with the Detroit-based J.L. Hudson chain, forming the Dayton Hudson Corporation. Headquartered in Minneapolis, it is now the nation's seventh largest nonfood retailer in the United States with 1980 revenues of more than four billion dollars.)

Through three generations of family management, and now as part of a publicly held company, Dayton's has earned a well-deserved reputation for imaginative marketing efforts designed to turn the great American pastime of shopping into something of an adventure. Not only will customers find the top American designer collections in the well-

known Oval Room, but also such European designers as Yves St. Laurent and Giorgio Armani in specially designed boutiques. And a professional visual merchandising staff makes use of creative lighting techniques, color and space design, and avant garde mannequins to provide store "theater."

Dayton's is known nationally as well as locally for its exciting and innovative events. From fashion shows and gourmet cooking to exotic import fairs and educational seminars, the ongoing events program is geared to current trends and consumer interests. Many events have featured personal appearances by celebrities such as Charlton Heston, Lauren Bacall, Cheryl Tiegs, Bill Blass, Gloria Vanderbilt, Arthur Ashe, and countless others from the areas of show business, fashion, and sports.

The store has also had many marketing "firsts" such as the use of touch-screen computer terminals for customers' shopping enjoyment, and the one and only Bell Telephone Phone Store to be installed within a department store.

Although Dayton's credo has always been quality, fashion, and value, the company also maintains a deep commitment to the communities in which it operates. Since 1946 Dayton's has allocated 5 percent of pretax earnings for charitable giving, primarily focused on social action programs and the arts. Dayton's contributions have totaled nearly $50 million in the past 36 years, and company executives have encouraged other firms to join the percentage philanthropy movement.

Now 80 years later, Dayton's strives to maintain the basic business philosophy of founder George Draper Dayton: to serve the community.

DERICKSON COMPANY

In 1879 G.P. Derickson and Company opened its doors at 107 Washington Avenue North, then the "business heart" of Minneapolis. It was an era when average home lots in the 23-year-old city sold for $250 to $1,000—plus enough lumber for the buyer "to build a small house." Home prices like that are now long-faded memories, but a century after its beginnings as a small hardware store, Derickson is one of the leading wholesalers of professional building supplies in the Upper Midwest. It has been at its present address on Linden Avenue since 1946.

Derickson has traditionally served the professional builder, rather than the do-it-yourselfer. It handles top-quality lines from famous-name manufacturers of kitchen cabinets and cabinet hardware, hand and power tools, appliances, laminates, builder hardware, millwork, and doors. Its more than 3,500 customers throughout Minnesota, the Dakotas, Iowa, and Wisconsin consist of home builders, remodelers, industrial and commercial contractors, and lumber dealers.

To meet their needs, Derickson stocks more than 22,000 items, specializing in cabinet and builder's hardware, also supplying the complete home from windows and doors, locks and hinges, built-in appliances, and kitchen cabinets, to complete wood and steel homes. The company helps preplan projects to complete structure of homes and commercial buildings. And it stays on top of the changing construction industry practices with computerized plans, energy-saving products, and all-weather materials.

Under the guidance of Vernon R. Wexler, Donald R. Yager, and Robert L. Wexler, Derickson has played an important role in a number of regional

and national areas. Vernon Wexler, who joined the company in the 1940s and now serves as president and chief executive officer, helped originate the "Reggie," the Oscar for home builders presented annually by the Minneapolis Builders Association. Wexler's testimony in 1957 before a U.S. Senate committee on small business tax problems contributed to the creation of the Small Business Administration. In 1963 he was chairman of Minnesota's trade mission to England and the Common Market; in 1980 he was appointed by Governor Al Quie to the Minnesota Commission on Small Business, created to represent the needs of small business at the state capital.

To commemorate the company's centennial in 1979, Derickson created two continuing scholarships: one awarded annually to a second-year architectural drafting student at the Dunwoody Industrial Institute, the other forming a fund to provide grants for graduate architectural students at the University of Minnesota, where Vernon R. Wexler serves

Vernon R. Wexler, president of Derickson Company, which is now located at 1100 Linden Avenue.

• • •

on the School of Architecture's advisory council. Both awards are symbolic of Derickson's continuing commitment to the state's home building industry.

G. P. Derrickson & Co.,
Hardware.

The Library of Congress added an "r" in this artwork of the east-central part of Washington Avenue in downtown Minneapolis.

DONALDSON COMPANY, INC.

In 1915 a Utah farmer had a problem. The salesman from the Twin Cities had the answer. Hiram Miller's new tractor from the Bull Tractor Company worked just fine during the rainy season, but as the summer sun turned his fields dusty his bright new machine sputtered to a stop. Twenty-six-year-old Frank Donaldson reasoned that dust was being sucked into the engine through the carburetor, so he cobbled up a wire cage wrapped with cloth, mounted it on an eight-foot pipe, and installed it on the tractor. It was the first effective air cleaner for the internal combustion engine and the genesis of Donaldson Company, Inc.

The start was anything but auspicious. Enthused by his new creation, Donaldson badgered his employer to produce the invention. He was fired on the spot. Undaunted, he went into business for himself in a corner of his father's sheet metal shop in St. Paul. In a few years he had five people working for him. By the end of the 1930s the firm was producing more than half the country's heavy-duty air cleaners. At his death in 1945, Donaldson held 22 patents (the organization holds more than 200 in 24 countries) and was posthumously elected to the Minnesota Inventors Congress in 1980. The family touch continues (although the company has been public since 1955) under chairman of the board Frank Donaldson, Jr.; William Hodder has served as president since 1973.

Donaldson today is involved in environmental protection—the inner environment of sensitive machinery and the outer one that people inhabit. Donaldson's filters clean the air that engines breathe, its silencers quiet industrial machinery, its liquid cyclones remove effluents from water and other fluids, and its dust collectors (produced by the Torit Division) clean the air for a healthier work environment.

Heavy-duty air cleaners protect mining, railroad, construction, and farm machinery which must be able to operate in the dirtiest of conditions. Since the 1930s, when Donaldson engineers developed the first successful oil-washed air cleaner, the firm has been a factor in the trucking industry.

From the tiny filter used in anesthesia-administration equipment and compact silencers for snowmobiles to complete filter houses handling large volumes of air for gas turbines and industrial silencers for power-generating plants, Donaldson products work in settings from sandy deserts to arctic ice. Headquartered in Bloomington, Donaldson has more than 3,000 employees in the United States and 10 countries around the world, an important source of the technology for a cleaner, quieter world.

• • •

Frank Donaldson, Sr., founder of Donaldson Company, Inc.

DORSEY & WHITNEY

The legal practice of Dorsey & Whitney (formally Dorsey, Windhorst, Hannaford, Whitney & Halladay) began in 1912 when Judge William Atwood Lancaster and Judge David Ferguson Simpson formed a legal partnership. Lancaster had served on the Hennepin County District Court. Simpson resigned as a justice of the Supreme Court of Minnesota to devote his full time to the practice. A short time later Judge Milton D. Purdy, a former U.S. district judge in Minnesota, joined the firm. James E. Dorsey, the first member of the Dorsey family to enter the practice, became an associate in 1913 following his graduation from Harvard Law School.

The original modest offices of Lancaster & Simpson were in the New York Life Building at Fifth Street and Second Avenue (now the site of First National Bank Plaza). Today the firm occupies the top six floors of First Bank Place East. From a small partnership, Dorsey & Whitney has grown into a full-service law firm with more than 180 attorneys and a total staff of nearly 500 persons. Major areas of specialization include probate, banking, pension and profit sharing, litigation, corporate and securities law, real estate, patent and trademark, municipal finance, tax, international, antitrust, health and labor law.

In recent years Dorsey & Whitney has established branch offices to handle more effectively the complex legal need of diversified, often multinational, clients. A first branch was opened in Rochester, Minnesota, in 1972 to serve the Mayo Clinic as well as other clients in that area. In the Twin Cities Dorsey & Whitney maintains offices in St. Paul and suburban Wayzata; on the national level there are branches in Washington,

D.C., and Great Falls, Montana. The firm took its first step internationally in 1980 by establishing an office in Paris, France, to handle legal work in Europe.

Over the years Dorsey & Whitney has watched a number of its alumni move on to service in other fields, most notably U.S. Supreme Court Justice Harry Blackmun, who was named to the nation's highest judicial body in 1970.

David R. Brink, a partner with the firm, is serving as 1981–1982 president of the American Bar Association.

GENEALOGY

Over the years, the firm has had various partnership names:
1912 Lancaster & Simpson
1913–1918 Lancaster, Simpson & Purdy
1918–1919 Lancaster, Simpson
1919–1927 Lancaster, Simpson, Junell & Dorsey
1927–1928 Junell, Dorsey, Oakley & Driscoll
1928–1931 Junell, Oakley, Driscoll & Fletcher
1931–1936 Junell, Driscoll, Fletcher, Dorsey & Barker
1936–1938 Junell, Driscoll, Dorsey, Barker & Colman
1938–1942 Fletcher, Dorsey, Barker, Colman & Barber
1942–1955 Dorsey, Colman, Barker, Scott & Barber
1955–1957 Dorsey, Owen, Barker, Scott & Barber
1957–1959 Dorsey, Owen, Scott, Barber & Marquart
1959–1961 Dorsey, Owen, Barber, Marquart & Windhorst
1961–1967 Dorsey, Owen, Marquart, Windhorst & West
1967–1976 Dorsey, Marquart, Windhorst, West & Halladay
1976–1982 Dorsey, Windhorst, Hannaford, Whitney & Halladay
1982 Dorsey & Whitney

DYCO PETROLEUM CORPORATION

In 1970 oil was selling for $2.50 a barrel and natural gas at 19 cents per thousand cubic feet—prices kept artificially low in light of inflated costs for other products in the United States. The percentage of U.S. oil imports, however, had risen from just 2 percent of the nation's needs in 1950 to over 25 percent 20 years later. It was at this point that the issues of supply and demand came into play, and domestic exploration became crucial to the nation's economy.

Jaye F. Dyer and Ronald G. Wade, two oilmen from Oklahoma, had watched these trends closely. They determined that private investment programs would provide the ideal framework for raising the capital needed for domestic exploration. Based on this information and the gamble that prices would rise, they decided to form an oil and gas program company. N. Bud and Harold I. Grossman of Gelco Corporation guaranteed the firm's initial bank loan and provided much of the seed capital for Dyco. On June 9, 1971, the four shook hands and Dyco Petroleum was incorporated in Minneapolis, Minnesota.

Dyco registered its first drilling program in July 1971. Dain Bosworth Inc. agreed to underwrite the young company's programs, and at the same time provide a marketing force in the brokerage community. From the beginning it was decided that investors would not just be used when extra capital was needed. Instead, Dyco would depend on the investments of others. The new organization would not drill for its own account; it would invest in its programs along with its participants.

That first year Dyco raised a total of $325,000; the majority came from investors in the Upper Midwest. Ten

years later, in 1982, the company registered $90 million in drilling programs with the SEC.

An investment in Dyco through common stock became possible when the firm went public in August 1976. Between 1978 and 1980 the performance of the stock enabled Dyco to declare four three-for-two stock splits. The company achieved another milestone with its listing on the New York Stock Exchange in January 1981, less than 10 years after it was formed.

Beginning in 1977, Dyco has concentrated its exploration activities in the Anadarko Basin of western Oklahoma and the Texas Panhandle. The company emphasizes the search for "deep" natural gas exclusively onshore in the United States. Activities are also conducted in the Rocky Mountain and Gulf Coast regions of the United

Jaye F. Dyer (foreground), president and chief executive officer; and (from left) Wayne O. Podratz, executive vice-president, program marketing and communications; Lendell Z. Williams, executive vice-president and general manager of operations; and Ronald G. Wade, executive vice-president and chief financial officer.

◆　　◆　　◆

States.

Corporate headquarters has been located in the Shelard Tower since 1975. Dyco's operations headquarters is in Tulsa, Oklahoma. Other operations offices is in Denver, Colorado, and Elk City, Oklahoma. The company, which at one time consisted only of Dyer and Wade, today employs more than 180 people, with 75 in the Minneapolis office alone.

EBERHARDT COMPANY

Providing services in real estate has been the business of Eberhardt Company since 1935, when Alex Eberhardt became a property manager for insurance companies renting back foreclosed Depression-era homes and businesses. In those days Walter Nelson, a St. Paul native, was supervising similar activities in Chicago for the Equitable Life Assurance Society and looking for a way to move back to the Twin Cities. He joined Eberhardt as a junior partner in 1939, acquiring the firm after Eberhardt's death in 1951.

The company engages in three interrelated areas, both commercial and residential: mortgage banking, real estate sales, and property management and leasing. Mortgage banking was the first fuel for growth, spurred by the housing boom in the years following World War II and Eberhardt's established working relationships with major

• • •

Eberhardt Company corporate offices at 3250 West 66th Street, Edina, Minnesota.

insurance companies. As a natural outgrowth of such activities the firm evolved into residential sales in the 1950s.

When the savings and loan industry grew to dominate residential financing, Eberhardt turned to the financing of income-producing property—both multifamily and commercial—in the Twin Cities and throughout the Midwest. It also moved into residential land development, putting together two dozen small subdivisions between 1954 and 1968, mostly in the western and southern suburbs of Minneapolis.

In the early '60s Eberhardt represented persons and companies who were acquiring land for many new developments. Acting over a period of eight years, it purchased the property which Dayton Hudson developed into Ridgedale Center. Its 8,500-acre purchases for the McKnight family became the "new town" of Jonathan. And Eberhardt acquired the property for the new Art Institute as well as other downtown developments. Walter Nelson's influ-

ence on the downtown was felt in other ways as well: he served two terms as president of the Downtown Council during the development of Nicollet Mall.

In recent years the Eberhardt profile in residential real estate has been extended through acquisition of a number of local firms, including Fox-Herfurth, McCanna Realty in Minneapolis, Dan Dolan Real Estate in St. Paul, and affiliation with Better Homes & Gardens for national relocation services. Acting for condominium associations and institutional investors, Eberhardt is also the largest residential fee property management company in the state.

From the Eberhardt Building near Southdale constructed in 1970, the company continues as a family business under the direction of James Nelson, who became president in 1976 when his father moved up to chairman of the board.

• • •

Walter Nelson, chairman of the Eberhardt Company.

FAEGRE & BENSON

The firm of Faegre & Benson has engaged in the general practice of law since December 20, 1886, when two young Maine-born attorneys, Albert C. Cobb and John O.P. Wheelwright, signed handwritten articles of partnership to combine their individual legal work. The two met while students at Bowdoin College in Maine and struck up a friendship that was to last half a century and travel half a continent.

While Cobb read law in his father's office, Wheelwright followed the lure of western opportunities, settling in Minneapolis and gaining admittance to the Minnesota bar in 1883. His first practice was at Third and Hennepin. Soon Cobb followed his friend west, and the two set up offices next door to each other on the sixth floor of the Temple Court, one of the most famous buildings of its day. Cobb, they agreed, would handle the office practice while Wheelwright took the trial work.

John Benson joined the firm in 1918, and it became Cobb, Wheelwright and Benson with three partners and three associates. Benson had headed the city's first legal aid bureau before joining the firm. In 1923 the firm of Hoke, Krause & Faegre joined forces with Cobb, Wheelwright & Benson, laying the foundation for the modern firm of Faegre & Benson.

The firm moved to its present address, the Northwestern Bank Building, the day the brand-new structure opened in 1930. The connection between bank and law firm was a strong one: Cobb was instrumental in the organization of Northwest Bancorporation (BANCO) in 1929. In the 1930s Faegre continued the firm's representation of the Bank and BANCO and also devoted much time to receivership matters. During this period Benson specialized in trial

COBB & WHEELWRIGHT
1886–1912

COBB, WHEELWRIGHT & DILLE
1912–1920

COBB, WHEELWRIGHT &
BENSON
1920–1923

COBB, WHEELWRIGHT, HOKE &
BENSON
1923–1928

COBB, HOKE, BENSON, KRAUSE
& FAEGRE
1928–1938

FAEGRE, BENSON & KRAUSE
1939–1940

FAEGRE & BENSON
1940–

matters.

The modern firm numbers more than 125 attorneys and at least as many paralegals, secretaries, and support staff. Faegre & Benson is noted for its expertise in corporate practice, from taxation, securities, and profit-sharing/pension plans to labor law, and in litigation from antitrust to product liability cases. A substantial amount of work continues to be done on behalf of nonprofit entities such as The Minnesota Orchestral Association, the Guthrie Theater Foundation, the Minneapolis Foundation, and the Walker Art Center.

•　•　•

Faegre & Benson's firm genealogy through the years, from 1886 to the present.

FAIRVIEW COMMUNITY HOSPITALS

It was the place they didn't build the original hospital that gave Fairview Community Hospitals its name. In 1905 Norwegian Lutheran immigrants and their pastors were hoping to build a hospital near Fairview Park in North Minneapolis. The United Church Hospital Corporation they formed did build a hospital, but it wasn't in North Minneapolis, nor was it originally called Fairview Hospital.

A man named George Christian, whose son died of tuberculosis, had offered $50,000 to any Protestant organization that would build a tuberculosis hospital, stipulating only that it be called Thomas Hospital after an Episcopalian bishop Christian admired. As a result, the hospital, which was opened in Riverside Park in 1908, predated the first to bear the Fairview name by eight years. In 1916, in large measure due to the fund-raising of the first women's auxiliary and the congregations of the founding group, full-service Fairview Hospital opened nearby.

Today Fairview Community Hospitals is the nation's largest nonprofit con-

A view of Fairview Hospital (left), Thomas Hospital (center), and Fairview Nursing School dormitory (right), early 1900s.

Fairview-Southdale Hospital was one of the nation's first satellite hospitals.

• • •

tract manager of hospitals, with more than 40 affiliated facilities spread from the Upper Midwest to the Pacific Northwest in addition to the four hospitals the system owns in the Minneapolis area—downtown Fairview, Lutheran Deaconess (which joined in 1973), Fairview-Southdale in suburban Edina, and Princeton Area Hospital to the north of the Twin Cities.

Over the years the Fairview name has been linked with many innovations in the management of health care, including the first full-service satellite hospital, Fairview-Southdale. Fairview president Carl Platou pioneered the concept of a hospital holding company in 1971 as a response to the need for medical cost containment. And Fairview has been a leader in the sharing of hospital services—pediatrics and open-heart surgery between downtown Fairview and nearby St. Mary's, dialysis equipment between Fairview-Southdale and Methodist Hospital in neighboring St. Louis Park, and pediatrics between the hospital element of the innovative Ridges health and human services campus and Minneapolis Children's Hospital when the former opens in Burnsville in 1984.

It took nearly 60 years to admit the first half-million patients, and just another 15 years to reach the one-million mark. Through it all, Fairview has remained true to its original intent—to provide high-quality health-related services in a spirit of Christian concern.

FIRST BANK MINNEAPOLIS

The Panic of 1857 broke like a thunderstorm over the little trading communities clustered along the banks of the Mississippi and Minnesota rivers. Gold disappeared from circulation. Real estate and business transactions fell apart. Merchants in Minneapolis, St. Anthony, and St. Paul were forced to issue their own scrip. It was a strange time for Jacob Kuntz Sidle and Peter M. Wolford to be starting a bank in rented space in Allen's Dry Goods Store. But 125 years later, that bank is better known as First Bank Minneapolis, the city's oldest surviving financial institution, one of the largest regional banks in America, and the largest member of First Bank System.

Since its earliest days the bank has concentrated on serving the corporate sector in the Upper Midwest. The 1900 acquisition of Nicollet Bank truly began First Bank Minneapolis' growth

The headquarters of First Bank Minneapolis is located at First Bank Place.

• • •

into a major regional financial institution. A year later deposits passed the $10-million mark. The realization that the bank's larger customers, particularly in the grain business, were fast outgrowing First Bank Minneapolis' ability to meet their needs led to the 1915 merger with Security National Bank which made First Bank Minneapolis one of the largest banks in the nation.

More acquisitions and further growth highlighted the 1920s. In 1929 First National Bank of Minneapolis and First National Bank of St. Paul created a jointly owned subsidiary that became First Bank System. Today First Bank System, with more than 90 member banks and trust companies, is one of the

20 largest financial institutions in the nation.

Since the 1950s First Bank Minneapolis has been firm in its commitment to a strong and vital downtown Minneapolis. Recently it opened First Bank Place, an important new anchor for the downtown area and a hub of the city's financial district.

A major source of financing and expertise for the region's wide variety of businesses, First Bank Minneapolis has in recent years substantially expanded its ability to meet the international banking needs of its customers. It was the first financial institution in the Upper Midwest to establish a correspondent banking relationship with the Bank of (the People's Republic of) China; it recently acquired a New York Edge Act subsidiary and London branch office, expanding its capacity to assist corporate customers with export financing.

FINGERHUT

Following World War II, a renewed economy caused a number of consumer-oriented industries to begin to boom, prominent among them the automobile industry. In those early days of America's love affair with the family car, many car seats came covered with fabrics that were easily torn or stained—the seats literally wore out before the car did. In 1948, in a garage in North Minneapolis, a man named Manny Fingerhut recognized opportunity when it came knocking. He also recognized the largely untapped potential of direct mail advertising, a discovery prompted by a necktie circular he received one day several months after launching his company's first product: seat covers made out of a sturdy fiber material. Given this marketing breakthrough Fingerhut could begin to expand his business by going beyond the local community and soliciting orders from car owners throughout the country. Today Fingerhut ranks among the top 10 of the estimated 10,000 mail order firms in the United States.

Mail order was far from a credible business in the early 1950s. Fingerhut, however, was successful by placing a high priority on capable business management and strong professional ethics. Through full-refund and customer satisfaction guarantees, based on 30-day free trial periods and strict attention to responsibly and promptly delivering its products, Fingerhut began to grow from a small, single-product firm to one offering more than 1,000 different items to American households. Today Fingerhut's catalog ranges from appliances and home furnishings to clothing and leisure items.

Fingerhut introduced its first true "best-seller" in 1954: clear plastic seat covers. It also began promoting an ex-

Theodore Deikel, chairman of the board and chief executive officer.

♦　♦　♦

tended payment plan which offered its predominantly lower- and middle-income customers a rarely found form of credit. Clear plastic seat covers, which in the beginning sold for less than $20, became popular for two reasons—they protected upholstery from wear and tear, and they provided an opportunity for the owner to show off and enjoy the original color and fabric of the car's interior.

The new line presented a number of challenges. Fingerhut had to overcome various technical problems in the manufacturing process—plastic then was still a relatively novel and unexplored material, especially the flexible variety—and customer acceptance of plastic fabric had to be won. But the solutions ultimately devised fueled the firm's growth into other product lines in the ensuing years.

The biggest step in this evolution was taken in 1957, when Fingerhut expanded its manufacturing and marketing operations to begin offering a casual coat for both men and women. In addition,

the organization started mailing advertising flyers for a small number of name-brand products to customers who had previously purchased (and responsibly paid for) seat covers.

Fingerhut's first coats were made out of a beige vinyl material, simulating the ever-popular leather look. The new product line, developed from the lessons learned cutting and sewing plastic seat covers, was founded on some early research which established that there was indeed a mail order market for such garments, previously available only through retail outlets. The coats turned out to be the most successful and popular single piece of merchandise in Fingerhut's history and remain important items in the modern, more diversified product line.

During the latter half of the 1960s, Fingerhut began to move into broader areas of apparel and domestic production and marketing. It also continued to expand its line of consumer hard goods. In the course of this steady and sustained growth the firm outgrew a succession of production and distribution plants—from the original garage to three rented offices on Hennepin Avenue South, to Washington and Broadway, and then Lake Street—before new facilities were constructed in Minnetonka in 1972. The headquarters complex on that site combines executive offices, staff services, and research, while operations and distribution activities are located in a number of towns throughout Minnesota.

In the modern era of sophisticated direct marketing, Fingerhut ranks as one of the industry's consistent leaders and innovators in the way it researches and reaches its customers. Sensitive to the growing consumer movement toward direct mail buying during the

1970s, Fingerhut's professional management team, under the direction of president Theodore Deikel, began to redefine the company's business strategy. Shifting its business emphasis from manufacturing to direct marketing, Fingerhut was quick to compile one of the nation's most comprehensive consumer data bases, allowing it to be a personal store for each of more than nine million past and current customers.

Today Fingerhut markets a full product line—everything from pantsuits to food processors, from tools to microwave ovens. One out of every six households in the United States has purchased from Fingerhut. Most of Fingerhut's products are acquired from outside vendors, both domestically and abroad, with less than 2 percent manufactured internally. The company creates, prints, and mails 250 million pieces of literature each year, processes more than 17 million payments, and fulfills over 6 million orders annually.

Through the use of its knowledge of consumer buying habits under a variety of economic conditions, Fingerhut continues to make a science of offering the right product at the right price to the right customer at the right time. The firm has already seized the opportunity to apply its direct response knowhow to the next revolution in consumer marketing—electronic shopping. Working closely with two sister companies in the electronic shopping field, HomServ and ViewMart, Fingerhut continues to broaden its base of marketing skills. And as the communications revolution expands, with cable television systems promising a world where consumers can shop and order merchandise at the press of a button, Fingerhut is poised for even stronger growth in the years ahead.

Over the years Fingerhut management has contributed to many civic and community activities throughout the state, including the innovative "Take a Cab on Us" program initiated in 1975 by Diekel, Fingerhut's chairman of the board and chief executive officer. Through this program, the company reimburses employees for cab fare should they find themselves—or observe another individual—in a position where driving would be unsafe.

Fingerhut converted from private ownership to a publicly held corporation in 1970. In 1979 it became a wholly owned subsidiary of American Can Company and continues to function as an autonomous division.

♦   ♦   ♦

Below Left
The product that first put Fingerhut in the driver's seat was its line of transparent Air-Flo seat covers, sized to fit every model and make of car and truck.
Below Right
Quality vinyl coats have been mainstays in Fingerhut's product line since the late 1950s.
Bottom
Fingerhut headquarters in Minnetonka, Minnesota.

FISHER PAPER BOX COMPANY

Fisher Paper Box Company was founded in 1893 when George A. Fisher, a native of Massachusetts, left his job with Heywood Paper Box in Minneapolis to start his own business. Over in St. Paul, brother Miles had his own Fisher Box Company.

It was an era when local merchants and manufacturers contracted with custom box suppliers for the packages used for everything from clothing to farm supplies. George Fisher began on the second floor of a building at 244 Hennepin Avenue. Within four years, larger quarters at 209 First Avenue North were taken. By the turn of the century the business was doing so well that George Fisher had a manufacturing plant designed to his own specifications. That structure, at 221 North First Street, was ready in 1905, and serves as the firm's home to this day.

Around 1900 Michael J. Kane came to the Twin Cities from LaCrosse, Wisconsin, where he had been part owner of the LaCrosse Paper & Box Company with Daniel Murphy. Murphy's brother, Mike, was in the drayage business—to be better known someday as Gateway Transportation—and his customers included both the LaCrosse company and Miles Fisher's St. Paul business. Before long, Kane was running the younger Fisher's operations, a state of affairs that continued until 1916, when the business was sold. The new owners didn't see eye to eye with the previous manager. Undaunted, Kane took his skills to Minneapolis and went to work for George Fisher. The two ran the enterprise together until Fisher's death in 1931, when Kane assumed sole responsibility until his own death in 1941.

By that time, a second generation of Fishers and Kanes had come along. G.L. Fisher and Paul Kane took things over and ran the company jointly until the former's death in 1960. In 1963 Kane purchased the remaining Fisher interests and continued operations with his own brother, Miles.

As the name implies, Fisher Paper Box designs, prints, and manufactures rigid boxes and folding cartons for retail and commercial customers. For many years, gift boxes for the Christmas season were a mainstay, with orders as large as 100,000 shirt boxes moving through the plant. In recent years, the concentration has shifted to small, custom runs as well as packages for local manufacturers such as 3M's tape and medical lines.

The plant specifically designed for the box business has long since proven its worth to the two families who have devoted nearly a century to Fisher Paper Box.

•　　•　　•

The office and manufacturing staffs of Fisher Paper Box Company posed for this photo on October 2, 1929. Michael J. Kane is at the far left, standing beside George A. Fisher.

GRAIN TERMINAL ASSOCIATION

Grain Terminal Association is an active trader on the floor of the Minneapolis Grain Exchange. A GTA employee, Ralph Hayenga, was instrumental in starting the sunflowers futures market in Minneapolis.

In the early days of the 20th century, as agriculture moved from a self-sufficient life-style to a production-oriented business, farmers faced more perils than simply bad weather and crop failures. Misgrading, low prices, false weights, and other practices were not uncommon. In 1916 alone, farmers estimated they lost $55 million because of marketing inequities.

It was in this climate that the seeds for marketing cooperatives were sown, and those seeds took particularly strong root in the Twin Cities. From the Equity Cooperative Exchange, and the Farmers Union Terminal Association which took its place, came the beginnings of the grain marketing activities that Farmers Union Grain Terminal Association was incorporated to handle.

GTA opened for business on June 1, 1938, with M.W. Thatcher as general manager, 121 affiliated member associations, and $30,000 of borrowed capital, plus another $1.2 million of credit—on Franklin D. Roosevelt's approval—from the Farm Credit Administration. Since that day the organization estimates it has saved its members more than $200 million.

Much of GTA's history has been written in small towns and river ports from Minnesota west through the Dakotas and Montana. Nearly 750 elevators and their local cooperatives and farmers have combined over the years to make GTA the fourth largest marketing cooperative in the nation.

GTA is a prominent member of the Minneapolis Grain Exchange, with traders active on the floor. Two retired GTA executives, Mel Werner and Ralph Hayenga, have served as Exchange president in the past decade; Hayenga was instrumental in the development of a futures market for sunflowers.

In recent years GTA has placed special emphasis on the development of

export markets and its own vertical integration, which is designed to help members control their produce from field to consumer's table. In 1981 the cooperative's grain marketing division handled an all-time record 459 million bushels destined for markets down the Mississippi River, east through Duluth-Superior, and west to markets in the Pacific.

Through GTA, farmers today process durum wheat to produce semolina and durum flours through their Amber Milling division, barley malt through Froedtert Malting, vegetable oils and protein feeds through Honeymead Products, consumer products through Holsum Foods, and livestock feeds through GTA Feeds; the Great Plains Supply division constructs homes and farm buildings. Together the various operating divisions help farm businesses keep pace with the tremendous changes confronting American agriculture.

◆　　◆　　◆

GTA's Elevator M is a familiar south Minneapolis sight.

GENERAL MILLS

I t began with one flour mill of doubt-ful promise on the banks of the Missis-sippi near St. Anthony Falls. Today it is one of the largest, most diverse corpora-tions in America, operating in five ma-jor business segments. Cadwallader C. Washburn would obviously be surprised by the size, scope, and success of Gen-eral Mills, the descendant of the com-pany he founded in 1866.

In the beginning people felt the new mill would do well just to survive. Washburn was gambling that demand for his flour made from midwestern spring wheat would keep the mill run-ning, despite the long-time dominance of winter wheat. The difference was whiteness—darker bran fragments clung to milled spring wheat, resulting in an unattractive and hard-to-sell grayish flour. It wasn't long before the mill on the riverfront came to be known as "Washburn's Folly."

But Washburn was an innovator, and soon he was producing a flour rivaling winter wheat in whiteness and offering superior baking qualities. Meanwhile, new partner John Crosby's administra-tive talent kept Washburn Crosby Com-pany moving forward. At the Miller's International Exhibition in 1880, Washburn Crosby flours were awarded the bronze, silver, and gold medals; the Gold Medal label, together with a repu-tation for quality and value, has been part of General Mills ever since.

The 1920s were critical years in the firm's history. The decade saw the crea-tion not only of General Mills, but also one of its most successful products and its most enduring and popular represen-tative. From her beginnings in 1921 as a pen name for the company's consum-er response department, Betty Crocker grew up to become one of the most in-fluential household authorities of all

"Washburn's Folly" the first flour mill built by Cadwallader C. Washburn near St. Anthony Falls in Minneapolis. Skeptics doubted the mill would survive.

• ◆ •

time.

General Mills was officially formed in 1928, when several milling companies merged, reflecting a nationwide trend in many industries toward consolidation. The merger promised greater efficien-cies, and with them, improved opportu-nities for growth in a changing industry. Within five months of its inception, General Mills included more than two dozen associated firms in 16 states, mak-ing it the largest flour miller in the world. For the next decade and a half, the company focused on expanding its milling and related activities, and on developing markets for a handful of con-sumer brands, including Gold Medal flour, Wheaties, Cheerios, and Bis-quick.

In the postwar period, General Mills continued to enlarge the scope of its consumer food business. The greatly in-creased movement of women into the work force helped to popularize conve-nience foods, and ready-to-eat cereals became widely accepted. Betty Crocker mixes and "Big G" cereals were increas-ingly familiar to millions of consumers.

Perhaps no strategic episode in the history of General Mills was as far-reach-ing and critical as the period soon to follow. Beginning in 1960, the company shifted its focus dramatically, first clos-ing half its flour mills and exiting from the feed business. Economic realism and a commitment to growth moved Gen-eral Mills away from other non-strategic businesses, including formula feeds, oil-seeds, electronics, and refrigerated bis-cuits. By 1966 the company had volun-tarily given up $200 million in sales through divestiture and realignment. The composition of General Mills at this stage was 94 percent food and 6 percent chemicals.

The organization's modern diversifi-cation accelerated greatly in the late 1960s, when General Mills changed from a consumer foods company to become a highly diversified consumer company with entries in many different areas. The diversification led ultimately to a focus on five industry areas: con-sumer foods, restaurants, toys, fashion, and specialty retailing.

The family of enterprises that com-prise General Mills today is a decentral-ized network of profit centers, responsi-ble for tens of thousands of products. The companies and their brand names are among the best-known in the coun-try, and include, in Consumer Foods alone, Gold Medal flour, Bisquick, Bet-ty Crocker mixes, "Big G" cereals, Tom's snacks, Gorton's frozen seafood, and Yoplait yogurt.

General Mills also owns and operates the country's leading dinner house chain, Red Lobster, which from a small base in 1967 has grown to over 300 res-taurants at the end of 1981. There are four other restaurant concepts in oper-ation. Similar growth has taken place in the toy group, which began with a

James F. Bell (seated), founder of General Mills, and other company pioneers view "products of the miller's art."

• • •

small acquisition in 1965. General Mills is today the world's largest toy company with Parker Brothers, makers of Monopoly and other board games, and Kenner, which produces *Play-Doh*, *Star Wars*, and *Strawberry Shortcake*.

Fashion and specialty retailing companies and brands include David Crystal, marketer of Izod/Lacoste alligator emblem-bearing apparel; Foot-Joy shoes; Monet jewelry; LeeWards Creative Crafts; Eddie Bauer clothing and outdoor gear; and The Talbots, a retailer of classic women's clothes.

One of General Mill's historic strengths has been the quality of its management, including three generations of the Bell family. James Stroud Bell, often called the greatest merchant miller of his time, became president of Washburn Crosby in 1888 and saved the mills from being sold to an English syndicate in the 1890s. His son, James Ford Bell, founded General Mills and helped to shape the firm during his presidency from 1925 to 1947. And Charles H. Bell, who served first as president and later as chairman (between 1952 and 1967), furthered the diversification.

The organization in the modern era

In 1936 the first official Betty Crocker portrait was commissioned from artist Neysa McMein.

• • •

has benefited from the leadership of General E.W. Rawlings, James P. McFarland, E. Robert Kinney, and Bruce Atwater, Jr. Atwater was named chairman of the board and chief executive officer in January 1982, following a 23-year career with General Mills. He

had served in a variety of marketing and management assignments and was named president in 1977 and chief executive officer in 1982.

General Mills is also known for the extent of its commitment to its employees and to the communities in which it does business. It has been in the forefront of support for nutrition education and information programs. Its American Family Reports, initiated in 1974, identify issues of concern to modern families. Direct philanthropy on the part of the General Mills Foundation, the corporation, and subsidiaries places General Mills among the top 30 corporate givers in the nation.

With sales in 1981 of more than $5 billion and over 70,000 employees, General Mills remains committed to products and services of quality and value, and to fulfillment of its responsibilities to shareholders, consumers, employees, and society.

• • •

General Mills headquarters in suburban Golden Valley.

GRAY, PLANT, MOOTY, MOOTY & BENNETT

Franklin D. Gray in the courtroom.

The law firm of Gray, Plant, Mooty, Mooty & Bennett celebrates its centennial during the 1980s. When during the decade, however, is open to some small discussion. In 1883 Joseph R. Kingman joined the law partnership of Charles H. Woods and William J. Hahn as office boy, clerk, bookkeeper, and law student (this in the days when aspiring lawyers "read law" with established practitioners, a combination law school and working apprenticeship). Three years later Kingman became a partner in the practice. But whether 1883 or 1886 is used as the official starting point for what was once colloquially known as "the Kingman firm," the modern descendant can lay claim to the longest continuing history of legal service in the city of Minneapolis.

Woods was a New Englander who came west after mustering out of the Union Army, where he had led a New Hampshire company. He served briefly as a justice of the peace and had several other early partners before linking up with Hahn, formerly of Lake City and then state attorney general. The firm specialized in real estate work in the fast-building city; examining abstracts, engaging in litigation over old, complicated titles, contesting liens, settling estates, and drawing wills.

By 1907 the name had become Woods, Kingman & Wallace, and the practice had moved to the new Security Building (now the Midland Bank Building). Next door was the law office of John Crosby, one of the family which participated in the creation of Washburn Crosby Company (now General Mills). Within a year Crosby was a full partner in Kingman, Crosby & Wallace,

but he left shortly thereafter to become general counsel of Washburn Crosby Company.

Kingman and Thomas Wallace might have continued their small partnership indefinitely but for two almost simultaneous occurrences in late 1914. Three of the four members of a larger firm which had once invited Kingman and Wallace to join died, leaving only Arthur Keith and three young associates. About the same time the partnership of Fiske & Cross was dissolved because the former wished to concentrate on his real estate business. Kingman and Wallace contacted Keith and Cross, and, on January 1, 1915, created the first major law firm in Minneapolis—Keith, Kingman, Cross & Wallace. When the founder of another prominent local law firm came to visit the new aggregation's spacious offices, he reportedly marveled, "I didn't know there was enough law business in Minneapolis to support such a layout."

•   •   •

Clinton A. Schroeder, president of the Minnesota State Bar Association from 1981 to 1982.

John W. Mooty joined the firm in 1945.

• • •

Thus, the modern-day firm emerged from the merger of three smaller practices whose roots trace back to the early days of the city.

Wallace left in 1918 to become president, and ultimately chairman of the board, of Farmers & Mechanics Bank (F&M). Keith died the same year. But Kingman continued active with the firm until shortly before his death in 1945 at the age of 85. There were 17 attorneys in the practice at the high point of the early era, but because of several untimely deaths, by the end of World War II only 11 were on board. From that point Gray, Plant, Mooty, Mooty & Bennett has grown to a firm of more than 60 lawyers, including over 35 partners, another 25 associates, and several lawyers "of counsel," including the dean of the University of Minnesota Law School. Its members were trained at more than a dozen of the nation's leading law schools. It has also branched out to open an office in Phoenix, Arizona.

Among those associated with the organization at the end of World War II were three of the modern-day senior partners: Franklin Gray joined the firm back in July 1929, Frank Plant first joined the firm in 1936 and returned in 1945 after a distinguished combat record with the Marine Corps, and John Mooty came directly from the University of Minnesota's law school in February 1945. In the early '50s they were joined by Melvin Mooty and Russell Bennett.

The current history of the firm began with its move to the Roanoke Building in 1955. The practice of law was changing in those days, ushering in an era of increasing specialization that was to contribute greatly to the partnership's growth during the '60s and '70s. In addition to traditional areas of expertise such as probate, estate planning, real estate law and litigation, complex problems of corporate organization, finance and taxation came to the fore. The firm expanded its professional staff and trained them to deal with these specialized areas of legal practice. By 1963 the entire third floor of the Roanoke Building had been taken over, and today the fourth floor as well. The firm's older members can remember second-floor offices that were vacated when the first skyway in Minneapolis (connecting the Roanoke and Cargill buildings) was built.

In recent years antitrust and product liability litigation have become significant to the firm's business. Partners have also taken special interest in the continuing legal education projects of the state bar association, in pro bono legal representation, and in local community service activities. Through it all, Gray, Plant, Mooty, Mooty & Bennett has seldom had time to contemplate its past. In the words of one senior partner: "We're too busy looking forward to the next hundred years."

Woods & Hahn (1881–1886)
Woods, Hahn & Kingman (1886–1888)
Woods & Kingman (1888–1896)
Woods, Kingman & Wallace (1896–1908)
Kingman, Crosby & Wallace (1908–1910)
Kingman & Wallace (1910–1915)
Merger of three firms:
 Kingman & Wallace
 Keith, Thompson, Evans & Fairchild
 Fiske & Cross
Keith, Kingman, Cross & Wallace (1915–1919)
Kingman, Cross & Cant (1919–1920)
Kingman, Cross, Morley & Cant (1920–1935)
Kingman, Cross, Morley, Cant & Taylor (1935–1950)
Morley, Cant, Taylor & Haverstock (1950–1953)
Morley, Cant, Taylor, Haverstock & Beardsley (1953–1954)
Cant, Taylor, Haverstock, Beardsley & Gray (1954–1961)
Cant, Haverstock, Beardsley, Gray & Plant (1961–1967)
Cant, Haverstock, Gray, Plant & Mooty (1967–1970)
Haverstock, Gray, Plant, Mooty & Anderson (1970–1973)
Gray, Plant, Mooty & Anderson (1973–1977)
Gray, Plant, Mooty, Mooty & Bennett (1977)

Genealogy of Gray, Plant, Mooty, Mooty & Bennett.

GREATER MINNEAPOLIS CHAMBER OF COMMERCE

Trading stopped for a minute when this photograph was taken of the trading floor of the old Chamber of Commerce Building in 1895. (Photo courtesy of the Minnesota Historical Society.)

Taken in 1885 at the intersection of Fourth Avenue and Third Street, this photograph shows the first headquarters building of the Minneapolis Chamber of Commerce. (Photo courtesy of the Minnesota Historical Society.)

The forerunner of the modern Chamber of Commerce began on October 28, 1868, as The Board of Trade of Minneapolis. C.E. Flandreau was elected first president along with four officers and 26 directors; there were 38 members in all. At its first annual meeting the next year, the Board officially incorporated and changed its name to Union Board of Trade of the Cities of Minneapolis and St. Anthony, continuing under that name until the cities combined as Minneapolis in 1872.

In 1881 a corporation known as the Minneapolis Chamber of Commerce was organized to serve the interests of the city's grain merchants. More general civic activities were carried on by the Board of Trade until 1911, when the Minneapolis Civic and Commerce Association was formed to unite the ef-

forts of the Board, the Publicity Club of Minneapolis, the Public Affairs Committee of the Commercial Club, and the Minneapolis Traffic Association. There were 650 local businessmen in attendance at Donaldsons' Tea Rooms on February 15, 1912, for the new organization's first formal meeting.

The Civic and Commerce Association operated across a broad spectrum, a tradition continued to the present. Notable among its original activities were the Committee on Benevolent Associations—formed to clean up waste, fraud, and mismanagement among charities active in the community—and the Smoke Prevention Committee, an early evidence of local environmental concern that visited 750 businesses in its first few months of existence, cited 66 "flagrant and persistent" violators, and even took a few of the worst offenders to court to make them clean up their acts.

On January 1, 1947, a novel name change was arranged. The grain-oriented Chamber of Commerce became the Minneapolis Grain Exchange. The next day the Civic and Commerce Association adopted the Chamber of

Commerce banner. The name was amended to Greater Minneapolis Chamber of Commerce in 1968 to reflect the growth of the metropolitan area.

Today the organization boasts nearly 3,000 members ranging from the largest businesses to individual professionals. Through volunteer activity and a professional staff the Chamber concentrates on business and community concerns beyond the reach of any one business or individual, including economic development, corporate responsibility, government-business relations, conventions and tourism, energy, world trade, and community service. The Chamber renovated and moved into the former NSP Building, now known as the Chamber of Commerce Building, in 1969.

HONEYWELL

An automatic control is a device that measures change and transforms the change into some useful work. Nearly anything that changes, no matter how slightly, can be controlled automatically. Modern concerns have focused attention on ways of controlling energy usage, but nearly a century ago those same concerns were basic to the founding of the company known today as Honeywell.

In 1883 Al Butz was a tinkerer with a struggling fire extinguisher business and the idea for a device that would automatically control boiler and furnace fires. The damper flapper he patented in 1885 launched the Consolidated Temperature Controlling Company; Butz recruited five employees and began operations in a shed near downtown Minneapolis. The firm eventually became the Minneapolis Heat Regulator Company, because most of the incoming mail was addressed that way.

The Minneapolis firm merged with one of its toughest competitors in 1927: the Honeywell Heating Specialties Company. William R. Sweatt, who had invested $1,500 in Butz's venture in 1891 and over the years guided it to national success, was named first chairman of the board. He was succeeded by his son, Harold W. Sweatt, who guided the company to worldwide prominence.

Through the years the Honeywell name has become associated with automation and productivity: controls to sense the temperature in a home or building and order heat from a furnace; controls to sense a deviation in the flight of a space vehicle and correct its course; controls to measure a patient's blood flow during a delicate operation; computers that increase the efficiency of control systems as well as improving the productivity of people through data

processing and office automation.

An international company with nearly 100,000 employees, Honeywell is divided into two operating organizations. Control Systems serves commercial and residential buildings, industrial markets, and aerospace and defense

markets throughout the world. Information Systems is responsible for Honeywell's worldwide computer business.

Honeywell's world headquarters has been located on the same site in the Phillips neighborhood of south Minneapolis since 1912, and the organization has been active in enhancing the area for both its employees and its neighbors. Through the Honeywell Fund and the firm's Neighborhood Improvement Program, as well as through the active involvement of generations of Honeywell people, the company has shown a deep and abiding commitment to the city and its people.

◆   ◆   ◆

In 1906 this clock thermostat represented the state of the art for regulating heat. Today Honeywell designs and makes powerful integrated circuit chips (up to 6,000 on one three-inch wafer) used in information systems and control systems.

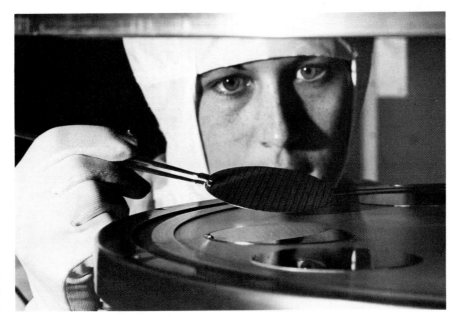

S.J. GROVES & SONS COMPANY

Many companies enjoy looking back on their humble beginnings, often pointing out that they started in nothing more than a hole in the ground. For S.J. Groves & Sons, the international heavy construction firm headquartered in suburban Plymouth, that's the literal truth. Between 1905 and 1908 the three sons of Steven Jasper Groves started bringing their teams of horses in from the family farm in Robbinsdale to excavate basements in Minneapolis. Winters they hauled ice for the Cedar Lake Ice Company. The excavation business proved so lucrative that the four Groves men moved into the city and set up a partnership: excavation and landscaping in the summer, ice hauling over the winter.

Quickly the excavation jobs became bigger and railroad grade construction was added to the family repertoire. In

A business that literally began in a hole in the ground—excavating basements in Minneapolis around 1910.

• • •

1912 the company took delivery of the first steam shovel to come to the Twin Cities, a five-eighths-cubic-yard "full revolving steamer" mounted on steel wheels. But since excavation also required hauling material away, horses remained the backbone of the family business until the advent of gasoline-powered trucks.

Gradually the firm took on the personality of the middle brother, Frank. Clarence, the oldest, sold his interest in 1914; the partnership converted to a corporation in 1918. S.J. Groves died in 1921 at the age of 82, but Frank and the third brother, Herbert, kept the business growing, with the former serving as president for more than half a century.

Franklin N. Groves, chairman of the board and chief executive officer, and his father, Frank M. Groves.

• • •

In 1920 Minnesota launched its first ambitious road-building program, and Groves was awarded the largest job let to that point, an eight-mile stretch of concrete through treacherous country west from Duluth. The Miller Trunk Highway established Groves as a seasoned hand at highway construction, and road work remains a company mainstay to this day, especially in developing nations around the globe.

In the early '20s Groves began to branch out regionally, then nationally. When it won the grading contract for approach roads through Camden, New Jersey, to the Delaware River Bridge connecting that city with Philadelphia, an area office was established in New

Jersey. It was the beginning of a consistent policy of decentralization that was to serve the firm well in the years to come and continues to the present. The Camden job also involved diverting the Cooper River through the city and constructing a tunnel under the river for the gas mains and telephone and electric lines serving South Jersey.

The Depression was a trying period for the building industry, but somehow Frank and Herbert Groves managed to keep their equipment busy. They moved west during this period, completing jobs in Yellowstone Park for the U.S. Park Service, dams for the Bureau of Reclamation, and highways for state highway departments from Montana and the Dakotas to Texas.

One of the company's best-known projects was built during the '30s: the toll highway connecting Marathon to Key West in the Florida Keys. The main structure, spanning 7.2 miles of Atlantic and Gulf of Mexico waters, was the longest bridge completely over water in the country. Groves also had a piece of the Pennsylvania Turnpike and the New York City Circumferential Parkway, the latter providing access to the 1939 New York World's Fair.

World War II brought a need for ordnance works, airfields, and improved transportation facilities; again Groves was quick to respond to new challenges. Its achievements included complete site preparation for the Gopher Ordnance Works at Rosemount and the Badger Works in Baraboo, Wisconsin; and airport work in Newark, Dubuque, Moline, and locally at Wold-Chamberlain Airport in Minneapolis. The '40s also saw Groves move into international construction through participation in U.S.-foreign joint ventures in Mexico, Venezuela,

and on the Island of Antigua, British West Indies.

Dams, highways, airfields, tunnels, and industrial site preparation continued to grow in the '50s and '60s, including plenty of work on the Interstate Highway system. Frank purchased his brother's interest in the company in 1942; declining health led him to turn the presidency over to his son, Franklin N. Groves, in 1969. At his death two years later, he left a legacy of caring that included—through donations of land, buildings, and money—helping United Cerebral Palsy of Greater Minneapolis create one of the largest and most successful sheltered workshops in the nation.

As America's road-building boom ended and gas worries began in the 1970s, Franklin Groves initiated diversification into mining, oil and gas exploration, real estate development, and (perhaps a most fitting tribute to the firm's origins) thoroughbred horse breeding. A subsidiary, Paul A. Laurence Company, specializes in paper mill and power plant construction as well as water treatment work, including the Metropolitan Waste Disposal Plant

on Pig's Eye Island in the Twin Cities area. Another, NCI Constructors of Minnesota, builds sophisticated concrete industrial structures and constructed the ski jumps and luge run for the 1980 Winter Olympics at Lake Placid, New York.

S.J. Groves & Sons entered its third era in 1981 with the appointment of O.E. Powers as president and chief operating officer, the first non-family member to hold that position in the privately owned firm. Franklin Groves remains as chairman of the board and chief executive officer, presiding over a company that began digging basements with horse-drawn equipment and now is world-renowned as a builder of dams, bridges, tunnels, highways, environmental waste treatment plants, and airports, in addition to mining coal and other minerals for itself and public and private sector clients throughout North America and overseas.

•   •   •

Modern construction projects for power plants, dams, and other complex structures are a far cry from basements and road building.

HOPKINS HOUSE

Harold Adolphsen left his family's small farm in South Dakota in the years just before the Korean War to go out on the road as a salesman for a music company. The company sold piano-accordions and Hawaiian guitars, and Adolphsen thought the haunting music of the Hawaiian guitar was the most beautiful sound he'd ever heard.

That is why the Hopkins House, some 4,000 miles from those sunny Pacific islands, is today the flagship of International Hawaiian Inns, Harold Adolphsen's growing lodging chain.

It isn't quite that simple, of course. But the combination of exotic island melodies and Adolphsen's observations as a professional traveler formed the foundation of the transformation he has brought about at the Hopkins House in recent years. It is also the theme uniting International Hawaiian Inns in Iowa City and Cedar Rapids, Iowa; Moorhead, Minnesota; and Phoenix, Arizona.

The Hopkins House and Harold Adolphsen's innkeeping career started at about the same time, but not together. The Hopkins House was opened in 1963 by several local businessmen to serve the industrialized suburban community growing up on Minneapolis' southwest side. The original inn boasted 54 rooms and an outdoor pool, compared to today's 169-room hotel and meeting and entertainment center.

About the same time, Adolphsen and his wife Carolyn ventured into the lodging business with the 39-room Voyageur Motel on Highway 18 in west Minneapolis. Later they ran the 80-room Biltmore in Edina before taking the helm for the Hopkins House's island odyssey in December 1978.

To Adolphsen, the essence of the International Hawaiian Inns concept is to tantalize, not inundate, guests with things Hawaiian. Rather than an overabundance of plastic potted palms and flowered shirts, he uses a subtle blend of foods, entertainment, and familiar visual accents such as handcarved Tiki gods.

In an era of large, homogenous hotel/motel chains, Harold Adolphsen believes International Hawaiian Inns will become as noteworthy for their individuality and quality as for their headquarters in the colder climes of the Upper Midwest.

•   •   •

The original outdoor swimming pool at the Hopkins House has been enclosed and transformed into the Kona Cove.

HORTON MANUFACTURING CO., INC. HORTON INDUSTRIES INC.

Not many companies have two different chances to succeed in business, but such is the history of Horton Manufacturing. Incorporated in 1902, the original firm first became known as a woodworking shop making truck bodies, then later (in the 1930s) as a manufacturer of hydraulic clutches for uses such as paper mill machinery and theater fans. But during and after World War II, the original Horton deteriorated and was eventually dissolved in 1951.

That same year the new Horton Manufacturing was formed when four investors—Hugh K. Schilling, his father P.A. Schilling (former chairman of the board of Hoerner Waldorf), N.H. Sandberg, and G.A. Cushman—purchased the drawings, jigs, and fixtures of the older firm and went back into the manufacturing business in cramped quarters at 3016 University Avenue. Within months the resurrected company had moved into its present factory building on 15th Avenue Southeast, although at first it shared the plant with four other businesses.

Since then, Horton has established itself as a primary producer of industrial clutches and brakes as well as a producer of specialized clutches for the cooling systems of heavy-duty trucks and off-highway equipment. Its original factory has been expanded many times, and now encompasses a city block. In 1973 an administration and sales building was constructed next to the plant. In 1975 a second plant was added in South Dakota for the fan clutch subsidiary, Horton Industries, Inc., and it too has since been expanded to equal the size of the Minneapolis plant. In 1981 a third plant was built in Wisconsin for added capacity for its industrial clutches and brakes. Horton products are also manufactured in Japan, Australia, and Scotland.

Not until 1981 did the modern company learn the background of the man who gave it his name. According to the granddaughter of Herbert Alonzo Horton, the business was started to manufacture either a Horton stove or a part for the original Franklin stove. During World War I, the plant was converted to make precision parts for the Gatling gun.

When the new firm emerged like a phoenix from the old, industrial clutches and brakes remained the main-

• • •

Hugh K. Schilling, president of Horton Manufacturing Co., Inc.

stay. More than 350 Horton products are now used to start and stop the machinery which manufactures the products millions of people use every day. A second automotive line includes a diesel engine fan clutch that helps conserve fuel and reduce noise on heavy trucks and off-highway equipment.

From two employees and no home of its own at its rebirth on September 28, 1951, Horton has grown into a diversified industrial manufacturer. The company is known for its commitment to youth development activities, especially Junior Achievement.

• • •

P.A. Schilling, one of the four founders of Horton Manufacturing Co., Inc., and father of Hugh K. Schilling.

HUBBARD BROADCASTING (KSTP)

The broadcasting traditions created by Stanley E. Hubbard (left), now chairman of the board, are carried on by his son, Stanley S., president.

University of Minnesota football coach Bernie Bierman watches his team practice on the first television set in the Upper Midwest. The picture is projected on a mirror below the screen.

• • •

First Lady Eleanor Roosevelt broadcasts on KSTP in the early 1930s.

• • •

In 1923, with $850 to his name, ex-barnstormer Stanley E. Hubbard returned to the Twin Cities where he had grown up and formed WAMD, the nation's first commercial radio station. He went on the air in early 1924 with 1,000 watts and the colorful slogan, "The Call of the North," but it wasn't the first time Minnesotans had heard his call. In 1913, at the age of 16, Hubbard had built the first amateur radio transmitter in the state.

Hubbard built much of WAMD's early equipment himself, indicative of both his talent for electronics (he conducted the world's first successful communication between planes in 1921 with a representative of the Marconi Company) and the state of his finances. A normal day involved selling in the morning, programming in the afternoon, announcing and directing in the evening—and sometimes sleeping in the studio afterwards.

In 1925 Hubbard developed the first live radio network in the Midwest. It operated during the night between Chicago and the Twin Cities, using two postal telegraph copper lines for which he paid $15 an hour.

The years up to 1925 saw little competition for the new Hubbard station. But in the spring of 1925, the Washburn Crosby Company began its operation of WCCO Radio, sparking a keen professional rivalry that continues to this day. Yet ironically, WCCO's first program had to be rebroadcast over WAMD because the latter station's signal blocked everything else off the crystal sets.

To compete with WCCO, Hubbard secured the backing of the National Battery Company in 1927 and purchased the license of St. Paul's KFOY. He then traded his two licenses for one: KSTP (STP as in St. Paul), conceived as the most powerful station in the country in those days. When WAMD's equipment

was destroyed in a fire, the new station had to be built from scratch. It was. Hubbard was back on the air in 60 days—and in style. From the White House, President Calvin Coolidge pressed the button that officially put KSTP in service.

Hubbard was one of the first to see the potential of radio news. In 1925, WAMD originated daily newscasts with Ruel Barlow, head of the University of Minnesota's school of journalism, at the microphone. When AP and UPI refused to sell their services to the few radio stations coming into existence, Hubbard created the Radio News Association to compete. His success convinced UPI to drop its opposition and extend its services to radio in 1930. In 1950, KSTP-TV became the first to schedule a regular 10 p.m. newscast seven days a week.

But radio was basically an entertainment medium. WAMD began with live broadcasts of name bands from the Marigold Ballroom in Minneapolis, later maintaining its own 35-piece orchestra. The Orpheum Theatre brought its

Early dispatches were carried by news planes of the 1920s and today, by the "Skycam" helicopter.

• • •

vaudeville acts over once a week, treating KSTP listeners to the likes of Jack Benny, Edgar Bergen, Kay Kyser, and the Marx Brothers. One of the first members of NBC's Blue Network, KSTP fed the Great Northern Railroad's "Empire Builder" show to the network, as well as the "Montgomery Ward Noonday Show," the first programming to originate from someplace other than New York, Chicago, or Los Angeles.

Sports also became a Hubbard mainstay. WAMD took midwestern listeners ringside for a live prizefight in 1925, and Hubbard himself did the play-by-

• • •

Sports coverage has come a long way since KSTP covered the National Open in Minneapolis via a wicker baby carriage (1930).

play of the first hockey broadcast in 1926. In 1930, KSTP packed its short-wave equipment into a wicker baby carriage to cover the National Open Golf Tournament in Minneapolis.

Given Hubbard's penchant for new technology, television was a natural addition. Hubbard bought one of the first RCA cameras in 1938, along with five television monitors, so he could experiment with the new medium. A year later his equipment was on display at the State Fair, introducing some 200,000 visitors to the coming revolution. That same year KSTP broadcast television's first parade, an American Legion march in Minneapolis, via closed circuit to the Radisson Hotel.

It was another nine years before KSTP-TV went on the air April 27, 1948, as the first NBC affiliate, the first station between Chicago and the West Coast, and just the third in the nation. In 1954, KSTP brought color to the Twin Cities; in 1961 it became the first all-color station in the country. The NBC era ended in 1979 when

affiliation was switched to ABC.

The Hubbard penchant for equipment continues to this day, most notably in the creation of the world's largest commercial meteorology service. When the station moved to new quarters on University Avenue, not accidentally directly astride the border between Minneapolis and St. Paul, Hubbard insisted the roof be designed to accommodate helicopter landing. At the time it seemed a pointless eccentricity, but today helicopters are mainstays in modern newsgathering.

In addition to covering news for more than 50 years, Hubbard has made his share. He was instrumental in the creation of the Metropolitan Airport Commission. In the 1950s a public information campaign on brucellosis, a disease carried by cattle, led to the eventual eradication of the disease in the state. And the "Secret Witness" program through which private citizens could help police investigators solve community crimes presaged the renowned "Crime Stoppers" program of today.

Hubbard Broadcasting operates eight radio and television stations in Minnesota, New Mexico, and Florida.

INTERNATIONAL MULTIFOODS

Feeding people—that was the basic business of the New Prague Flouring Mill Company in 1892, when Francis Atherton Bean, Sr., rented a vacant mill in the small town south of Minneapolis to make a second start at milling. It is the same basic business that chairman and chief executive officer William G. Phillips presides over nearly a century later, as International Multifoods moves into new headquarters atop the 50-story Multifoods Tower in the City Center development in downtown Minneapolis.

Through the years, the small-town milling operation has grown into a truly international producer and marketer of many diverse foods—"multifoods." Its more than 8,500 employees on four continents continue to be united by the kind of family traditions so typical of Minnesota's milling industry.

If not for the determination of its founder, Multifoods might never have happened at all. Francis Bean began his first milling business in Faribault in 1872 when he took charge of the flour mill his father had purchased after the Civil War, the Polar Star Milling Company. The business prospered until about 1890, when plummeting flour prices and discriminatory railroad freight rates brought about the firm's collapse. Bean was $100,000 in debt when Polar Star Milling died. He was still in debt two years later when, at the age of 52, he approached his brother-in-law, J.H. Mallory, for a loan so he could lease the closed Zimmer flour mill at New Prague. Mallory took a second mortgage on his Rice County farm to stake Bean to $1,000. By 1896 the operation was doing so well that the original owner decided to take it over himself. Undaunted, Bean built his own mill. New Prague remains an important part of the com-

pany's milling operations to this day.

Bean's activities became international in scope in 1908 with the purchase of Saskatchewan Flour Mills Ltd. of Moose Jaw. Within a few years International Milling was distributing Robin Hood flour the length of Canada, building and running mills north and south of the U.S.-Canadian border, and putting in an ocean shipping dock in Vancouver, British Columbia, to provide an outlet to the Pacific.

Transportation and other urban efficiencies brought about the move to Minneapolis in 1923, and with it, a

At the turn of the century, Multifoods, then called the New Prague Flouring Mill, purchased several small local mills to serve a growing Midwest market.

•　•　•

commitment to the city's center that has continued through the years. Through those years, under the strong leadership of Atherton Bean, grandson of the founder, the Twin Cities became the home of this ever-growing international firm—jumping south to Venezuela in the 1950s, later to Brazil and Mexico as well, and spanning the Pacific more recently with franchise operations principally in Japan, Thailand, and Malaysia. Six years after going public and setting out on a systematic program of diversification, International Milling became International Multifoods in 1970; a year later the firm was listed on the New York Stock Exchange. In 1973 Multifoods broke the half-billion-dollar-mark in sales. Today it is a billion-dollar-a-year enterprise.

The transition from family business to modern multinational came in the 1960s when Atherton Bean hired Phillips. Through some 45 acquisitions and planned growth into new areas, Multifoods has become a broadly based food manufacturer, processor, and marketer, feeding people all over the world.

The company operates in four areas. In industrial markets, Multifoods supplies basic foods sold to other food companies and institutions in the United States, Canada, and Venezuela, including bakery and export flour, durum flour, and prepared bakery mixes and supplies. The consumer segment con-

• • •

Today, ultra-modern methods, which are faster and more efficient, assure traditional high-quality flours.

centrates on manufacturing and marketing retail food products in the same three countries, plus Brazil. In the United States, principal products include Robin Hood flour and mixes, Kaukauna cheeses, Kretschmer wheat germ, Reuben specialty meats, Smoke Craft snack meats, and Adams peanut butter.

Farmers and producers of livestock and poultry know Multifoods for its broad line of formula feeds and animal health products, primarily under the Supersweet label, Lynks seed corn, and Osborn and Tevco veterinary products. Away-from-home diners can find Multifoods behind nearly 1,000 shops and restaurants—Mister Donut coffee shops in Japan, the United States, and Canada, Boston Sea Party restaurants in the United States, and pizza shops and restaurants under the Pizza Patio and Pizza Delight names in Ontario, Canada.

Multifoods was a founding member of

• • •

The modern consumer is offered a variety of Multifoods products in the grocery store (below center), and in snack shops and restaurants, such as this Boston Sea Party in Bloomington, Minnesota (below right).

the innovative Minnesota Business Partnership and has made a firm commitment to the state's renowned Two Percent Club, the nearly two dozen Minnesota businesses which each year contribute that much or more of their pretax earnings to community activities. It is a policy in keeping with the ideals of the company's founder, a man who made a very special Christmas trip back in 1911, when his second venture in the milling business was thriving.

Unannounced and enjoining secrecy on each man he visited, Francis Bean instructed the creditors of the old Polar Star Milling Company to dig through their records to determine what portion of its $100,000 debt was due them— even though he was under no obligation to make payment and most of the men he visited had long forgotten the debt's existence. But not only did Bean pay each bill, he added six percent interest over the 21 years since his original business failed. "Like a business romance with a Dickens Christmas tale ending," marveled the *Minneapolis Journal* of the day, after one of Bean's friends got wind of what was going on and tipped off a newspaper reporter.

InterNorth, Inc.

The beginning of the Great Depression was an inauspicious time to start a new business. The Midwest was caught in the iron grip of a severe drought. Crops shriveled and died. Businesses everywhere were failing. But one company's founding fathers went ahead anyway, incorporating Northern Natural Gas on April 23, 1930. Today, more than 50 years later, that struggling little pipeline company has grown into one of this country's largest and most diverse energy businesses. Now known as Inter-North, Inc., the corporation has operations throughout much of the United States, in Canada, and in a number of Caribbean countries.

All that was far in the future a half-century ago, however. From headquarters in Omaha, Northern Natural Gas began to develop plans to pipe natural gas from Kansas to Nebraska, Iowa, and Minnesota. In the beginning it looked southwest to the Hugoton Field of Kansas, Oklahoma, and Texas for supplies. That field was to become the largest, most productive natural gas field in the world.

More than a supply source was needed, however. Building pipelines was back-breaking work in that era, and the techniques of welding, coating, wrapping, and bending steel pipe were still in the early stages of development. Construction crews worked 12-hour days, seven days a week, often through dust storms and blizzards, but they reached Emmons, Minnesota (just south of Albert Lea), in 1931.

At first what Northern Natural Gas found throughout the Midwest was doubt. The engineering technology for building and operating long-distance, high-pressure pipelines was brand-new, and so was the very idea of natural gas. Consumers were often reluctant to try the unfamiliar fuel, but imaginative marketing techniques, including countless demonstrations of the effectiveness of gas appliances, gradually overcame the initial reluctance. In town after town, people became convinced that natural gas was indeed cleaner and more efficient than coal.

InterNorth's activities today are divided among seven separate operating companies and their subsidiaries. All have an impact, either directly or indirectly, on the energy available to Minnesotans.

Northern Natural Gas, the original enterprise, still delivers natural gas. Today it operates a sophisticated 21,500-mile pipeline system, one of the most extensive in the nation. This energy artery stretches from southwest Texas to Michigan and supplies 74 utility companies in nine states. In Minnesota, Northern Natural Gas operates 2,875 miles of pipeline and supplies 20 utility customers, including Minnegasco, which serves Minneapolis, and Northern States Power Company, which serves St. Paul. As one of Minnesota's largest single energy suppliers, Northern Natural Gas provides all of the natural gas used in the Twin Cities area and about 95 percent of the total consumed in the state.

Peoples Natural Gas, the corporation's retail arm, serves gas customers in more than 300 communities in eight states. It is the third largest gas utility in Minnesota, supplying nearly 90 cities and towns, including Rochester, Eagan, and Farmington.

Northern Plains Natural Gas Company is responsible for the design, construction, and operation of the Northern Border Pipeline, a major new energy transportation system which will soon bring Canadian natural gas and, ultimately, Alaskan supplies to midwestern homes, businesses, and factories. Scheduled for completion in 1982, the major leg of this project will extend more than 800 miles from the Montana-Saskatchewan border, across the Dakotas and southwestern Minnesota, to Iowa.

Northern Natural Resources Company manages the corporation's Canadian subsidiaries and its interests in the Alaskan and Trailblazer-Overthrust pipeline projects. Both pipelines will eventually make more natural gas available to Minnesota.

Northern Liquid Fuels Company produces, transports, and markets natural gas by-products—propane, butane, gasoline, and helium. It is the largest company of its kind in the United States and two of its subsidiaries are active in Minnesota. HTI pipes propane to its terminal near Rosemount and wholesales it to area distributors, among them Northern Propane Gas Company, two of whose 10 retail outlets in the state are in the Twin Cities.

Northern Petrochemical Company produces a wide range of plastics and PEAK-brand car care products. The company's National Poly Products Division operates a plant in Mankato, where it manufactures plastic bags and gloves.

Nortex Gas & Oil leads exploration efforts to find new supplies of energy for both the corporation's natural gas and fuel and chemical operations.

InterNorth has grown and changed considerably since Northern Natural's beginnings during the Depression. Total gross investment in plant facilities now stands at more than $3.5 billion, and the work force has increased from 461 to about 11,000. The corporation has been publicly owned since the mid-1940s when, in compliance with the Holding

Company Act, the corporation's three original owners divested themselves of control of Northern Natural Gas stock.

InterNorth's commitment to Minnesota has changed and grown as well. It now has nearly 600 employees at some 70 locations around the state, busily providing their neighbors with energy and energy-related products. Clearly, InterNorth will play a significant role in Minnesota's energy future.

◆　　◆　　◆

Top Left
At the time of Northern Natural Gas Company's founding, pipeline-building techniques were in their infancy, presenting a multitude of construction problems as the system was extended northward from Kansas through Nebraska, Iowa, and into Minnesota.
Top Right
Nortex Gas & Oil Company, an InterNorth subsidiary, is searching for new energy supplies offshore in the Gulf of Mexico, as well as onshore in the southwestern and Rocky Mountain states.
Center
The Northern Border Pipeline, being built by an InterNorth subsidiary, is a major new energy transportation system which will bring Canadian and Alaskan natural gas to the Midwest.
Right
Northern Natural Gas Company, now known as InterNorth, Inc., began serving communities in Minnesota in 1931, a year that saw more than 1,000 miles of pipe added to Northern's system.

INTER-REGIONAL FINANCIAL GROUP

In 1974 Inter-Regional Financial Group was a brand-new holding company created to allow the securities firm of Dain, Kalman & Quail to venture into new areas of investment and finance. Less than 10 years later it has become one of the nation's premier diversified financial service companies, part of the trend toward "financial supermarkets" capable of providing a broad range of investment vehicles for individual, corporate, institutional, and government clients in 24 states from coast to coast.

The oldest and largest member of Inter-Regional is Dain Bosworth Incorporated, the largest regional investment banking firm in the United States. The organization serves 14 Midwest and Rocky Mountain states through 44 branch offices. It provides a full range of investment products for individuals and institutions; handles corporate needs through underwritings, private placements, and other financial services; and serves municipalities and other public entities with underwriting and financing for capital projects.

Dain Bosworth is the descendant of a number of regional investment companies, the oldest of which, Kalman & Company, was founded in St. Paul in 1909. The Rocky Mountain contingent originated in Denver with Bosworth, Chanute, Loughridge and Company in 1916 and Sullivan and Company in 1927. Many of the Iowa offices trace back to Quail and Company, organized in Davenport in 1922. The Dain name derives from J.M. Dain and Company, founded in Minneapolis in 1929.

The Denver firms merged to form Bosworth, Sullivan & Company in 1946. In 1967 Dain and Kalman merged, and the subsequent acquisition of Quail produced Dain, Kalman &

Thomas E. Holloran, chairman and chief executive officer

♦   ♦   ♦

Quail. This firm grew through the acquisition of Nebraska-based J. Cliff Rahel and Company in 1969, of Platt and Tschudy (an advisory and asset management firm which is now Inter-Regional's Investment Advisers, Inc.) in 1970, and of Woodard-Elwood & Company of Minneapolis in 1972. That same year Dain, Kalman & Quail went public. Bosworth, Sullivan was acquired a year later, and in 1978 the operations of the two firms were combined, resulting in Dain Bosworth in 1979.

Rauscher Pierce Refsnes became part of the family in 1981. Headquartered in Dallas, Texas, it includes 23 brokerage offices in seven southwestern and western states, a trading office in New York City, and an options clearinghouse in Chicago. The Sun Belt's premier investment banking and brokerage firm was formed in 1933 when Mercantile National Bank of Dallas spun off its municipal bond department to John H.

Richard D. McFarland, president.

♦   ♦   ♦

Rauscher, Sr., vice-president of the department, and Charles C. Pierce, Sr., his assistant.

Rauscher and Pierce had just $1,500 between them when they opened the doors of Rauscher Pierce & Co.; the balance of their start-up capital came as a $50,000 loan from their former employer. Over nearly half a century Rauscher Pierce Refsnes compiled an impressive track record in public and corporate finance and investor services as well as particular expertise in the emerging growth companies of the Southwest, especially in energy and technology.

IFG Leasing Company began as All-States Leasing Company in 1964 when the Lorenz family of Billings, Montana, started a small car leasing firm. Four years later the business was moved to Great Falls and expanded into office equipment. In the early '70s the family went looking for a broader capital base at the same time Inter-Regional was looking for an established business with

Inter-Regional Financial Group and its Minneapolis-based subsidiaries are housed in the Dain Tower at Sixth Street and Marquette Avenue.

• • •

less volatile earnings than those common in the securities industry. All-States Leasing was acquired in 1974 and ultimately merged into IFG Leasing, its wholly owned subsidiary, in 1980. The firm now leases capital equipment from small copy machines to multimillion-dollar oil drilling rigs to commercial, agricultural, industrial, government, and professional users in virtually every state of the union. Its headquarters remain in Great Falls.

Midwest Life Insurance Company was formed in 1906 in Lincoln, Nebraska, and currently is admitted to do business in 27 states, primarily in the Midwest and West Acquired in 1980, Midwest underwrites specialized insurance products oriented to the investment business and marketed through Inter-Regional's securities firms and others.

Dain Corporation was organized in 1973 to provide and supervise real estate investments for individuals, institutions, and corporations throughout the United States. It concentrates on existing properties in selected markets and makes its services available to brokerage and investment banking clients of Inter-Regional's securities firms.

Investment Advisers, Inc., was founded in the late 1940s as Platt & Tschudy and was acquired in 1970. It provides portfolio management services to employee benefit trusts, individuals, trustees, endowment funds, foundations, and other organizations needing securities management assistance. In addition, it manages several no-load stock and bond funds.

IFG Information Services, the newest Inter-Regional member company, was formed January 1, 1982, to provide expertise in system design, computerized applications, communications systems, and computer resources to the growing number of firms in the Inter-Regional family.

Under the guidance of chairman and chief executive officer Thomas E. Holloran and president Richard D. McFarland, Inter-Regional employs more than 2,200 men and women throughout the western United States. Indicative of its rapid growth, the company was listed on the New York Stock Exchange in 1981. Inter-Regional Financial Group, Dain Bosworth, Midwest Life Insurance, Dain Corporation, Investment Advisers, and IFG Information Services are all headquartered in the Dain Tower in downtown Minneapolis.

• • •

This picture of Dain Tower, taken when the building was opened, shows the art deco interior and the statue "Wings" which was commissioned by the builder to depict his interest in aviation.

INVESTORS DIVERSIFIED SERVICES

The disastrous Panic of 1893 was a tough time for Minneapolis and the growing agricultural and industrial region it served. A dozen large banks in the Twin Cities were forced to close, and many smaller country banks were wiped out in frantic runs by panicked savers. Many people lost their life's savings, and those who had never put away a nickel were in dire straits.

In the aftermath of the national panic, a lot of first-class new timber was seeded, not the least of it the 1894 incorporation of Investors Syndicate, which grew up to become Investors Diversified Services (IDS), a nationwide financial services firm with an impact in many areas of the economy.

Investors Syndicate was launched in a one-room office in the Lumber Exchange Building by John E. Tappan, a 26-year-old law student whose only previous business experience had come from collecting on bad debts during the day to finance his night school studies. Tappan learned the only way to settle overdue accounts was to help people organize a regular payment plan that would, over time, clear up the amount owed. Why, he reasoned, couldn't the same system be used to help people who weren't in financial trouble save for the future? With $2,600 and abundant confidence, he went into business.

Tappan began by offering a fixed-return investment known as a face amount certificate. Investors made small, regular payments until the certificate matured, usually in 10 years, in order to collect the face amount of the certificate. This figure came from their payments and the interest Tappan earned for them by investing their premium dollars, primarily in first mortgages on homes.

Within a year Tappan had invest-

John E. Tappan, founder of IDS.

• • •

ment contracts with 150 people in the Twin Cities. Within 20 years his reserves had grown from the initial stake to $88,000. During that time, despite two depressions, he was able to pay off every matured certificate in full and on time, establishing a reputation for reliability that would be basic to all the success that followed. The company passed the million-dollar mark in 1918; by 1925, when Tappan sold his interests at the age of 57, Investors Syndicate had assets of more than $12 million.

Investors Syndicate spread from coast to coast during the 1920s and 1930s, its growth based on individual salespeople who offered investment programs face-to-face to the little guy— farmer, merchant, worker, homeowner —mostly in small towns. From 1929 through 1939, during the worst days of the Depression, with many banks closing their doors, Investors Syndicate paid out $101 million on time to hold-

ers of matured certificates.

After World War II the artificial wartime interest ceilings were removed and Investors Syndicate (now IDS) began to grow faster, putting money into industrial and construction loans in the postwar growth years and guiding the early years of Investors Mutual, the mutual fund started in 1940 that today ranks among the world's largest. New York-based Alleghany Corporation acquired full ownership of IDS in 1979 after 30 years as a minority investor.

In Minneapolis, of course, the IDS name is most frequently linked to the distinctive 57-story IDS Center, the single most visible element in the rejuvenation of the downtown. Originally conceived as a 12-story, quarter-block office building, the IDS Center grew in the planning stage to occupy the entire city block bordered by Nicollet Mall, Seventh, Marquette, and Eighth. The renowned Crystal Court, the spectacular promenade area under a canopy of interlocking plexiglass pyramids that links the IDS Center to the four surrounding business blocks via the city's Skyway system, has drawn international acclaim. The IDS Center remains company headquarters.

From a simple certificate, IDS has grown in nearly a century to offer an extensive range of financial services to consumers and businesses of varying income levels and needs. Financial planning, insurance and annuity products, investment certificates, and mutual funds are its principal products. Its associated mutual funds form the largest group of stock and bond funds in the world. IDS Life Insurance, established in 1957, now ranks among the top U.S. life insurance companies. IDS Advisory, created in 1972, provides investment management services to large corporations and institutions for their pension and other tax-exempt funds. IDS Trust Company, formed in 1978, helps corporations meet the fiduciary and investment responsibilities of employee benefit and other programs.

Nearing a century of dedication to meeting the changing needs and aspirations of Americans, IDS stands today as an industry leader providing comprehensive financial services ranging from

•   •   •

Right
Walter D. Scott, president and chief executive officer of IDS.
Below
The Lumber Exchange Building, where IDS was born in 1894.

simple accumulation of money to solutions for the most complex problems of estate conservation and business continuity.

With $12 billion of assets owned or managed, 1.5 million individual and corporate customers, and 3,700 sales people in 160 sales offices around the country, IDS continues successfully to do what John Tappan set out to do in 1894—help people manage money safely . . . and profitably.

•   •   •

Below
Rising gracefully along Nicollet Mall in the heart of downtown, the IDS Center is Minneapolis' best-known modern landmark.

LITTON MICROWAVE COOKING PRODUCTS

Litton Industries was founded in California in 1953 as the Electro-Dynamic Corporation. Almost from the beginning Charles B. Thornton, first president and past chairman of the board, anticipated that the company would be in the microwave business someday. Litton's initial interest in the development of microwaves for cooking was based on the potential it saw while developing components for defense-related radar applications.

In 1963 the Atherton Division was formed in Palo Alto, California, to investigate the potential microwave oven market. Later that year it acquired the Bruder Company of Cleveland, Ohio, a manufacturer of infrared sandwich heaters for the vending industry. Its

owner, Robert Bruder, was already developing a microwave at Franklin Manufacturing Company in Minneapolis for sale by his company. Franklin, founded in 1929 as the Franklin Transformer Manufacturing Company, made a variety of products, including transformers, electrical motors, garage door openers, and battery chargers.

In early 1964 the first microwave ovens using the Litton magnetron tube and built by Franklin were ready; based on their potential, Litton acquired Franklin in August of that year. Over the next several years the division developed the Model 700, the first all-Litton-engineered oven, and the Models 500 and 550, the beginning of real growth in the commercial microwave oven market.

Canadian operations were established in Toronto in 1966, the division offices consolidated in Minneapolis a year later.

In the summer of 1971 the first consumer oven with the Litton brand name—Minutemaster—was introduced. European marketing operations were launched in 1972 and the division's new consumer plant in suburban Plymouth was completed. The division name was changed to Litton Microwave Cooking Products in 1973, and has since become one of the best known of Litton's more than 100 divisions.

Under the direction of William W. George, and now Wayne L. Bledsoe, new microwave oven models have been introduced almost annually, including the new Litton-Aire over-the-range model which outstripped early market expectations from day one. Accessories for consumer microwave ovens have also played a significant role in the division's growth, in keeping with the firm's original concept of selling a complete system rather than just another kitchen appliance.

In its less than 20-year history, division sales have increased 630 times, from $300,000 in 1963 to $189 million in 1981. Litton Microwave Cooking Products has more than 50 distributors and 8,000 dealers in the United States and over 40 distributors worldwide; it employs nearly 2,000 people at three facilities in Minneapolis and Sioux Falls, South Dakota.

•   •   •

Already one American home in five has a microwave oven, and the number is expected to double through the mid-1980s; in 1981 Litton Microwave Cooking Products outperformed the industry.

LUTHERAN BROTHERHOOD

Lutheran Brotherhood, a fraternal benefit society, ranks in the top 5 percent of U.S. insurance companies in terms of its more than $11 billion of life insurance in force. Among fraternal benefit societies, Lutheran Brotherhood ranks second in assets and third in life insurance in force. It operates on a not-for-profit basis for its contract holders and also aids communities and the Lutheran Church through a variety of programs.

The society sprang from a church convention held in the Twin Cities in 1917. Two delegates to the session, J.A.O. Preus and Herman L. Ekern, submitted a proposal (in Norwegian) for the formation of an insurance society for Lutherans. It met with far from universal agreement. Some objected to the very concept of insurance, believing it to be incompatible with faith in God's providence.

•   •   •

Arley R. Bjella, chairman of the board of Lutheran Brotherhood.

Despite these concerns, a study committee headed by the Reverend Thor Eggen approved the concept and articles of incorporation were signed on June 17. The new society was named Luther Union at first, but was changed to Lutheran Brotherhood in 1920 following the formation of a partnership with the Lutheran Brotherhood of America, an organization founded during World War I to tend to the spiritual needs of Lutheran servicemen.

Through the strong leadership of its founders—Eggen, Preus, and Ekern—and their successors, Lutheran Brotherhood developed into a major fraternal benefit society with nearly one million contract holders. Today it offers a broad range of life and health insurance benefit contracts to help provide members with financial security: protection of life value and earning power, retirement planning (including Individual Retirement Arrangements—IRA), es-

•   •   •

The Lutheran Brotherhood Building, Minneapolis.

tate planning, and meeting personal business needs through pension planning and profit-sharing programs. A subsidiary, Lutheran Brotherhood Securities Corp., was formed in 1970 and currently distributes five mutual funds, including a money market fund.

Lutheran Brotherhood has always remained loyal to its Minneapolis roots, a commitment visibly evidenced by the dedication in 1982 of its new 17-story headquarters building in the downtown across Fourth Avenue South from the Hennepin County Government Center.

Under Arley R. Bjella, chairman of the board, and Clair E. Strommen, president and chief executive officer, Lutheran Brotherhood employs 650 men and women in its home office and has approximately 1,000 district representatives serving Lutherans throughout the 50 states.

•   •   •

Clair E. Strommen, Lutheran Brotherhood's president and chief executive officer.

MARQUETTE NATIONAL BANK

In the 1920s Ralph W. Manuel, founder and first president of Exchange State Bank, began assembling the group of small banks that would ultimately become the Marquette National Bank of Minneapolis. Each had been founded primarily to serve small businesses and consumers, and as Marquette grew to become the fourth largest bank in the city of Minneapolis, that strong consumer orientation has been carefully preserved.

Although some of the banks that became Marquette were started as early as 1890, the true foundation was laid in 1916 when Manuel organized the Exchange State Bank. At about the same time another bank, the State Institute

for Savings (chartered in 1889 as the Guaranty Savings and Loan Company) was hunting for a merger partner. Under Manuel's guidance, the two became the Marquette Trust Company. In 1922 the Pay Day National Bank, which had been formed two years earlier and was also headed by Manuel, changed its name to Marquette National Bank and became affiliated with Marquette Trust Company. Both institutions took their names from their Marquette Avenue addresses.

Within a few years the assets of the Industrial State Bank (formerly the Continental State Bank) were consolidated into the growing institution, and a few years later still the Transporta-

tion National Bank had joined Marquette. In 1934 Manuel received a national charter for the merger of Marquette National Bank and Marquette Trust Company into the Marquette National Bank of Minneapolis.

On Manuel's retirement in 1945, Russell L. Stotesbery became president. It was he who introduced economy checking accounts and installment loans as part of Marquette's continuing small customer focus. In 1955 he moved the ever-growing bank from its old brownstone at 517 Marquette Avenue to the newly remodeled LaSalle Building at Seventh and Marquette, renaming it the Marquette Bank Building. Like his predecessor, Stotesbery quintupled the size of the bank during his tenure.

Carl R. Pohlad became only the third president of Marquette after Stotesbery's death in 1955, a position he has now held for more than a quarter of a century. His contributions include the introduction of national credit card services to the Minneapolis area as well as the shepherding of detached facilities and automatic teller machines to keep the bank abreast of the continuing surge toward electronic banking. Pohlad has also carried on the tradition of the office, quintupling again the size of the institution.

Marquette Bank now occupies sites on both sides of Marquette Avenue, part in the former Baker Arcade Building, part on the original site—which is now part of the IDS Center complex.

•   •   •

The original Marquette National Bank Building at 517 Marquette Avenue. Erected in the 1920s, it is one of the few fine examples of Egyptian Revival architecture in the country.

MARSH & McLENNAN

The year was 1909 when Donald McLennan came to Minneapolis to open an office of his Chicago-based insurance brokerage firm. He had secured the account of F.H. Peavey Company, and more than 70 years later the Peavey account continues to be a major client of the firm's Minneapolis operations.

The Minnesota connection, however, began with McLennan's boyhood in Duluth. By the time he moved to Chicago in 1904, he was one of the country's recognized experts on railroad insurance, largely as a result of his work for two Twin Cities-based lines: the Northern Pacific and the Great Northern. This move to Chicago was as a co-owner of the Duluth-based Manley-McLennan Agency. At about this same time, Henry W. Marsh was building his reputation in New York and Chicago as a co-owner of the Marsh-Ullmann Company. In 1905 they merged their interests, forming the firm of Burrows-Marsh & McLennan which in 1907 became Marsh & McLennan.

In its early days the Minneapolis office grew through the acquisition of major local insurance agencies which provided local identification and were able to capitalize on the ever-growing national capability provided by the en-

◆　◆　◆

The present management team of Marsh & McLennan, Minneapolis office.

Henry N. Marsh (above) and D.R. McLennan (above right), founders of what would become the world's largest insurance brokerage firm.

◆　◆　◆

ergy and leadership of Donald McLennan and Henry W. Marsh.

The milling and grain industry has always been a mainstay of Marsh & McLennan's Minneapolis operations. Since World War II the expansion of the Minneapolis office has been through not only its identification with the expanding agribusiness of the Twin Cities, but identification and brokerage involvement in the airline industry, hospital and health care field, the computer and data processing industry, as well as manufacturing businesses headquartered locally which required the national and international capability of Marsh & McLennan. The resulting growth places the Minneapolis office as one of Marsh & McLennan's five largest U.S. operations.

Marsh & McLennan was the first

Minnesota firm to offer actuarial services to its clients and took an innovative role in the design and management of self-insured workers' compensation plans for many local employers.

As an insurance broker, Marsh & McLennan analyzes the activities of its clients and advises them on the best ways to meet their insurance requirements, suggesting ways to reduce risk as well as determining the type and amount of actual insurance coverage needed. That has led to the development of sophisticated risk management and computerized loss projection programs in addition to insurance evaluation.

Under Managing Director George C. Wright, Marsh & McLennan's Minnesota offices include more than 150 employees in Minneapolis and St. Paul, plus another 70 who work for William M. Mercer, a separate company created in 1976 to administer employee benefit plans. Marsh & McLennan is the world's largest insurance brokerage firm.

MEDTRONIC, INC.

For most Americans the late 1950s and early 1960s will be remembered for the "space race"—the great technological spurt that landed a man on the moon by 1969. But for more than one million people the world over, a more important thrust was being made inwards, toward the fragile engine that sustains life itself. In 1960 the first implantable heart pacemaker was successfully demonstrated on a 77-year-old inspector for an optical company. Later that year, on October 24 to be exact, Palmer Hermundslie flew to Buffalo, New York, to meet with the two men who had designed the device and get their signatures on a contract giving Medtronic, Inc., of Minneapolis exclusive rights to produce and market their implantable pulse generator. Production began in November; by December Medtronic had orders for 50 of the units, which sold for just $375 in those days.

It was a major step for a modest company which began in a refurbished garage in northeast Minneapolis in 1949. Earl Bakken and Hermundslie were brothers-in-law who had formed a medical equipment repair company on the basis of a conversation at a family birthday party. Bakken, a graduate student in electrical engineering at the University of Minnesota, had become a familiar figure at Northwestern Hospital due to his skill at repairing sensitive medical laboratory equipment. Hermundslie had been working for a local lumber firm. Both recognized the opportunity in the growing field of medical technology.

They started with a garage workshop, the walls built with lumber from refrigerator boxcars, the windows protected by steel bars salvaged from an old bank. One month they billed a total of eight dollars for repairing a centrifuge. But

Medtronic's first office building and manufacturing facility at 818 19th Avenue Northeast.

•   •   •

gradually the business began to grow—to a second garage, eventually to an apartment on Central Avenue. And as it grew, equipment repair and the income obtained representing several manufacturers in the five-state area fostered some sophisticated tinkering. It was not uncommon for Bakken to modify equipment for researchers at area medical centers or design and build new devices for special uses. In all, Medtronic built nearly 100 different devices during the 1950s, although only 10 were ever made a part of the product line.

Through its sales and service activities, Medtronic came to the notice of Dr. C. Walton Lillehei, a pioneer in open-heart surgery at the University of Minnesota Medical School. Lillehei and other researchers had encountered a significant problem, especially with younger patients: in about one in 10 cases corrective surgery resulted in a blockage of the heart's electrical impulses, causing abnormally slow rates.

Physicians as early as 1803 had dis-

covered that the heart could be stimulated by electricity, but the pacemakers of the 1950s were cumbersome devices which literally had to be plugged into a wall outlet. A power failure was a constant worry, mobility was severely limited, and the higher voltages necessary for such external shocks frequently proved traumatic.

By 1958 researchers at the university, including Medtronic engineers, discovered a way of combining a pulse generator with a wire electrode at-

•   •   •

The first external pacemaker, developed by Earl Bakken.

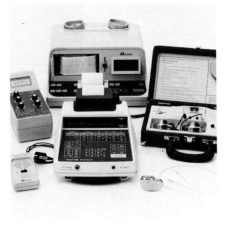

The implantable Spectrax pacemaker in the foreground surrounded by follow-up and monitoring instruments.

• • •

tached directly to the heart. That left the problem of the power source. Within a very short time, Bakken had designed a relatively low-voltage, transistorized pulse generator that was battery-operated and could be worn by the patient.

In the next two years the technology evolved significantly and Medtronic was well-established as a pioneer manufacturer of these medical devices. The system's greatest drawback was that it was still external—wires could become snagged or dislodged, their passage through the skin presented an opportunity for infection, and the system simply wasn't convenient for patients forced to "wear it" 24 hours a day.

The implantable device developed by Dr. William Chardack, a surgeon, and Wilson Greatbatch, an electrical engineer, was the long-awaited breakthrough. It was Medtronic that brought the device into production, complementing it with a number of other medical electronic products. From 1962 sales of $500,000 Medtronic jumped to

$12 million by 1968, establishing itself as the world leader in the field.

Today Medtronic, with annual sales over $300 million, is the world's leading producer of implantable medical devices. That includes not only the design and manufacture of heart pacemaker systems, but also neurological devices for the treatment of pain and the prevention of muscle disuse atrophy, plus computer systems for diagnostic imaging and mechanical heart valves. The company employs nearly 4,800 men and women around the world and does business in more than 75 countries.

The pacemaker has come a long way in the past 20 years. Medtronic's Spectrax-SXT is a multiprogrammable device with telemetry which can be adjusted by a physician using a computerized programmer without additional surgery. Its microelectronic circuitry and lithium batteries good for up to 10 years are contained in a package weighing just an ounce and one-half,

nearly five times lighter than pacemakers of just 10 years ago. The latest generation of pacemakers can speed up or slow down the pulse rate according to the dictates of the body, compared to past generations which had to be set at a fixed rate. Also on the horizon at Medtronic are implantable devices which will administer drugs to a localized site or organ—morphine to control chronic pain, chemotherapy for cancer patients, and insulin for diabetics.

Medtronic's philosophy is embodied in the first of its six corporate objectives adopted early in the company's history: To contribute to human welfare by application of biomedical engineering in the research, design, manufacture, and sale of instruments or appliances that alleviate pain, restore health, and extend life.

• • •

Rice Creek Tower, part of Medtronic's largest facility in Fridley.

MINNEAPOLIS STAR & TRIBUNE COMPANY

John Cowles and President Eisenhower in 1956.

The *Minneapolis Tribune* was launched in 1867 when a pre-Civil War paper, the *State Atlas*, merged with the postwar *Minneapolis Chronicle*. In the 1890s and early 20th century, under the ownership of William J. Murphy, the *Tribune* brought the first Mergenthaler typesetting machines to Minnesota, published its first cartoon and first half-tone engraving, and even experimented with color. Murphy's will left $350,000 to the university in supporting journalism education.

The *Minnesota Daily Star* was also born of turbulent times, founded in August 1920 by the head of the Non-partisan League and a former Socialist mayor of Minneapolis. After a one-month receivership in 1924, the paper reappeared as a more orthodox afternoon daily. It was this paper—third then among the city's three dailies—that the Cowles family purchased in 1935.

John Cowles moved from Des Moines to Minneapolis to take charge, and the *Star*'s success led to its purchase, in 1939, of the city's other afternoon paper, the *Minneapolis Journal*, founded in 1878. The approach of World War II, meanwhile, combined with the *Star-Journal*'s continuing success, resulted in 1941 in a merger of the *Tribune* with the Star-Journal Company. The two competing Sunday editions combined under the *Tribune* name, and later in the 1940s the *Star-Journal* once again became *The Minneapolis Star*.

The Star and Tribune newspapers' publishing plant, originally constructed in 1921, has been rebuilt and enlarged four times since 1939. Each paper has maintained separate news and editorial staffs, between them winning four Pulitzer Prizes and hundreds of other awards and honors. In addition to its publishing responsibilities, the company has taken an active role in the community, including membership in the Five Percent Club (the more than 40 Minnesota companies which annually contribute 5 percent of their pretax earnings to a broad range of public service activities).

The firm has also expanded into other parts of the communications industry, including network and cable television, daily and weekly newspapers, commercial directories, and commercial printing.

In recent years, MST has participated in several experiments transmitting its data base information to home or business terminals. *Advertising Age* magazine, in its December 1981 report on the 100 leading media companies, ranked by advertising and circulation revenue, placed the Minneapolis Star & Tribune Company number 29 in the United States.

Headquarters is in the IDS Tower.

• • • •

The Minneapolis Star & Tribune Building and the adjacent newsprint facility and office building.

MINNESOTA TWINS

The 1965 Minnesota Twins.

•   •   •

On October 26, 1960, Calvin Griffith, president of the Washington Senators, announced the historic decision to move his American League baseball franchise from the nation's capital to the Twin Cities, giving birth to the Minnesota Twins. Well over a million fans turned out during the team's first season at Metropolitan Stadium in Bloomington. They saw a struggling team that finished seventh out of ten, but one with a nucleus that promised big things for the future. In 1962 the Twins jumped from seventh to second, the first of many pennant runs in the '60s—a decade in which Minnesota led the American League in attendance.

The banner year was 1965, when the Twins rebounded from sixth the year before to win the American League by seven games over the Chicago White Sox. (The Met also hosted the 1965 All-Star Game.) Shortstop Zoilo Versalles was named the league's Most Valuable Player. Jim "Mudcat" Grant led the league with 21 victories. Al Worthington and Johnny Klippstein anchored a top-notch bullpen. And studded through manager Sam Mele's line-up were names like Harmon Killebrew, Tony Oliva, Bob Allison, and Jimmie Hall.

Allison's sprawling catch in left field in the World Series against Los Angeles that fall is still remembered as one of the all-time great plays. The Twins jumped to a 2-0 edge by beating Dodger aces Sandy Koufax and Don Drysdale in the first two games at the Met. Los Angeles came back to sweep three straight at home. Mudcat Grant's pitching and hitting sparked the Twins' sixth game victory, but the dream ended one step short when Koufax proved overpowering in the Dodgers' seventh game win.

When divisional play came to baseball in 1969, the Twins won the first Western Division crown under fiery Billy Martin, then repeated the next year with Bill Rigney at the helm. Killebrew was the league's MVP in 1969 with 49 home runs and 140 RBI, and Rod Carew's .332 pace led the league in hitting. In both years, however, the Baltimore Orioles swept the best-of-five playoffs to earn the trip to the World Series.

The '70s brought leaner days for Minnesota, but there were plenty of memorable individual moments. Carew won six batting championships. Oliva and Killebrew made their last appearances before local fans (Killebrew's #3 is the only Twin jersey ever officially retired). In the later years of the decade, attention increasingly turned to the new era to be initiated on Opening Day 1982 in the Hubert H. Humphrey "Metrodome." More hospitable playing conditions and a bright new crop of promising young players may someday soon return Calvin Griffith's charges to the prominence they enjoyed in the '60s.

•   •   •

Calvin Griffith, president of the Minnesota Twins.

MINNESOTA GAS COMPANY

On February 21, 1870, the Minneapolis Common Council voted an exclusive 40-year right to manufacture, distribute, and sell gas in the city to the Minneapolis Gas Light Company, an enterprise headed by the city's first elected mayor, Dorilus Morrison. Nine months later, on November 22, gas manufactured from coal was flowing through a single wooden main that stretched from the new gas works on 14th Avenue near the Mississippi River down to Nicollet Avenue and 192 waiting customers.

In the beginning gas was used solely for illumination. The original users were billed six dollars for each thousand cubic feet, *more* than customers in the early 1980s paid. But gas wasn't the only source of lighting. Electric wires were strung in Minneapolis in 1882. Intense competition often found both gas and electric lights on the same streets.

The late 19th and early 20th century period was truly a gas-light era. During the Exposition of 1886, Nicollet Avenue was alive with gaslights from Second to Sixth streets; bright red, white, and blue globes sat pyramid-style on each post and arched over intersections. It was also the era of the Rand family, three of whose members served as company presidents between 1876 and 1928.

Like Morrison before him, Alonzo Cooper Rand was both mayor and company president. He succeeded Charles E. Vanderburgh, judge of the Fourth Judicial District.

By the 1890s Minneapolis Gas Light Company was doing more than just lighting the streets. The Minneapolis Omnibus and Carriage Company was the first to use gas to fuel boilers. The gas range had also arrived, and more than 1,000 were installed in Minnea-

polis homes and restaurants in 1893 alone. By the turn of the century there were nearly 150 miles of gas lines in service, and the population had climbed past 200,000.

The gaslight era peaked in 1910; by 1924 all 8,700 gaslights had been removed. Gas had evolved from a source of outdoor illumination to an indoor fuel suitable for cooking, laundering (there was a gas iron on the market), water heating, commercial power, and—slowly but surely—room heating. In 1916 Dr. Alfred Owre, dean of the University of Minnesota's School of Dentistry, became the first Minneapolis resident to heat his home with gas.

The Roaring '20s brought a strange inkling of the turbulence of modern times. The city, which regulated rates, reduced the amount the gas company

To meet peak wintertime energy demands, Minnegasco maintains liquefied natural gas and standby propane supplies.

•   •   •

could charge in 1920—and the Minneapolis Gas Light Company went into voluntary receivership until 1924, when the dispute was settled. Soon the firm was growing again, expanding to suburban St. Louis Park in 1926, and a year later to Brooklyn Center and Columbia Heights.

"Natural" gas did not come to Minneapolis until 1934, when it was first blended with manufactured gas to produce a higher heat value fuel for approximately the same price.

Minneapolis Gas Light Company changed its name to Minneapolis Gas Company in 1948, also ending its affiliation with a utility holding company

Prior to the arrival of natural gas, manufactured gas was stored in holders like this one in northeast Minneapolis. The last of the company's holders was dismantled in 1961.

• • •

and commencing its independent corporate status. A year earlier straight natural gas had finally replaced the manufactured gas mix. As a result, more than 350,000 household gas appliances had to be converted—a task taking 225 servicemen and costing $650,000. As new appliances replaced old, a new image and corporate symbol was also born—Minnegasco, a young Indian maiden created in 1959, portrays the modernity, friendliness, and informality the firm emphasizes.

While operational changes in the post-World War II era were substantial,

Minnegasco's growth—in geography, new customers, diversification, services, and leadership—changed more dramatically in the 1970s and early 1980s.

Between 1974 and 1976, the company merged with or acquired three regional natural gas utilities and took the mantle "Minnesota Gas Company." Its gas operations now span several hundred miles—from Brainerd, Minnesota, in the north to Lincoln, Nebraska, in the south, and total more than a half-million customers.

The organization diversified under the direction of current board chairman Paul W. Kraemer. There were new ventures: a centralized downtown Minneapolis heating-cooling plant, acquisition of small manufacturing firms, and ownership and development of a 1,200-acre planned community. This non-

Minnegasco's new corporate headquarters is in downtown Minneapolis.

• • •

utility activity is one of the firm's cornerstones as it seeks further expansion in the 1980s, partially as a response to government regulation and also to maximize the abilities of its management and 2,200 employees.

As the oldest and largest energy supplier in Minnesota, Minnegasco is still an energy-marketing company. In the energy-conscious '80s, the company emphasizes the wise use of energy in consumer programs. That continued allegiance to its customers is an attitude that folks like Dorilus Morrison would appreciate.

MODERN MERCHANDISING, INC.

Harold Roitenberg, founder and chairman of Modern Merchandising.

Modern Merchandising, Inc., traces its beginning to 1961 when Harold Roitenberg, chairman of the board, formed Creative Merchandising & Publishing to produce catalogs for the emerging catalog showroom industry. Two decades later the major source of revenue is the operation of more than 70 showrooms in 17 states. However, Modern Merchandising, Inc., is also the largest publisher of catalogs for the catalog showroom business through its publishing subsidiary.

Most showroom companies of the early '60s were not large enough to publish high-quality catalogs independently. Instead they relied on black-and-white illustrations supplied by manufacturers. By combining their resources, Roitenberg found he could produce attractive four-color catalogs at a reasonable cost—and realize substantial savings due to united buying power as well. Now a wholly owned subsidiary, Creative Merchandising & Publishing annually prints more than 13 million fall catalogs for the more than 300 outlets of some two dozen catalog showroom companies around the country.

The retail side of the business was entered in 1966 with the opening of the first LaBelle's showroom (in partnership with Leonard LaBelle, now senior vice-president) in downtown Minneapolis. LaBelle's has since grown to eight showrooms in the Twin Cities metropolitan area with nearly 30 more in eight western and Rocky Mountain states. In addition, Modern Merchandising operates multi-store showroom chains under the names of Jafco in the Pacific Northwest, and Dolgin's in Missouri, Kansas, and Illinois, as well as smaller divisions in Idaho (Great Western), Ohio (Miller Sales), and Michigan (Rogers Distributing).

Modern Merchandising's rapid growth has been fueled by two significant advantages of catalog showrooms: the chance to pre-shop and compare prices at home, then purchase from a streamlined retail/warehouse outlet whose minimal overhead and large inventory help keep prices low. Through LaBelle's and its other showrooms, Modern Merchandising offers fine quality jewelry and giftware along with name brands of small appliances, consumer electronics, cameras and stereos, gifts, toys, sporting goods, and housewares, all at competitive prices.

Modern Merchandising was formed in 1971 with the merger of LaBelle's and Creative Merchandising & Publishing. Nationwide, the company employs more than 6,000 men and women including nearly 1,000 employees in the Twin Cities. The company moved its modern headquarters and distribution complex to Minnetonka in 1978.

•　　•　　•

Attractive showrooms displaying one of every item held in inventory have become familiar sights to the millions of Americans who have made catalog showrooms one of the fastest growing segments of modern retailing.

NASH FINCH COMPANY

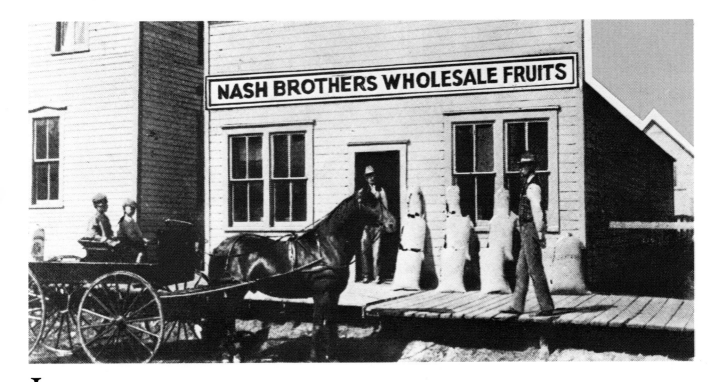

NASH BROTHERS WHOLESALE FRUITS

I t all started when the Nash family moved to Minneapolis in the early 1880s from Vermont, where the father ran a general merchandise store. In 1885 Fred, the eldest of the three brothers, gave up a brief attempt at homesteading in North Dakota and opened a small confectionery in Devils Lake, North Dakota. He sent for his two younger brothers, Edgar and Willis, to join in the first "Nash Brothers" merchandising venture. The three lived in the back of the store, cooking their meals from food in stock until the business began to grow. By 1889 they were marketing fresh fruit to other retailers in the region.

Thirty years later the brothers returned to Minneapolis and established the company's base for expansion. Growth continued and the operation spread to Canada, the Pacific Northwest, and south to Texas.

The Nash's first non-family employee was 14-year-old Harry B. Finch, hired in 1889. In 1921 the various acquisitions and operations were consolidated through the incorporation of Nash-Finch Company and F.P. Nash became the organization's first president. Harry B. Finch became president in 1926.

The Depression sowed the seeds for the modern supermarkets. As they developed in the Midwest, Nash Finch altered its distribution pattern and began to concentrate on serving these supermarkets. In 1954 the firm entered the retail food business with corporate ownership and franchising of supermarkets. Membership markets were added in 1964. From that first confectionery, Nash Finch grew to serve more than 350 affiliated and independent markets, plus 100 additional company-owned supermarkets, warehouse food stores, and membership markets. A subsidiary, Nash DeCamp, owns and operates packing, shipping, and cold-storage facilities in California and Arizona.

In 1916 the Nash brothers bought the Caldwell Importing Company of Minneapolis, which for 15 years had supplied its private label. The business was named Nash's Coffee Company and was eventually sold in 1960.

For over 96 years the business has continued to grow. In 1981 the volume exceeded one billion dollars, placing the company among the top wholesalers in the United States. The firm's executive offices remain in Minneapolis, where approximately 175 employees are based.

•   •   •

The original Nash Brothers wholesale house, established in 1885 in Devils Lake, North Dakota.

MUNSINGWEAR

Eighteen eighty-six. The Statue of Liberty is dedicated. Ty Cobb is born. Coca-Cola is the newest headache remedy. Bloomingdale's opens at 59th Street and Third Avenue in New York City. And Sears, Roebuck and Co. is launched in North Redwood, Minnesota.

Against this backdrop, the Northwestern Knitting Company was organized in 1886 by three young men. One of them was named George D. Munsing. He had developed a method of plaiting silk over wool to eliminate the itch of underwear. Munsing's itchless underwear set his young company on a path that would take it into the next century and beyond.

Outgrowing its tiny quarters in the loft of a saddlery building in downtown Minneapolis, the venture moved to a new plant—the first poured concrete building to be constructed in Minnesota. That structure, actually composed of seven interconnected buildings constructed between 1891 and 1912, served as the company's headquarters for 91 years.

Northwestern Knitting changed its name to Munsingwear Inc. in 1919. Four years later it became the first Minnesota company to be listed on the New York Stock Exchange. By that time, innovation, being first, had become a way of life at Munsingwear.

Other early firsts include having placed the first underwear advertisement in a national magazine—an 1897 edition of *Ladies Home Journal*—and invention of the famous union suit. The underwear ad may have shocked the world, but the union suit revolutionized the industry and put Munsingwear at the forefront.

The 1930s and 1940s were years of dramatic growth. Sales more than doubled. Product innovations, too, abounded. The company developed the first flexible corset when a designer took pity on the bound, boned, and buckled contraptions suffered by ladies of the day. The first whirlpool-stitched bra came out in 1933 and stayed in the line for almost 40 years. Men's briefs benefited from introduction of the horizontal fly and the kangaroo pouch. And the first insulated underwear was developed in 1945.

A leader in advertising throughout its history, Musingwear shocked the world by placing the first underwear ad in an 1897 edition of Ladies Home Journal.

• • •

Also during that time, the firm opened sales offices and showrooms in New York, Chicago, and Los Angeles. In 1933 the first research and development department in an apparel firm began at Munsingwear. And 1947 saw installation of the first electronic data

Munsingwear relocated its corporate headquarters in 1982 to this downtown office building at 245 Marquette Avenue.

• • •

processing equipment.

Later innovations included the first nylon-reinforced T-shirt neckband which in 1950 provided Munsingwear's entry into the T-shirt business; development of hot-pack fabric for Sister Kenny's polio treatment; reflectorized kids' clothing; underarm gussets in sport shirts; establishment of a golf pro advisory board; first backless and strapless bra in 1960; first non-twist yarn and T-shirt.

While innovation has been the life's blood of Munsingwear's growth, acquisition too has played a big part, beginning in 1912. That was the year Munsingwear first purchased the Vassar Swiss Underwear Company. The move was, at the time, not a good one, and the companies parted after six years . . . destined to meet again more than 30 years later. In the interim, Munsingwear acquired Wayne Knitting Mills, David Clark Company, and Rollins Hosiery Mills.

The Vassar Company was reacquired in 1951 and operated as a separate division producing women's lingerie. In 1957 it was merged with the newly purchased Hollywood-Maxwell Company, a nationally known bra and girdle manufacturer. The emerging Hollywood-Vassarette division of Munsingwear that year introduced the industry's first color-coordinated line of intimate apparel for women.

Acquisition of two small companies

in 1978 and 1981 provided additional fabric production capability in Fairmont and Red Springs, North Carolina. In 1982 those facilities absorbed the production of the closing Minneapolis plant.

Innovation and acquisition have been two important means of growth and success for Munsingwear. A third is expansion. Worldwide demand for its products led the company to begin in 1952 to build a network of licensees. Today Munsingwear has licensees in Australia, Canada, Japan, Mexico, South Africa, Thailand, and Turkey. Nearly the entire globe is served by agents, representatives, distributors, and direct sales of the organization's products.

While international business was booming in the 1970s, domestic business flattened. Munsingwear struggled to stay competitive while remaining a domestic producer. Simultaneously, three of the company's Japanese associates—Toyobo, C. Itoh, and Descente companies—were looking to strengthen their ties with Munsingwear. A new issue of stock in 1981 made each of the companies 10 percent owners of Mun-

singwear and raised needed capital for the company.

Its balance sheet strengthened, Munsingwear took steps to improve its operations. A series of plant closings corrected the imbalance of manufacturing capacity and sales demand. The company instituted profit improvement programs which saved almost $5 million in just the first two years.

Even at its centennial, Munsingwear is as new, modern, innovative, and revolutionary as it was in 1886. Its product lines meet and even create today's consumer desires, just as they did then. In the 1980s Munsingwear moved aggressively into new product areas such as kids' wear and branded Pro Shop sports apparel lines. Introduction of the large-size Lady Vassarette line is another example of the company's unabated attention to consumer needs.

Munsingwear is on the right track for the 1980s. And the future never looked more promising.

• • •

This historic facility housed Munsingwear's manufacturing and corporate headquarters operations for 91 years, from 1891 to 1982.

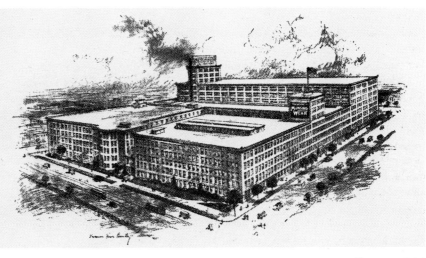

NAPCO

*Ed Rappaport, founder of
Northwestern Auto Parts Company.*

*Max E. Rappaport, chairman of the
board and president, 1954 to 1965.*

◆　　◆　　◆

By almost any standard, it was an extraordinary meeting the top executives of Napco held back in early 1977. Locked away at L'hotel Sofitel with a handful of outside consultants, the management team had the novel task of deciding what business the company, founded nearly 60 years before, should be in. With $12 million in the bank, mostly from the sale of its heavy-axle manufacturing business, and two strong operating divisions still active, there was no need to hurry. It was an opportunity that might come only once in a firm's lifetime, and the decision called for a good deal of deliberation.

The decision? Napco chose to enter the service merchandising field and put its hard-earned bankroll behind Mass Merchandisers Inc. of Harrison, Arkansas. That was in June 1977, and over the next few years more than a dozen related acquisitions followed.

As one of the nation's leading service merchandisers, Napco distributes nationally advertised nonfood consumer products through supermarkets, drug stores, convenience stores, and other retail outlets in the Midwest, South, and West. Nonfood items may represent approximately 6 to 7 percent of an average grocer's volume, but they typically account for 25 to 30 percent of profits. One main reason for that is the emergence of sophisticated service merchandisers, who provide prepriced goods, stock and maintain the shelves, and supervise inventories and merchandising. Computerization from route salesperson to warehouse provides a constant data base for tracking what is selling, what isn't selling, and what to do about it.

For Gary Rappaport, chairman of the board and chief executive officer, it represents quite a transition from the company his grandfather founded—and in which the grandson spent summer vacations from college sweeping the plant floors. Edward Rappaport was a journeyman tinsmith when he left his native Rumania in 1899. How he came to Minneapolis is unclear, but in 1918 Northwestern Auto Parts Company (hence the acronym NAPCO) opened its doors at 310 Plymouth Avenue. Through the next 30 years, Northwestern grew from a small parts distributor and salvage firm to a major supplier of service parts for vehicles no longer in service and for uncommon contemporary models of passenger cars, trucks, and construction equipment. The business moved to a larger shop at 834 North Seventh Street about 1929.

As an auto parts supplier, Northwestern was the first to produce a catalog of its replacement inventory. The Rappaport family spent evenings around the dining room table putting the first ones together by hand. But early on Ed Rappaport, and soon his sons Max, James, and Fred as well, realized there was only limited profit potential in the individual auto wrecking or truck dismantling business. So they began purchasing entire lots of more marketable parts from large eastern salvage yards. By the end of World War II, Napco's over-the-counter business had reached $2,000 a day, more than its 10 closest competitors combined, and it was supplying customers throughout the Upper Midwest.

After the war, Napco's understanding of parts wholesaling led it into the military surplus market. Military and foreign markets had yet to develop at that time, but there were great shortages of transportation equipment, and leftover jeeps, trucks, and other vehicles were quickly sold in the civilian market.

Before long the United States began selling military hardware overseas, but not until the Korean War did the necessity of keeping this equipment supplied with spare parts become widely recognized. When it did, Napco was ready. The firm's international division continues to distribute, service, and sell repowering kits for vehicle modernization (such as converting gasoline-fueled vehicles to diesel), as well as special-purpose vehicles, aircraft spares, communications equipment, automotive replacement parts, quartermaster supplies, and soft goods.

The '40s to the '60s brought a second-generation Rappaport, Max, to the helm and took Napco into a second

business configuration: manufacturing. In 1949 the company had developed a front-wheel-drive axle; through the next 25 years it carved out a niche producing axles, universal joints, and gears for forklift tractors, mining equipment, steamrollers, street sweepers, rail maintenance trucks, tanks, military transport planes, and other large vehicles. In 1955 the company went public and in 1963 it purchased Electro-Craft Corporation, a maker of high-performance DC servomotors and related amplifier and control systems for computers and office machines. (Electro-Craft was sold in 1980 to provide cash for further acquisitions in the service merchandising field.)

For Max Rappaport, 1955 was important for family reasons, too. In that year, his father and his brother James both died from heart disease. Max, a founder of Mt. Sinai Hospital in Minneapolis, established a foundation to fund research on such practices as bypass surgery a full decade before the practice was performed on humans.

Upon the death of Max Rappaport in 1965, his son Gary was named president and chief executive officer. During the next 10 years Napco saw a number of acquisitions and sales, but it became increasingly apparent that a

small manufacturer was at a disadvantage in large, capital-intensive and high-technology industries. In 1976, after much soul-searching, the decision was made to sell the industrial products division and seek a new direction for Napco.

Napco's transition from a family-run manufacturing business to major service merchandiser has benefited from the expertise of an unofficial family as well. Current president Frank Trestman joined the firm in the 1950s as an accountant and has since risen through the management ranks to the top operating position. Erwin Kelen ran Electro-Craft during most of the 17 years it was part of Napco, and has remained involved as a director of the organization. Henri Jacob, president of the International Marketing Group, has been instrumental in guiding that division of the company to its position of prominence.

And that is how the company's top management happened to be in the position to invest its future in becoming the nation's leading service merchandiser.

•　　•　　•

Napco's corporate headquarters at 1600 Second Street South, Hopkins.

NATIONAL CAR RENTAL SYSTEM, INC.

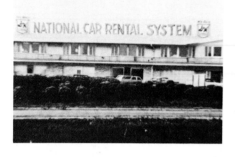

Above Left
National's first offices in Minneapolis were in a remodeled furniture store at the intersection of Highway 100 and 50th Street.

Above
National Car Rental's international headquarters, located in the Minneapolis suburb of Edina, was ready for occupancy in 1980.

Company legend has it that when National Car Rental System left New York City for Minneapolis in 1965, the move involved just seven employees and seven boxes. That year the company lost about three million dollars, and there were those who thought Minneapolis would be National's final resting place. The business that had been founded in 1947 as an informal association of 24 independent car rental operators who wanted to share ideas about the relatively new but promising field was in very real danger of going under.

It didn't. Instead, Minneapolis proved to be the right medicine. Today National Car Rental, now a wholly owned subsidiary of Household International of Chicago, numbers 13,000 people worldwide and ranks a solid third in the fiercely competitive car rental field.

But when two Minneapolis businessmen—Kenneth Glaser and William McKinstry—bought the struggling firm and moved it into a remodeled furniture store at 50th and Highway 100, survival was the primary concern. And survive National did, mainly by working to establish a reputation for outstanding service, both for the cars it rents and for the customers it rents them to. And as the dramatic growth of air travel and the nation's expanding economy brought fi-

nancial muscle, new lines of business have been added, bringing National attention to auto leasing, truck rental and leasing, even the dredging of waterways.

Minneapolis is actually the fourth headquarters city National has had since officially incorporating in St. Louis in 1961. Shortly thereafter, the firm was moved to Jackson, Mississippi, and then to New York City in 1963. From seven employees and seven boxes, the growth of National is reflected in the new 19-acre international headquarters facility in suburban Edina that the organization moved into in the summer of 1980. The location provides a central focus for reservation calls from across the country and around the world.

National was the first in the car rental industry to introduce computerized central reservation service. That same year, 1969, was important internally as well. That was the year Household International, one of the nation's largest multi-industry corporations, acquired a majority interest. In 1974 National became a wholly owned subsidiary of Household.

Automobile rental activities account for about 70 percent of National's business. In addition to the familiar green-bannered counters in airports and cities around the world, National is active under the Lend Lease name in the fleet leasing of cars and trucks. Another division, Mud Cat, provides environmental reclamation services through the sale and lease of portable

National Car Rental's counter, a typical sight across the country.

• • •

dredging equipment that can remove sediment, weeds, and other accumulations from lakes, canals, reservoirs, and industrial settling ponds. Internationally, travelers find National's car rental affiliates under the Europcar name in Europe, Africa, and the Middle East; to the north it's Tilden, Canada's largest rental car operation. National also has licensees in Latin America, the Caribbean, and the Pacific—more than 100 countries and territories in all, making Minneapolis truly an international headquarters.

Under National presidents Joseph James and Bemiss Rolfs, quality has

Car condition is an important factor to most car renters, so National concentrates on keeping its fleet in the best maintained condition of any car rental company.

• • •

become the watchword at National. When a company survey of rental car customers revealed that the condition of the car was far and away the most important consideration for people planning to rent a car, National created a position for a vice-president in charge of maintenance and established strict service standards. The result? Surveys conducted by the United States Auto Club consistently rated National number one in the overall condition of its rental fleet, which now numbers more than 75,000

vehicles in the United States alone.

Despite its size and stature in the car rental industry, National still believes field management is a key ingredient. That's why it gives its field managers the opportunity and the responsibility for making decisions that allow quick reaction to competition and the marketplace.

Because so much of its growth and maturity has come since the company moved to Minneapolis, National supports many community programs, including the University of Minnesota's Executive Development Center, which provides top and middle management assistance for regional businesses, and many civic activities such as the Minneapolis Aquatennial.

NATIONAL CITY BANK OF MINNEAPOLIS

W hen National City Bank of Minneapolis first opened its doors on the ground floor of the Sheraton Ritz Hotel in June 1964, it was determined not to become "just another downtown bank." With an initial capitalization of $3 million (the largest of any bank opened in the region in that era), the first new national bank organized in the downtown since 1920 set out to be an innovative force in commercial banking. And its short but successful history is evidence of how well it has lived up to that ambition: under the direction of C. Bernard Jacobs, chairman of the board, and James H. Hearon III, president and chief executive officer, National City has grown to rank fourth in the city of Minneapolis, seventh in the state, in terms of deposits, with assets approaching $400 million.

In its aggressive and flexible response to its commercial banking customers, National City quickly outgrew the Sheraton Ritz. In 1975 its activities were consolidated in its current headquarters, the former Federal Reserve Bank Building at Fifth and Marquette, a financial landmark in the city since

Selmer Jerpbak, founder of National City Bank of Minneapolis (left), the late Whitney Eastman, one of the original directors of the bank (center), and C. Bernard Jacobs, then executive vice-president and currently chairman of the board of the bank and president and chief executive officer of National City Bancorporation.

•   •   •

its completion in 1925. The bank also maintains facilities in the Sheraton Ritz and opened a Southdale branch in 1978. In 1981 National City Bancorporation, its parent bank holding company, acquired the five-year-old National City Bank of Ridgedale in Minnetonka.

National City is a full-service bank offering more than 100 different customer services, from commercial, real estate, and personal installment loans to trusts, bond trading, and direct equipment lease financing. International banking is available through National City's branch in Georgetown, Grand Cayman Islands, established in 1974 to facilitate participation in the Eurodollar market and international financial ac-

tivities. A representative office in Budapest, Hungary, opened in 1979 to serve the increasing level of export and import activity to and from Eastern Europe.

National City is known in the community for its sponsorship of the long-running "Business Scene" weekly television program as well as the publication of a newsletter by director Walter W. Heller, one of the nation's most respected economists. National City introduced free checking accounts and the first drive-up television tellers to the Twin Cities; it has, from its first day of business, paid daily interest on regular savings accounts. Its unique Money Manager statement shows checking, savings, and loan information on one convenient form while Executive Line services, introduced in 1979, give special attention to the credit requirements of upper-income and professional customers.

•   •   •

National City Bank of Minneapolis' move to its newly remodeled headquarters was completed in 1975. The former Federal Reserve Bank Building has been a city landmark since 1925.

NORTH MEMORIAL MEDICAL CENTER

In 1954 the northern and northwestern sections of Minneapolis and the dozen suburbs developing beyond faced a crucial problem: one small hospital, few doctors, and virtually no medical services. Emergency treatment was a particularly pressing concern. Three decades later North Memorial Medical Center meets those multi-faceted needs, but emergency services remain the core.

North Memorial began by assuming ownership and management of Victory Memorial Hospital, a 30-bed, one-doctor facility built in 1939 just 500 yards from the Minneapolis city limits in Robbinsdale. Vance C. DeMong was hired as the first administrator, a position he would hold for more than 25 years.

Many members of the original board of trustees stayed with the hospital through the years: George Mellin, Kenneth Nesseth, C.R. Baker, Harry DeZiel, Jr., Julian Paradise (the first chairman of the board), Charles Wallace, and A.R. Wolff. The modern medical center they helped nurture now includes an acute care medical institution with nearly 550 beds and a staff of more than 300 physicians, fully developed outpatient programs, and the neighboring Oakdale Medical Building. In addition, North Memorial provides its own ambulances.

As the northern communities grew through the 1960s, the hospital also grew. The first three stories of the north wing opened in 1960, turning the country hospital into a 165-bed facility. In 1963 a four-floor addition increased the bed total to 302. The west addition provided better ancillary service facilities and nursing stations, with final construction bringing the hospital to the 550-bed mark.

In the '70s, however, medical services began to change. No longer could a hospital be measured merely by beds. Increasing emphasis was placed on outpatient services and home care, and North Memorial was quick to respond. In 1972 it began providing services for senior citizens in area high-rises; open-heart surgery was first performed in the hospital that year. A complete spinal cord program and evening diabetes education classes were added in 1975, along with community education seminars in the hospital's 409-seat auditorium.

In 1977 two North Memorial nurses developed the I CAN COPE cancer education course, since adopted by the American Cancer Society. The existing home care department was expanded to include hospice services, and an inpatient hospice opened in 1980 to provide support to the dying and their families. That same year an innovative joint venture was formed with Health Central, Inc. (which operates three smaller hospitals in the northern communities), to help all four competing institutions coordinate medical services for the people they serve.

♦　　♦　　♦

Emergency services have always been a priority for North Memorial Medical Center.

NORTHERN PUMP COMPANY

John B. Hawley, Jr., 1899–1980.

They called him a Renaissance man because there seemed to be nothing he couldn't do. As a high school senior in Forth Worth, Texas, he built a home wireless set so powerful that the local newspaper ran a story about the evenings he spent listening to coded instructions being broadcast to the German Army from Berlin toward the end of World War I. In 1921 he took his civil engineering degree from Cornell University a full five months ahead of his class. He personally held 29 patents, mostly in hydraulics and oil pumping machinery, and many of them helped make Northern Pump Company, and its wartime subsidiary Northern Ordnance, the U.S. Navy's largest ordnance producer during World War II.

By any standard of measurement, John Blackstock Hawley, Jr., was a human dynamo. In some ways it ran in the family. Major John Blackstock Hawley, Sr., was an engineer who bid (but lost) on the Panama Canal at age 28 and later ran the water system for the U.S. Army in France in World War I. Confined to a sanitarium in Colorado for treatment of tuberculosis after his graduation from Cornell, the younger Hawley emerged $27,000 richer from several inventions he sketched out during his stay.

He came to Minneapolis (not far from the family's original home in Red Wing) in 1924 with a bundle of new inventions and ideas, including an improved pump for oil wells that he wanted Northern Pump to manufacture. Four years later he earned $100,000 for his ideas and inventions and exchanged that for ownership of the company. Under his guidance Northern Pump became a leading producer of commercial pumps and an established manufacturer of naval ordnance.

Northern Pump's roots go back to 1907, when a group of Minneapolis insurance men formed the Northern Fire Apparatus Company to make light firefighting equipment. That involved substantial use of pumps, which brought the firm into contact with machinist and inventor Theodore Pagel and his Pagel Pump Company; Northern Pump resulted from the merger of the two organizations in 1913.

The company began working for the U.S. Navy as early as 1932. One early contract was for a vibration dampener for submarines. Another was a submersible pump whose best predecessor weighed 400 pounds; Hawley's weighed 93 pounds but pumped twice as much water. In the mid-1930s Northern Pump made power drives for elevators aboard the Navy's first aircraft carriers. A 1936 visit to Europe convinced Hawley that war was inevitable, so he was ready when the Navy's call for large-scale production came in September 1940.

• • •

During wartime, Northern Pump's plant was served by 35 commissary wagons bringing hot food and coffee to the workers. This photo from 1942 shows plant workers' enthusiastic support of War Bond purchases (as well as the slacks worn by female workers).

When that call came Northern Pump was still a little company in a little plant. Within months 400 acres of cornfield in the northern suburb of Fridley were transformed into one of the nation's premier defense plants. Hawley vowed that the initial order—for 100 five-inch anti-aircraft gun mounts—would be filled by Christmas 1941, months ahead of the Navy's peacetime expectations. The 100th gun mount was delivered three days before the attack on Pearl Harbor.

Northern Ordnance's early days bore the unmistakable stamp of Hawley's strong will and impertinent personality. Told it would take 90 days just to draw up plans for the new facility, Hawley set out to have the building itself up and running in 60—which he did. He called it his "running start" style of getting things done. That style permeated the more than $300 million of defense work Northern Ordnance performed during the war. At one point the company was two years ahead of its own production schedules, prompting the Navy's resident inspector to describe the operation as "two months ahead of the unbelievable."

To motivate his workers, and keep them from things that might distract them from their work, Hawley offered unlimited overtime (at time-and-a-half) plus War Bonds raffled off on hard-to-fill shifts. Lunch trucks circulated throughout the plant day and night, with free coffee and meals at below cost (25 cents for a quarter-chicken or a 10-cent ham sandwich built around a slice of meat a quarter-inch thick). In emergencies employees could borrow money from the company without interest. There was a fully equipped hospital on site. Hawley was years ahead of modern ride-sharing pro-

grams—he ran three red, white, and blue streetcars to carry workers between the plant and Minneapolis. For its wartime efforts, Northern Pump won six Navy "E" awards and Hawley received the Navy's Distinguished Public Service Award, its highest civilian honor.

Not that turbulence wasn't also encountered: Hawley unabashedly confessed to charges that he pirated workers away from other employers, even paying $10 bounties to employees who brought in new machinists. He was the Peck's Bad Boy of defense contractors, constantly feuding with the government bureaucrats who "renegotiated" Northern Ordnance contracts long after the materiel was delivered to skin Hawley of the profits he earned from beating production schedules instead of piling up cost over-runs.

In the mid-1940s Hawley began to look ahead to peacetime and the changes that would be necessary to keep Northern Pump profitable. He became the nation's number one wildcat oilman, claiming anyone from Texas had an innate ability to find oil. At first he earned the unenviable nickname "Dry Hole" Hawley, but his con-

On September 4, 1956, the Navy's highest civilian honor, its Distinguished Public Service Award, was presented to John B. Hawley, Jr. (at the microphone), in recognition of Northern Ordnance's wartime efforts.

◆　　　◆　　　◆

fidence and persistence paid off—he struck it big in Montana, and again in Texas.

When a friend approached him with a group of failing farms, near McHenry, Illinois, Hawley bought them and then proceeded to build an award-winning herd of purebred Herefords. In the 1970s he supported research into producing methanol from coal, corn, and wastes, and he backed efforts to ascertain the effects of fructose on victims of hypoglycemia. His support of local hospitals included having a company plane standing by in case word of a kidney donor was received.

Northern Ordnance eventually became a casualty of the governmental red tape Hawley so detested. The plant was sold to FMC Corporation in 1964, and it continues to perform defense work. Northern Pump today is operated by a trust for the Hawley family.

NORTHLAND ALUMINUM PRODUCTS, INC.

In 1951 three women from Hadassah, the Jewish women's organization, came to Northland Aluminum Products in suburban Minneapolis with a request. They had a very old European cake pan they wanted to duplicate and sell to raise funds—could the company form a pattern and make a few hundred pans? Brothers David and Mark Dalquist, who'd realized a long-cherished dream in 1946 with the founding of their own firm, thought they could. Today there are 31 million BUNDT* pans in kitchens around the United States and Canada, making the BUNDT* the single most successful baking pan ever made in America.

The Dalquists, along with longtime friend Donald Nygren, had started Plastics for Industry on nothing more than $500 and a wooden workbench in Mark's basement on Colgate Avenue in Minneapolis. The new company made plastic prototypes for General Mills (which was starting its own line of appliances) and patterns for tractor parts made by Minneapolis Moline Foundry. They had invested their modest bankroll in a small lot in St. Louis Park and borrowed money from their father to build a 40-foot by 50-foot shop.

In 1949 the Dalquists purchased a small plant called Northland Aluminum and its trade name NORDIC WARE® for steak platters and griddles. Both names were extended to their own growing line of gourmet cookware, some designed for ethnic Scandinavian foods: Krumkake and Rosette irons, Ebelskiver and Platte pans. Ads in foreign-language newspapers proved so successful that a mail order division, Maid of Scandinavia, was created. The original partnership was superseded in 1962 by two small corporations, Northland Aluminum Products, Inc., and Maid of Scandinavia Company. Respective presidents were Dave and Mark Dalquist.

The BUNDT* was not an immediate sensation. In fact it wasn't even a major product through the '50s, as Northland's sales steadily grew to the million-dollar mark by 1964. However, by that time the BUNDT* was enough of a minor phenomenon that several women's magazines sent photographers and writers to report on this small factory in Minneapolis that was making a different kind of cake pan. The real explosion came in 1972, when Pillsbury introduced cake mixes for the BUNDT* with a premium offer of an authentic pan. Within weeks Northland Aluminum's plant was the scene of 'round-the-clock frenzy, turning out 30,000 BUNDT* pans a day, seven days a week!

One of the original Teflon licensees appointed by Du Pont, Northland Aluminum's line grew in the '70s to include many items of aluminum cookware and bakeware, Belgian waffle irons, omelet pans, small electrical appliances, custom die-casting and coatings, baked-on enamels, industrial teflons, and (through its Vikron subsidiary) magnetic tape heads. The plant includes 450 employees, five modern factory buildings, and annual sales near $40 million.

More recently the company's growth has been fueled by 24 items of microwave cookware introduced in 1978, including the Micro-Go-Round, a patented automatic turntable for microwave ovens, widely seen on national television.

* Reg. U.S. Patent Office

•   •   •

From the classic BUNDT pan to electric kitchen appliances like the wok, to other accessories for modern microwave ovens, Northland Aluminum's NORDIC WARE® is found in millions of kitchens from coast to coast.*

NORTHWESTERN NATIONAL BANK OF MINNEAPOLIS

It all began with a deposit of $2,315, made by William Hood Dunwoody in 1872. In its second century of service, Northwestern National Bank of Minneapolis today is the largest bank in the Ninth Federal Reserve District with deposits of more than three billion dollars and six branches of its own.

The 1870s was a decade of tremendous construction. Minneapolis was being called "the new sawdust town" because so many sawmills were in operation. The Milwaukee Road and the Northern Pacific were building railroads. Millers with names like Pillsbury and Dunwoody were building their first mills. When Northwestern opened its doors at Marquette and Washington, the heart of the financial district in those days, it had $200,000 in working capital and the city's first mayor, Dorilus Morrison, as its president.

As the city's industrial base expanded and the region's farmers prospered, Northwestern's strength also grew and Minneapolis became the financial center of the Upper Midwest. While 1929 is generally bleakly remembered, Northwestern celebrated two major achievements: groundbreaking for its present headquarters at Seventh and Marquette, and the organization of Northwest Bancorporation to formalize financial services throughout the region. The system has grown to more than 87 affiliated banks in seven states, plus a number of bank-related service companies. Northwestern National Bank of Minneapolis remains its largest affiliate bank.

As the region has changed, so has Northwestern. Worldwide demand for food and agribusiness products has strengthened the region's agricultural sector. The Twin Cities have become a leading supplier of high-technology computers. Reliance on our nation's

own natural resources has fostered growth in energy-related industries, many of which are located within the Upper Midwest region. Northwestern Bank is intimately involved in the area's growth and continues to be committed to supporting the city's and the region's economy.

Symbolic of Northwestern's strength and community service is its nationally known Weatherball, which was installed in October 1949—78 tons of sign and support anchored to the 15th floor of the Northwestern Bank Building at Seventh and Marquette. A massive steel

The largest free-standing sculpture in Minneapolis, Mark di Suvero's "Inner Search" graces the Northwestern Operations Center in the historic Gateway area of downtown. (Photo courtesy of John Louis Anderson.)

•   •   •

sculpture of a more abstract nature stands on the site of Northwestern Operations Center just a few blocks away. "Inner Search," by Mark di Suvero, provides further visible evidence of Northwestern's dedication to the culture of the community it serves.

NORTHRUP KING CO.

Chester A. Arthur was president in 1884. The U.S. Department of Agriculture was just 22 years old. The fountain pen, the adding machine, and the cash register debuted. In New York, the cornerstone for the Statue of Liberty was laid; in Washington, D.C., for the Washington Monument. And in Minneapolis, Jesse E. Northrup and Charles P. Braslan rented the first floor and basement at 22 Hennepin Avenue and issued their first price list of "Polar" seeds. Northrup King will be 100 years old in 1984, and it will celebrate its centennial as the world's largest general seed house.

For Northrup and Braslan, two young men who headed west from seed company jobs in New York and Massachusetts, respectively, success came quickly—at first. A 12-page catalog, generously illustrated with wood engravings, was issued in 1885, and the extra business it helped stimulate prompted the two entrepreneurs to move next door a year later, expanding to three floors and the basement at 18 Hennepin. The next year additional needs moved them another door down the block to 10-12 Hennepin, and A.H. Goodwin joined in the incorporating of Northrup, Braslan & Goodwin: Northrup handled production, Braslan sales, and Goodwin organized the administrative side of the business. Braslan's contributions were especially original—he sent traveling salesmen throughout the Midwest attired in Prince Albert coats and silk hats.

But the business that had begun so auspiciously fell on equally hard times in the next decade. Overextended, financially injured by the national Panic of 1893, and staggered by a fire that destroyed its market building, Northrup, Braslan & Goodwin declared bankruptcy in May 1896.

Northrup King seed salesmen spent a lot of time on the road in trucks like this one, sometimes camping out at night to stretch their $2.50 per diem for lodging.

◆   ◆   ◆

Six months later, Northrup started over. Joined by Preston King as treasurer and Charles C. Massie as secretary, a young man from Scotland who had started trucking seeds for the original firm in 1892, Northrup, King & Co. was incorporated on November 4. The first few years were rocky, since Northrup was left with a number of bad accounts from the first venture, only a small stock of seeds, and very little ready cash after buying out the creditors of the old firm. But by 1900 the company was beginning to grow again. It entered the feed business with chicken feeds and other brands. It introduced field seeds such as clover, timo-

thy, and millet to midwestern farmers. And it began its ambitious packet seed marketing, setting up display cases in stores in the region. By 1911 the firm could celebrate its first truly prosperous year.

Through all this time, Massie was working his way up through virtually every department. When Preston King died in 1914 and Jesse Northrup retired that same year, the Scots-born trucker and utility man was elected president. Charles Massie would hold that post for 34 years.

One of the first actions of the Massie era was the purchase of a 17-acre site along the railroad tracks (an important consideration) at 15th Avenue Northeast and Jackson Street. The next year ground was broken for a modern plant and office complex to consolidate the company's operations. It

Jesse E. Northrup, president of Northrup from 1896 to 1914.

*   ♦   ♦

has been Northrup King's home since October 1917.

Over the years the firm grew, both geographically and in terms of the seed lines it carried. Branch operations sprang up in Idaho and Utah, and Pacific markets were reached with the purchase of Bomberger Seed Company of Berkeley, California. Modern operations involve subsidiaries in Argentina, Australia, Canada, Mexico, and Europe; a half-interest in Betaseed, which concentrates on sugarbeet sales, research, and development; and nearly 20 U.S. testing and research facilities.

The seed business is not simply a matter of selling seeds. Development and production of those seeds is a complex and exacting process. It is not uncommon for 10 years to pass between the first breeding of a new seed variety and the production of marketable seed. For Northrup King, the practice is as old as the company. Back in 1887 it began breeding to produce varieties suitable for southern Minnesota. In 1922 it started working on hybrid corns, but not until 1933 did the first strains arrive on the market. The radish varieties developed in the 1930s account for almost half of the nation's radish production. Alfalfa blends introduced in the '50s ensured uniform yields under wide variations in climatic conditions. Northrup King has proven particularly adept at developing corn types for the North Central states, not only increasing average yield per acre, but also extending the "corn belt" farther north.

As a general seed house, Northrup King produces a broad line of seeds: for vegetables and flowers, for lawn and turf, for all kinds of farm needs from pasture and forage crops to hay and seed grains. Twin Citians annually enjoy the rows upon rows of flowers which bloom during field trials at the company's Eden Prairie research facility. A larger field research center south of the Twin Cities near Northfield watches over new strains of vegetables, hybrid corn, forages, soybeans, and sunflowers.

Northrup King markets nearly 1,000 different varieties of vegetable seeds to commercial growers and processors worldwide, and packet seeds are sold to home gardeners through thousands of retail outlets coast to coast. Rare hybrid flower seeds sold to commercial growers and florists often command prices as high as $15,000 per pound.

Northrup King was acquired by Sandoz, a Swiss firm, in 1976. The seed company's international headquarters, however, remains where it first started, firmly rooted in Minneapolis. The basic need for food makes the seed industry one of the most vital in the world, but that is a position of prominence that hasn't changed much from the day Jesse Northrup opened shop on Hennepin Avenue a century ago.

NORTHWESTERN NATIONAL LIFE INSURANCE CO.

Northwestern National Life Insurance Co. (NWNL), in terms of assets and insurance in force, ranks among the top 50 of more than 1,800 life insurance companies in the United States.

NWNL began as the Northwestern Aid Association, a mutual assessment organization, on September 15, 1885, in two small rooms on the upper floor of the old Minnesota Loan and Trust Building. The name was changed to Northwestern Life Association in 1892; nine years later it merged with National Mutual Life Insurance to become Northwestern National Life Insurance Co. (NWNL).

The firm has been headquartered in Minneapolis since its founding. After renting space in various buildings in downtown Minneapolis, NWNL, in 1905, built a home office at 11th and Nicollet, moving in 1942 to a second new home office at 430 Oak Grove on Loring Park. By 1960 the company had outgrown its Oak Grove building, and at the time an opportunity arose to participate in the Minneapolis Housing and Redevelopment Authority's large-scale

The Northwest Aid Association began in two rooms on the upper floor of the old Minnesota Loan and Trust Building (A), just a short distance away from its current home at 20 Washington Avenue South (B). Northwestern National Life moved to the building, designed by noted architect Minoru Yamasaki, in 1964.

♦   ♦   ♦

renovation of the Gateway, Minneapolis' oldest business district. Thus, in 1960, NWNL, the Sheraton Corporation, and IBM jointly announced plans to construct buildings in the Gateway, launching a program which has seen the redevelopment of the entire district.

NWNL's Yamasaki-designed home office, occupied in 1964, has since become a landmark in downtown Minneapolis. In 1981, 100 Washington Square, a 22-story office building, owned and developed by NWNL, was completed. In addition to a number of outside tenants, several of NWNL's large departments are officed there.

The company has insured both men and women since its founding; many life insurance companies did not insure

women because of the higher mortality risks which then prevailed. NWNL was also a pioneer in the group life insurance business, having written its first group policy in 1916.

Over the years NWNL has marketed a wide range of individual participating (dividend-paying) and non-participating (guaranteed cost) life insurance products and services as well as group life and health insurance for employee benefit programs. Currently it offers a number of flexible life insurance products, including Adjustable Life, and will introduce Universal Life in 1982. Other products include disability income policies, fixed and variable annuities for pension and profit-sharing plans, Individual Retirement Annuities (IRAs), and mutual funds.

The company owns and operates two life insurance subsidiaries—North Atlantic Life Insurance Company (Jericho, New York) and Northern Life Insurance Company (Seattle, Washington). Other subsidiaries include the NWNL Financial Corporation, which owns NWNL's non-life insurance businesses; the NWNL Management Corporation, a securities/broker dealer specializing in the sale of mutual fund shares and variable annuities; the NWNL Investment Services Corporation, an investment adviser; NWNL Reinsurance Company (NWNL RE), a reinsurer of risks insured by other property casualty insurance companies; NWNL General Insurance Company, a direct-writing property-casualty insurer; and Three Arches Managers, Inc., an intermediary (a broker for reinsurance) which negotiates reinsurance business for NWNL RE.

NWNL's consolidated insurance in force and assets as of December 31, 1981, totaled $32 billion and $2.2 billion, respectively.

NORTRONICS COMPANY, INC.

On November 1, 1954, Leonard Kronfeld formed a company to enter into the manufacturing of electronic products. This was the launching of Nortronics, which now has become the world's largest manufacturer of magnetic read-write heads. Kronfeld was an electrical engineer, and he shared the dream of many talented people in the infant days of the Electronic Age—to have his own business to pursue the many promising products that seemed to lack nothing more than a designer to become real. His brother Mervin and uncle Harry Glasgall helped finance the venture, which began in his apartment before moving to offices on Wayzata Boulevard.

With a handful of colleagues, among them Joe Dundovic, Kronfeld experimented with several products and in 1956 developed a magnetic head for high-fidelity recording and reproduction of both stereo and monaural applications. From that point Nortronics quickly became a world leader in the design and manufacture of magnetic tape heads and advanced magnetic technology.

By 1960 Nortronics had produced a four-track stereo conversion kit and a successful series of amplifiers for stereo playback and recording, as well as the first miniature magnetic tape heads for mini-recorders. Two years later more than 100 employees made the move from the old Strutwear Building in Minneapolis to the present manufacturing and headquarters facility in Golden Valley. For the next few years the company grew with the booming consumer electronics industry, developing the head that made eight-track tape systems possible.

Leonard Kronfeld became chairman of the board in 1967. John A. Yngve, an attorney who had served as secretary and a board member since the firm's incorporation in 1956, was elected president. Mervin Kronfeld moved west from New York to become director of marketing. As the consumer electronics industry began to shift to Japan, Nortronics initiated a shift of its own. The people at Nortronics designed, developed, and built a line of magnetic read-write heads for the then rapidly emerging data processing and computer industry for applications such as desk top computers, programmable calculators, word processors, and other applications in the computer field.

As the '70s progressed, the requirement by the computer industry for high-density storage grew rapidly. Nortronics' technology and development kept pace and it is now in the forefront of supplying those heads as well as single and double flexible disk heads.

As the 1980s begin, Nortronics and its people are developing thin film technology to serve the next advancement in magnetic storage required by the computer industry.

♦   ♦   ♦

Below Left
Leonard E. Kronfeld, founder and chairman of the board of Nortronics Company, Inc.
Below
Magnetic head research and development laboratory at Nortronics.

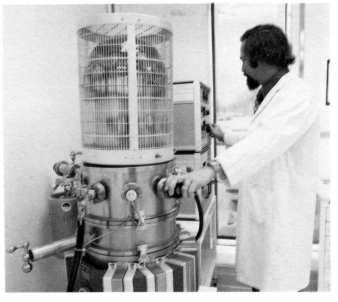

OXFORD DEVELOPMENT MINNESOTA, INC.

The Roanoke Building (the corner of Seventh Street and Marquette Avenue), as it appeared shortly after its completion in 1927.

The IDS Center's dynamic octagonal tower and delicate Crystal Court have become landmarks for the entire Twin Cities metropolitan region.

• • •

An architectural model superimposed on the cityscape shows Minneapolis City Center phase one as it will appear when completed. The 52-story Multifoods Tower is on the left and the 32-story, triangular Amfac-City Center Hotel is on the right.

• • •

Oxford Development Minnesota is a relative newcomer to the Minneapolis business scene. At the same time, it provides an important link to the business heritage of Minneapolis through its ownership of some of the city's most notable downtown landmarks. Moreover, Oxford's development of Minneapolis City Center—an anchor block in the downtown bordered by Hennepin and Nicollet avenues and Sixth and Seventh streets—and St. Paul's Town Square will keep it deeply involved in the future business history of the Twin Cities through the remaining years of the 20th century and beyond.

Oxford Minnesota's parent, Oxford Properties, Inc., was incorporated in Denver, Colorado, in 1974. Today Oxford is one of the largest real estate de-

velopment and management firms in North America. As it entered the 1980s the company owned, operated, or had under development more than eight million square feet of prime commercial real estate in the United States.

Oxford Minnesota was formed in 1977 and began operations with the purchase of a major segment of IDS Properties. A subsidiary of Investors Diversified Services, IDS Properties was the developer of the IDS Center as well as a major owner of commercial property in downtown Minneapolis. Oxford's initial acquisition included the management organization built by IDS Properties and the buildings on the Baker and Northstar blocks.

As a result, Oxford Minnesota's roots

go back much further than 1977. Robert V. Hovelson, president of Oxford Minnesota, has been active in Twin Cities real estate since 1964 as an employee of Baker Properties. He moved to IDS Properties when that firm acquired Baker Properties in 1968, became president of IDS Properties in 1970, and vice-president of development for Oxford Properties in 1977.

What attracted Oxford to the Twin Cities were the significant efforts taken from the late 1950s on to revitalize the downtowns, especially the creation of Nicollet Mall to preserve the retail corridor of Minneapolis. In addition, the concentration of corporate headquarters in the metropolitan area gave strong indication that the local community would be able to sustain the type of development projects Oxford specializes in: large-scale, mixed-use properties in the downtowns of key financial centers. That formula has also taken Oxford to such dynamic cities as Denver, Phoenix, Los Angeles, and Louisville.

The IDS, Baker, and Northstar blocks are unique locations in downtown Minneapolis' central business district, around which the bulk of the city's major office buildings, department stores, and hotels are concentrated. The three blocks are also central locations on the city's growing skyway system.

The IDS Center blends office, retail, hotel, and restaurant space into a full city block—the 55-story office tower, which has become the city's most distinctive modern landmark; the eight-story Annex building; the 19-story Marquette Hotel and the two-level Woolworth's building—all arranged around the popular Crystal Court. Designed by internationally recognized architect Philip Johnson and completed in 1972, the IDS Center was purchased by Oxford in 1981.

The four buildings comprising the Baker Block (Baker, Multifoods, Peavey, and Roanoke) are interconnected by walkways, arcades, escalators, and tunnels and linked to three surrounding blocks by skyways. The Baker Building was opened in 1926, the Multifoods and Roanoke buildings a year later.

The Northstar Block, which contains the Cargill, 608, and Northstar buildings, is a multi-use facility including office, retail, restaurants, almost 1,000 stalls of garage parking, and the 226-room Northstar Inn. The 608 Building, formerly the Pillsbury Building, was

erected in 1916, the other structures in the early 1960s.

On the development front, Oxford's Minneapolis City Center is a two-phase project. The first phase, for which ground was broken in 1979, includes the following: the 52-story Multifoods Tower, which will house the headquarters of International Multifoods and of Target Stores Division of Dayton-Hudson Corporation in addition to numerous other businesses; a new, five-level Donaldsons Department Store; the Amfac-City Center Hotel, a 32-story, 620-room hotel and convention facility; a 636-car covered parking structure housing the new Nankin Cafe on its street level; the reconstructed Scottie's bar and restaurant, an art deco city landmark; and at the heart of the development, a three-level retail mall featuring more than 100 stores, shops, and restaurants.

With the completion of Town Square in St. Paul, which opened in late 1980, and phase one of Minneapolis City Center, slated for completion in 1983, Oxford Minnesota will own or manage more than five million square feet of commercial and office space in the heart of the Twin Cities.

♦   ♦   ♦

Past and present: William Baker (left) and Oxford senior vice-president Robert V. Hovelson (right). Baker's father, Morris, founded Baker Properties in 1926, and William served as chairman of Baker Properties and later as president and chairman of IDS Properties, which Oxford acquired in 1977.

PAKO CORPORATION

The equipment and systems that process the increasingly wide variety of photosensitive materials in industrial, government, and personal use are complex combinations of modern electronics and mechanical technology. No company in the world has had a greater impact on the design and manufacture of equipment for the photographic, motion picture, X-ray, and graphic arts industries than Pako Corporation.

The firm began in 1910 as a one-man photo print shop in a tiny, third-floor room in the old Times Building in Minneapolis. The one man was Glen M. Dye, in 1968 named one of four charter members of the Hall of Fame of Photography for his contributions, which helped transform the photographic industry from manual to automated systems.

Dye started by making and selling photo postcards produced on a homemade mechanical printer. Soon he was

In 1919 Pako's mechanized print dryers were state-of-the-art. Modern technology makes equipment like the CP-6000 Series Color Paper Processor (lower right), capable of handling hundreds of prints per minute.

•   •   •

processing film and prints for a growing number of photo film dealers. The venture, originally known as Photo Advertising Company, then Photographic Appliances Corporation, became better known by its initials: Paco. In 1918, at the suggestion of Kodak's George Eastman, Dye changed the acronym to Pako. Over the years, that name came to be associated in the Twin Cities with high-quality photo finishing services. But in 1981 Pako sold its filmshops to concentrate on what has always been its primary line of business: photo technology.

The roots of that business go back to Dye's printer. By 1921 the demand for

photographic printers, washers, and dryers brought a move to a plant on North Lyndale Avenue, home for nearly 40 years before Pako built its present headquarters complex in suburban Golden Valley in 1960. Photographic equipment soon included machines which mechanized other steps in the processing of prints and film.

The World War II use of X-rays to examine munitions and aircraft parts created a need for a mechanized way to process X-ray film; Pako met that need, and subsequently expanded into medical X-ray processors. Processors for Graphic Arts and sophisticated systems for motion picture processing are more recent additions. Pako's modern line of film processing equipment ranges from small, neighborhood-scale "mini-labs" to totally automated, high-volume machines which can produce more than 10,000 prints per hour.

They operate eight international subsidiaries—in the Common Market nations, Australia, and Japan—in addition to their North American activities and important efforts in the rest of the world. After 20 years as a publicly held company, Pako again became privately held in 1980.

PEAT, MARWICK, MITCHELL & CO.

One of Peat Marwick's first homes—Temple Court Building at Hennepin and Washington avenues. (Photo courtesy of the Minnesota Historical Society.)

In the early days of the Minneapolis office of Peat, Marwick, Mitchell & Co. ("Co." as in co-partnership), it was not uncommon to see a young accountant arrive, British bowler jammed down over his ears, steamer rug thrown over one shoulder, lugging a miniature trunk and inquiring—in a thoroughly English accent—if Mr. Benjamin Franklin was in. James Marwick and Simpson Roger Mitchell, classmates at the University of Glasgow in their native Scotland, had crossed the Atlantic to open an accounting practice in New York in 1897. One of their first branch offices was Minneapolis, much of whose early history was written by one Benjamin Franklin, Jr. (no known relation to the prominent Philadelphian). For years many accountants of British origin and training were posted to Minneapolis for their first American experience. The practice was further reinforced when Marwick and Mitchell merged with the distinguished British firm of W.B. Peat & Co. in 1925.

Both Marwick and Mitchell took a deep personal interest in Minneapolis operations, Marwick especially maintaining a long-running correspondence with the local partners-in-charge and dropping in when an occasion presented itself. What originally interested the partners in the Twin Cities was the thriving grain businesses. Their confidence was speedily justified: the young firm was successful in signing up most of the major grain companies in town, including the Minneapolis Grain Exchange (the forerunner of the Greater Minneapolis Chamber of Commerce). Franklin started as an assistant to Frederick A. Ross, the first office manager, in 1906; later the two were named copartners-in-charge and Franklin stayed on to oversee the operation's growth through the early '20s.

The first office, officially opened December 1, 1904, was in the Temple Court Building at Hennepin and Washington, one of the true landmarks of downtown Minneapolis. Today the headquarters is in another downtown landmark, the IDS Center. Peat Marwick also has another office in St. Paul's Town Square. The contrast between the original and present-day locations is no less marked than the contrast between old style accounting firms and their modern descendants. In addition to accounting and auditing services, Peat Marwick today offers tax, management consulting and private business advisory services, the latter geared to the special needs of smaller, emerging, or privately held enterprises.

Under the direction of managing partner Merlin E. Dewing, the Minneapolis office ranks among the firm's top 10 U.S. offices (there are more than 300 offices worldwide). Peat Marwick serves companies reflecting the full range of Minnesota business, with concentrations in high technology, manufacturing, banking and insurance, not-for-profit organizations, and agribusiness.

• • •

Peat, Marwick, Mitchell & Co.—Twin Cities partners.

PILLSBURY

In 1879 Charles A. Pillsbury announced plans to construct the largest and most modern flour mill in the world. When completed in 1881, it became a showplace of Minneapolis.

On June 4, 1869, Charles A. Pillsbury spent $10,000 of his father's and Uncle John's money for a one-third interest in the Frazee & Murphy mill on the west bank of the Mississippi River below St. Anthony Falls. Some 112 years later Pillsbury moved into its brand-new corporate headquarters, the 40-story Pillsbury Center in downtown Minneapolis—overlooking the site of the original mill as well as the historic "A" Mill on the east bank of the river. The contrast between the mills of the late 19th century and the gleaming high-rise in which Pillsbury will chart its course through the latter years of the 20th century is no less pronounced than that between the company's business, then and now.

From its roots as one milling concern

in "the Mill City," Pillsbury has become an international marketing company participating in three major segments of the modern food industry: Consumer Foods, Agri-Products, and Restaurants. And for all the romance and color of its first century, probably no period in Pillsbury's past is more important to the present-day firm than the decade of the 1970s. In 1970 Pillsbury reported sales of $674 million; in 1980 that figure had passed $3 billion. From fewer than 19,000 employees, the company grew through those 10 years to employ more than 60,000.

What happened was a decade of transition which added balance and greatly strengthened Pillsbury's ability to compete in the world marketplace. In all, 13 businesses which did not fit into the firm's long-term strategy were divested and 14 others, most notably Green Giant Company, were acquired. The result: a compounded growth of 18 percent in sales, 26 percent in net income, over the 10-year period.

Pillsbury today is known the world

Located in the 40-story north tower of Pillsbury Center in downtown Minneapolis, Pillsbury World Headquarters houses more than 1,500 employees.

• • •

over under a variety of names. In Consumer Foods, its Pillsbury and Green Giant labels are complemented by American Beauty pasta products, Poppin Fresh refrigerated foods, Totino's frozen pizza, Hungry Jack, and Figurines. When America dines out, it turns to Burger King, the world's second largest restaurant system, Steak and Ale, and Bennigan's. And in Agri-Products, Pillsbury's Best Flour and mixes and Pioneer Foods rice milling extend the firm's reach from grains to bakery products, feed and grain ingredient merchandising, bulk commodities handling and storage, and allied distribution and transportation systems.

It is a distance of more than a century but less than a mile from Charles Pillsbury's first milling venture to the diverse and dynamic corporation that is Pillsbury today.

PRUDENTIAL

changed the conduct of Prudential's business more than those incredible machines.

Modern computers in Minneapolis and around the country help pay claims, handle service requests, underwrite and issue business, monitor the budget, and conduct market studies. So well did Prudential's Minneapolis people master the computer that the North Central office subsequently took on computer work for the Indiana/Illinois region, plus more than half the company's pension processing.

From the beginning, Prudential people took an active role in supporting community groups, such as the United Way, Junior Achievement, and the Special Olympics. In 1975 the Employee Community Service Committee was formed to facilitate employee volunteerism. The work of this committee is indicative of the way more than 3,000 North Central employees have helped Prudential stay close to the people it serves, bringing to life the vision of a transplanted Minnesotan more than 30 years ago.

• • •

Prudential's North Central home office headquarters building, located on Wayzata Boulevard and Theodore Wirth Parkway, has become a familiar landmark to Minnesotans.

While Prudential has had sales offices in Minneapolis since 1899, it was in 1953 that the North Central home office was established as part of a systematic decentralization of the New Jersey-based insurance company. That strategy, masterminded by Carrol Shanks (Prudential's then-president and a native of Fairmont, Minnesota), envisioned a major corporation composed of essentially hometown operations.

The North Central office in Minneapolis began with a core group of 140 families transferred from Newark headquarters. Orville Beal was the first senior officer in charge and later became Prudential's president. Within a year a thousand Minnesotans had joined their ranks and plans for a permanent home office building were nearly complete.

In 1953 New Jersey employees prepared for their move to Minneapolis to set up operations at the North Central home office.

• • •

Faced in Mankato limestone and completed in January 1955, the striking new building on Wayzata Boulevard was nestled in parklike grounds and offered an eye-catching view of the growing downtown to the east.

At formal dedication ceremonies that summer, a time capsule predicting the world of 1975 was closed. In it, local leaders foresaw many things—nosteer cars with electronic controls, a cure for cancer, world peace—but strangely enough no one mentioned the computer. Yet since that sunny day in 1955, no single development has

ST. MARY'S HOSPITAL

In April 1882 the former mansion of the late Captain Edward Murphy was converted into a 20-bed hospital run by the Sisters of Mercy. Financial difficulties forced the closing of Mater Misericordia Hospital in early 1887. The building and grounds were sold to Archbishop John Ireland for $30,000. Two months later, Mother Seraphine Ireland (the Archbishop's sister) sent five Sisters of St. Joseph of Carondelet to reopen the mansion as St. Mary's Hospital. The original medical staff included Dr. Horatio B. Sweetser, whose medical family would be a major part of the hospital's history for the next 100 years, and Dr. A.A. Ames, mayor of Minneapolis from 1876 through 1900.

The mansion, however, was ill-equipped to serve as a hospital, and within three years, with the city's population approaching 165,000, St. Mary's was embarking on the first of several significant building programs. In 1915 that first 100-bed hospital gave way to a newer, more extensive structure three years in the building. By the time it opened in 1918, the University of Minnesota Medical School had formalized an internship program which

One of St. Mary's early nursing school graduation classes, taken around 1900. St. Mary's is owned and operated by the Sisters of St. Joseph of Carondelet, and has been operative at the same site since 1887.

• • •

required at least six months' experience in one of the area's hospitals (students from the "U" had been informally training at nearby St. Mary's since 1905) and the government had chosen St. Mary's to care for World War I veterans. Two years later St. Mary's was a busy 315-bed, full-service hospital with more than 80 physicians and interns on staff, and its nursing school was celebrating its 20th anniversary.

Through the years family practice has remained a primary concern, and that emphasis continues through family-oriented care ranging from obstetrics and pediatrics to counseling for chemical dependency, cancer, and heart disease. A pivotal point in the hospital's history was reached in the early 1950s, when consideration was given to moving St. Mary's to the western suburbs. The combination of community needs, the hospital's deep roots in the Cedar-Riverside

area, and the close association developed through the years with the University of Minnesota's nearby medical school resulted in a decision to remain committed to serving the central city. Subsequent expansion has raised the hospital's capacity to some 500 beds, added sophisticated services such as open-heart surgery, and fostered a close working relationship with neighboring Fairview Hospital.

Today the St. Mary's complex includes the hospital, St. Mary's Rehabilitation Center, plus the combined St. Mary's and Fairview Medical Office Building, which connects to the former via a skyway. Despite government regulation and an inflationary economy, St. Mary's continues to preserve the values of a voluntary, church-sponsored hospital.

• • •

Heart surgeries have been performed at St. Mary's for many years. Drs. Joseph Garamella (left) and John Kelly perform open-heart surgery at St. Mary's Hospital in Minneapolis. In 1981 approximately 150 open-heart surgeries were performed at the hospital, included in more than 7,000 surgical procedures done at the hospital annually.

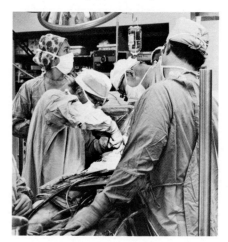

SKARNES INCORPORATED

Reubin F. Skarnes faced a serious challenge in 1956. The business he had founded in 1923 in the back room of his brother's hardware store took all the attention he could give it, but a traffic accident in Europe that summer had left him unable to make the rounds of his customers. Determined to keep the business going, he turned to his nephew and future son-in-law. Both had sales experience, albeit not in the material handling equipment Skarnes Engineering and Supply Company represented. John Kilby had been selling for U.S. Rubber. Tom Wanous was on the road for Johnson Wax. Neither knew the other at that point. Both gave the matter a lot of thought before joining the family business. It was to prove a business marriage made in heaven; in 1961 Skarnes sold the firm to the former partners-by-chance. Today Skarnes Incorporated is nearing its 60th birthday just a couple of blocks from where the firm started.

The modern company represents more than a dozen major lines of material handling equipment, ranging from simple casters and wheels (for Bassick-Hamilton-Divine) to 20-ton overhead cranes (for Cleveland Tramrail). Its clients are spread throughout Minnesota, the Dakotas, and western Wisconsin.

In addition, Skarnes continues to sell its ROL-A-LIFT, which puts hard-to-handle loads of up to six tons on wheels. Reubin Skarnes bought the original idea back in the 1940s, then greatly improved on the design and contracted manufacturing to Midland Welding and Manufacturing of Minneapolis. There are now seven different sizes—all still produced by Midland—used to handle everything from storage tanks and heavy equipment to fragile and sensitive machinery such as computers and electrical panels.

None of this was predictable when Reubin Skarnes returned to his native Minneapolis from Chicago in 1923 after his father suffered a stroke. He answered ads seeking representatives and solicited the job of representing The Chicago Rawhide Company, which sold leather belting, rawhide gears, and shoe leather. His first office was the back room of Skarnes Hardware. A nail keg served as an office chair, rent was minimal thanks to the understanding landlord, and correspondence was taken down to the Curtis Hotel, where a stenographer employed to do typing for guests could be hired part-time.

The business moved to its present location on Franklin Avenue after World War II. Under Kilby and Wanous, additional product lines have been added and a systems engineering division started to help customers ranging from Fortune 500 giants to small businesses design efficient materials-handling layouts and select the proper equipment to get the job done.

•   •   •

T.K. Wanous, president (left), and John Kilby, secretary-treasurer (right), of Skarnes Incorporated.

SOO LINE RAILROAD COMPANY

The Soo was formed in 1961 through the merger of the Minneapolis, St. Paul & Sault Ste. Marie (the Old Soo) with the Wisconsin Central and the Duluth, South Shore & Atlantic. The new Soo (the name derives from the pronunciation of "Sault" in Sault Ste. Marie) was in the black the first year and has been ever since, a railroad whose sole concentration is railroading.

The bloodlines of the Old Soo trace back to the 1880s, some 20 years after railroads first came to Minnesota. Unlike the early land grant roads and their colorful, even infamous, Rail Barons, the Old Soo was built largely with private funds and purchased most of its original right of way. Its purpose was competition—to challenge railroad pricing practices on eastbound shipments of Minnesota products via Chicago, then the only existing route east.

William Washburn and other local businessmen identified a shorter route to the eastern seaboard and built the Old Soo's first line via Sault Ste. Marie,

Michigan. At Sault Ste. Marie the Old Soo connected with the growing Canadian Pacific System, creating strong ties between the companies that exist today. Enterprises such as W.D. Washburn and Company (now part of General Mills) would use the new gateway as an alternative for moving products east to ports like Boston.

The Duluth, South Shore & Atlantic is the oldest segment of the Soo. Its earliest component, the Iron Mountain Railroad, built a 12-mile plank railroad in 1855 and moved ore cars with horses and mules. While the Old Soo was building east, the South Shore was created to consolidate lines in Michigan's upper peninsula and connect with the Canadian Pacific at Sault Ste. Marie.

The third component, the Wisconsin Central, was built in the 1870s to carve a north-south route through the state to Lake Superior. In 1909 the Old Soo leased properties of the Central and continued to lease or operate them as part of

the Soo system until the 1961 merger.

Old and new, the Soo has always been a Minneapolis company with corporate headquarters downtown and operations based at Shoreham Yard on the city's northeast side. Today the freight handled over Soo's 4,500 miles of track is both international and regional in scope: fertilizer, machinery, and harvested grains for agriculture in the Midwest; lumber, pulp, paper, and food products from Wisconsin and Upper Michigan; forest, petrochemical, and mining products through busy Canadian interchanges to the nation; and construction materials for the downtown revitalization of Minneapolis and St. Paul.

•   •   •

Each year the Soo's more than 230 locomotives and 11,000 freight cars handle some 10 billion-ton miles of service.

TARGET STORES

Target Stores, a division of Minneapolis-based Dayton Hudson Corporation, was conceived with the knowledge that while there will always be room for full-service, high-fashion department stores at the upper end of the merchandising spectrum, there will also be people who place a priority on convenience and low prices available through the economies of mass merchandising. When Target was launched in 1961, that was still a largely untested assumption; 20 years and 151 stores later, it has long since been validated. With annual sales exceeding $2 billion, Target now ranks among the top five discount operations in the country and expects to move up the scale another notch or two as some 100 additional stores come on-line through the mid-1980s.

The first Target store opened in Roseville in early 1962, just months after the new division was formed by what was then the Dayton Company. Under the initial guidance of Douglas Dayton, it quickly established itself as a unique form of discount store: brand-name merchandise, careful attention to customer amenities from the general cleanliness of the store to the courtesy of the staff, and a firm commitment to quality that today includes independent consumer product testing. Since 1974, when Target's all-out toy safety campaign began, more than 1,250 toys have failed that inspection and been rejected as store merchandise.

The first year Target was a specifically Minnesota phenomenon, with three other Twin Cities and one Duluth store beginning operations. But by 1966 Target had leaped halfway across the continent to Denver, Colorado. The next significant steps were taken in 1969 and

1970, when the company opened stores in Dallas and Houston, Texas, while also acquiring more than a dozen stores from a chain that had been operating in Iowa, Illinois, and Nebraska. A more recent expansion step was taken in 1980 with the acquisition of 40 Ayr-Way stores in the Midwest.

Such rapid growth has placed a premium on efficient, centralized planning and operations extending outward from the Minneapolis headquarters. Computerization has been a major element in handling that growth, so much so that many of the programs developed by and for Target have contributed to the rapid success of Dayton Hudson's B. Dalton Bookseller since that division was launched.

Today Target is concentrated in the central corridor of the country, from Minnesota and the Upper Midwest down the Mississippi to Texas, with growing clout in the South. Floyd Hall is chairman of the board and chief executive officer of Target, which is the

largest division of Dayton Hudson, one of the 10 largest nonfood retailers in the nation.

•   •   •

Above

New Target Stores incorporate contemporary design inside and out and utilize the latest energy conservation devices and programs.

Below

A Target Stores interior features a convenient self-service shopping environment with wide aisles and bright interior design and lighting.

SUPER VALU STORES, INC.

A modern Super Valu store in Minneapolis.

• • •

P rior to the 1920s, food distribution was perhaps the most inefficient of retail enterprises. Consumers routinely made their purchases from many small specialty stores—the butcher, the grocer, the baker, the fruit and vegetable vendor—which meant stores carried only limited numbers of items which were sold in relatively low quantities, thus increasing the cost of food on the table.

From this inefficiency was born the chain store concept: larger, more diverse operations with more purchasing power, greater efficiency and productivity, and therefore lower prices. At first independent retailers were hard pressed to compete. By the end of the 1920s the average chain food store had

annual sales of $46,000 compared to the independent's average of just $17,380. To make matters worse, the wholesalers, from whom the independents procured merchandise, refused to recognize they had any role to play in helping the individual operators survive.

Today, under the leadership of Super Valu, the world's largest food wholesaler, that state of affairs has been completely reversed. Under a corporate creed that recognizes that "the future success of both Super Valu and its retail-

ers is relative to, limited by, and dependent upon the future success of each other . . . ," the company has developed the industry's most extensive list of retailer support services to supplement its basic wholesale product supply responsibility to over 2,100 stores in 25 states. The result: sales in the 1970–1980 decade grew from under one billion dollars to over four billion dollars.

Super Valu can trace its beginnings back to the B.S. Bull Company, an early wholesale grocer in 1870's Minneapolis. Hugh G. Harrison was one of its organizers, and in 1871 he joined with George R. Newell to form the Newell and Harrison Company. The partnership split up several years later, but the Harrison and Newell names were to reunite in the next century.

The two businesses proceeded along somewhat similar paths in the interim. Both prospered during the late 1800s before Harrison sold out to an associate and a new partner, F.G. Winston, in 1893. By 1916 the business was known as Winston, Harper and Fisher—and banker Perry Harrison of the original family had bought into the firm.

In the '20s the rise of the chains inspired a plan to merge all the wholesalers in the Upper Midwest into one large organization which could be more competitive. Unfortunately, only two of the prospective members of the super-firm were sufficiently profitable to make the merger work: the George R. Newell Company and Winston, Harper and Fisher. The complex merger never came off, but on January 1, 1926, the two profitable Minneapolis operations united to become the Winston and Newell Company. Two years later the firm affiliated with the Independent Grocer's Alliance (IGA), the first successful attempt to allow independent retailers to face chain competition as a united group while still maintaining their valued autonomy.

In the years to come, president Tom Harrison's leadership would give added impetus to the "voluntary" concept, so much so that in 1942 Winston and Newell broke ties with IGA to start two voluntary organizations of its own—one called U-Save, the other named Super Valu. There were 420 members at the outset constituting a small percentage of Winston and Newell's total business. Yet, over the next 10 years, sales to affiliated stores became an increasingly dominant part of the organization's business, bringing the realization that the marketing dynamics of the voluntary group had made the independent retailer competitive with his chain counterpart. It was also evident that the partnership between the company and its affiliated retailers was an interdependent one.

Thus, in 1954, the name of the firm was officially changed to Super Valu to identify it more closely with the stores it served. Within a year, Super Valu had embarked on a second era—one marked by acquisitions.

It began in 1955 with the Joannes Brothers Company of Green Bay, Wisconsin. Over the next two decades other firms were drawn under the Super Valu umbrella: the Eavey Company of Xenia, Ohio, in 1961; J.M. Jones Company of Champaign-Urbana, Illinois, and Food Marketing Corporation of Ft. Wayne, Indiana, in 1963; Chastain-Roberts Company of Anniston, Alabama, in 1964; the Lewis Grocer Company of Indianola, Mississippi, in 1965; Charley Brothers Company of Greensburg, Pennsylvania, in 1977; and Ryans of Billings, Montana, in 1980.

The effect of this systematic growth

was to propel Super Valu from a compact, five-state operation into a major food wholesaler with operations in half of the 50 states. From a ranking of 16th among food distributors, Super Valu was on its way to the top. In 1967 the company celebrated the 25th anniversary of its voluntary group and for the first time was listed on the New York Stock Exchange.

Super Valu's third era came in the 1970s, largely under the direction of president and chief executive officer Jack Crocker, who joined the company in 1972. During this period, sophisticated new services designed to increase the sales and profitability of affiliated independent retailers were introduced, wholesale operations matured and broadened, and, for the first time, Super Valu began diversifying into nonfood lines.

On the nonfood front, Super Valu acquired Shopko Stores of Green Bay, Wisconsin, in 1971. The self-service discount department store chain has since grown to a family of 32 stores in four states.

In 1973 the company opened its first County Seat store. The leisure wear chain grew to 250 stores throughout the country by the decade's end, making it one of the most successful new retailing efforts of the decade.

In response to the growing need for support services to its retailer affiliates, Super Valu established Studio 70, an interior design firm specializing in retail supermarkets; Planmark, an architectural design and engineering group; and Risk Planners, an insurance agency whose services are focused on the special needs of supermarkets and owners. Other services include retail accounting, advertising, site location, training, consumer research, energy

management, and dozens of other critical support services.

At the beginning of the '80s, Super Valu also acquired Cub Food Stores, a low-margin, high-volume chain whose own family roots trace back to 1870s Stillwater.

As Michael Wright, current chief executive officer, and his management group look to the future from their new headquarters complex in suburban Eden Prairie, their prospects are perhaps best summed up in a statement of philosophy authored by chairman Jack Crocker in 1974 that states the company's "total commitment to serving customers more effectively than anyone else could serve them . . . the pursuit of this meaningful goal is the continuing and overriding responsibility from which every corporate activity must evolve. We value today's success as merely the beginning of a constantly expanding level of achievement."

◆   ◆   ◆

A plaque bearing the Super Valu corporate philosophy hangs in the lobby of the new corporate headquarters.

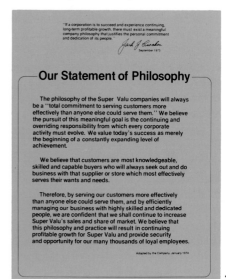

TENNANT COMPANY

If Irish-born George Henry Tennant could see the company he founded in 1870, he wouldn't recognize anything except its name. What began as a small manufacturing business of wood products has grown, through a series of twists, turns, and happenstance, into a world leader in the manufacture of powered, industrial floor-maintenance machines and floor coatings.

Tennant opened his small woodworking shop in northeast Minneapolis to make wooden rain gutters and downspouts. By the turn of the century, his firm was one of the leading manufacturers of hardwood flooring in the Upper Midwest. But as the forests receded, wood shortages prompted other ways to keep the saws running—silos, milk cartons, even toilet seats (which, legend insists, were "dadblamed uncomfortable").

Then, during the Great Depression, the organization happened upon a product that was to change its character and, in the decade that followed, would result in the development of a machine that would create a new industry. Ben Casper, a junior high school janitor who was tired of wet-mopping and hand-buffing his floors, fashioned from an old washing machine motor and a wad of steel wool

wrapped around a coffee can, a machine that would "dry clean" his floors. He showed it to his neighbor, who was Tennant Company's shop foreman. The company acquired the rights to manufacture the machine, and by 1938 its entire effort focused on manufacturing floor-care machines.

During the '30s, Lloyd Hale, who had married one of George Tennant's granddaughters, virtually created the market for the floor-maintenance equipment that Edward McMaster "Mac" Pennock, one of Tennant's sons-in-law, had developed from the janitor's coffee can contraption. The business was down to the proverbial shoestring by the end of the decade, but then along came World War II, defense plants, and the need to keep those defense plants very clean. From $330,000 in sales in 1938, Tennant Company hit the million-dollar mark in seven years.

In 1947 Ralph Peabody, a company engineer, invented the first vacuumized powered sweeper and, with it, a new industry. It revolutionized industrial floor maintenance and formed the genesis of a still-growing line of sweepers, scarifiers, scrubbers, and replacement parts that propelled Tennant Company

to industry dominance worldwide. Today the firm's product line also offers urethane floor coatings, designed to protect floors from wear, and epoxy floor coatings, designed to repair eroded floors.

The venture went public in 1969, but it still has the strong involvement of Tennant descendants, 112 years after the founding date. George Pennock, a grandson of George Tennant, joined the business in 1934 as an accountant and proceeded up the ladder to president in 1963. In 1976, after 13 years in which sales rose at a compound annual rate of 16 percent, Pennock turned over the chief executive officer's job to Roger Hale, a great-grandson of George Tennant.

In its second century, Tennant Company is a worldwide leader in the design, manufacturing, and marketing of specialized industrial and commercial floor-maintenance equipment and related products. Its operations include wholly owned subsidiaries in the Netherlands and Brazil, a joint venture in Japan, and export sales throughout the world. It moved to its present headquarters in Golden Valley in 1957 and has manufacturing operations in Golden Valley and Maple Grove, Minnesota.

Tennant Company has achieved recognition for an unusually profitable growth record, excellent personnel relations, and company-wide emphasis on quality programs.

•   •   •

Tennant Company developed the TENNANT™ maintenance system, which results in a neat, clean floor that is easy to maintain. The company meets the needs of industry with floor-cleaning machines and floor coatings.

THE THUNDERBIRD MOTEL

When Metropolitan Stadium—now affectionately remembered as "the Met"—first opened in 1956, Rod Wallace was involved in the opening day ceremonies: specifically traffic control at the intersection of 78th and Cedar Avenue as head of the Hennepin County Sheriff's Rescue Squad and Shrine Cycle Corps, organizations he had been instrumental in founding. He couldn't have predicted then that one day soon he would be hosting visitors to the Met and the Twin Cities just two blocks away.

The I-494 Strip was still well over the horizon in those days, when Wallace opened the doors of his Thunderbird Motel on Monday, May 20, 1963. The now-thriving entertainment and lodging corridor connecting Minneapolis-St. Paul International Airport and downtown Minneapolis consisted of one small hotel and a nearby restaurant. Since then, the distinctive 263-room motor inn Wallace and 18 other local businessmen had pioneered has become one of the most familiar landmarks along the Strip. Wallace acquired full ownership of the Thunderbird in 1967.

Innkeeping was a second business challenge for Wallace; his first success was in construction. That line of work brought him into contact with the owners of another Thunderbird—in Miami Beach, Florida. From that came an interest in building and running a first-class hospitality and convention/meeting facility near the airport and stadium complex. (The Thunderbird name is doubly significant for Wallace, since it had been on the stern of every sailboat he's ever raced.)

Over the years, the Thunderbird has acquired and commissioned numerous additions to its renowned collection of Native American art and artifacts, Wallace's way of preserving and showcasing the Upper Midwest's rich Indian heritage. The theme is extended throughout the motel using a decor scheme marked by Indian motifs, soft desert colors, and the Thunderbird totem, with a reflecting pool and suspended stairway leading to the spacious "Hall of Tribes" banquet hall and ballroom.

The Thunderbird has seen six expansions since it opened with 108 rooms nearly two decades ago. In January 1969 it survived a disastrous fire that gutted the cocktail lounge and main dining room, doing more than a half-million dollars' damage. By the next day the inn's staff had set up temporary food and beverage service in the lobby; and by the opening of baseball season, it was business as usual again.

Through the years, Wallace has played an active role in local affairs, organizing Bloomington's Hospitality Association and Convention Bureau and presiding over the Greater Minneapolis Hotel Association. He also helped to found the Minneapolis Aquatennial's AquaJesters, as well as the Hennepin County Sheriff's Water Patrol and the University of Minnesota's Golden Gopher Club.

♦ ♦ ♦

The Thunderbird Motel combines Native American art and artifacts with high-quality lodging and meeting/convention facilities.

TOUCHE ROSS & CO.

The seeds of the Minneapolis office of Touche Ross & Co. were sown in 1908, when John Ballantine Niven was appointed coreceiver of the Pillsbury-Washburn Flour Mills Company. Niven, who had formed a partnership with fellow Scotsman Sir George Alexander Touche in 1900, was sent to Minneapolis to represent British interests during the nine months of the receivership. His firm subsequently established an office in the city in 1913, primarily to serve the firm organized after the receivership: Pillsbury. From that day to this, the Touche Minneapolis office has always been close to Pillsbury, now residing in the new 40-story Pillsbury Center complex.

Up to 1921 the Minneapolis office

had only three clients other than Pillsbury, and annual billings of about $2,000. The next year, however, growth began in earnest when the firm was engaged to make an investigation of a small bus company in northern Minnesota. From that and other bus companies around the country came the organization of the Greyhound Corporation.

William Bechert became the first partner-in-charge upon his promotion to partnership in 1926, five years after coming to Minneapolis from New York headquarters. It was Bechert who shepherded the initial investigation of an Iron Range bus company for Piper, Jaffray & Hopwood, and rode along as the resulting firm grew to national promi-

nence.

George Ludolph took over in 1944. Remembered as a taskmaster, he also indulged an artistic side, polishing his style at the Minneapolis College of Art and Design. Palmer Tang, a University of Minnesota graduate, succeeded Ludolph in 1957. When the Financial Accounting Standards Board was created to replace a former governing body, Tang was chosen as one of six practicing public accountants to serve on the initial advisory council. Carl Pohlman, named associate partner-in-charge in 1980, is another with a long record of service in Minneapolis, his dating back to the 1950s.

When the Minneapolis office celebrated its 50th anniversary in 1963, it was staffed by four active partners and 46 other professionals and support personnel. By contrast, its new offices in Pillsbury Center, and the St. Paul office created in 1962, are home to 26 partners and nearly 300 staffers. From one client, Touche has grown to serve some 1,200 Minnesota businesses in such fields as agribusiness, finance, health care, manufacturing, retail sales, real estate and construction, transportation, utilities, and the public sector. A member of Minneapolis' Five-Percent Club, the city's Touche office serves more publicly held clients than any other firm in the Twin Cities.

• • •

A hallmark of Touche Ross is the unusually large number of local talents who have risen through the ranks in the Minneapolis office to full partnership. Members of the "Twenty Year Club" include (seated, left to right) Ron Bach, Palmer Tang, and Carl Pohlman (standing, left to right); Joe Buchan, Einar Ross, Ken Stocke, and Alan Murphy.

THE VALSPAR CORPORATION

Valspar had its origins in Boston, Massachusetts, in a paint store established in 1806. Lawson Valentine joined that firm in 1832, his brother Harry years later, and in 1870 the two moved the Valentine Company, as it had come to be known, to New York City.

About the same time a Swiss immigrant came to Minneapolis, drawn by the area's potential as a source of high-quality flax. Minnesota Linseed Oil Company was created to convert flaxseed into linseed oil, a drying oil used as a primary component of paints and floor coverings in those days. In 1904 the company—eventually known as Minnesota Linseed Oil Paint Company, and finally Minnesota Paints—moved from 10th Street and Washington Avenue to the location Valspar still occupies at 3rd Street and 11th Avenue.

At its inception, the forerunner of Minnesota Paints processed linseed oil; paint was first manufactured in Minneapolis in 1882. Meanwhile, the Val-

which emerged a diversified, modern entine brothers evolved from paints to varnishes. Their claim to fame was the development of a varnish that would not turn white. It was called "Valspar," and became known for a demonstration test first inadvertently photographed at the World's Fair, when boiling water poured on a floor coated with varnish amazingly did not ruin the clear finish. That same varnish was on the *Spirit of St. Louis* when Charles Lindbergh crossed the Atlantic.

During the '30s both Valentine Paint and Minnesota Paint began periods of growth and acquisition, the latter under the guidance of Valentine (no relation to the eastern family) Wurtele, who became president in 1931 shortly after the death of his uncle, W.A. Ramsay, the driving force behind the firm for many years. Wurtele was succeeded by his son, Angus, in 1965. Angus Wurtele continued as Valspar president after the 1970 merger, from firm with operations spread throughout

the Midwest, East, and Mountain States.

Further acquisitions continued Valspar's growth through the '70s. Today the company is known for national (Colony) and regional (Valspar, Minnesota, Masury, and Elliott) brands of paints and coverings, plus quality private-labeled paints for retail and hardware wholesalers and farm cooperatives. From independent roots in linseed oil and varnishes, The Valspar Corporation has become one of the top 10 paint and coatings producers in the nation, specializing in consumer coatings; chemical coatings used on farm and construction equipment, precoated building materials, office equipment, and toys; and resins, colorants, stains, and marine finishes.

•   •   •

This float represented the Minnesota Linseed Oil Paint Company, a forerunner of today's Valspar.

WCCO RADIO

When the call letters WCCO were first broadcast on October 2, 1924, there was no reason to believe they would become any more distinguished than those of other fledgling stations in those early days of radio. Yet, over the decades, WCCO became much more than just another radio station. Regionally, it came to be an institution whose signal covered much of Minnesota and significant portions of Wisconsin, Iowa, and the Dakotas. Nationally, within the broadcasting and advertising industries, it became something of a legend.

The call letters came from the name of the station's owner in 1924, the Washburn Crosby Company (now known, of course, as General Mills). It was purchased from the milling company in 1929 by a young man named William Paley, who was assembling a network of stations with the equally impressive initials CBS. WCCO Radio is now one of the family of broadcast properties owned locally by Midwest Radio and Television, Inc.

Charlie Boone and Roger Erickson have brought their lighthearted morning reporting to everything from the weather to the wedding of Prince Charles (aired via satellite from London) during their more than 20 years on WCCO Radio.

◆   ◆   ◆

From those first days when its signal could only be heard by the few people who owned radio sets, the station's audience grew until WCCO became the dominant station in the Upper Midwest. Now WCCO frequently leads the nation in "share" of audience, and only a handful of stations in New York and Chicago can surpass the number of listeners who tune in WCCO's prime morning programs.

On-air personalities have been an important element in the station's success. Cedric Adams joined WCCO in 1931; his popularity was so great that in the '40s airline pilots flying over the Twin Cities claimed the metropolitan area abruptly went dark every night at 10:15—when Adams finished his eve-

ning newscast. Over the years other WCCO announcers became household words: Clellan Card, Bob DeHaven, Darragh Aldrich, Maynard Speece, and Jergen Nash, to name but a few. Today, Boone and Erickson, Howard Viken, and Steve Cannon are every bit as well-known.

News, information, and sports have all contributed greatly to WCCO's success over the years. The station's news bureau has won countless accolades for broadcast excellence, including such prestigious awards as the Peabody and du Pont-Columbia. Every game of the Minnesota Twins since the team came to this region in 1961 has been heard on WCCO, and the station also broadcasts the Minnesota Vikings and the University of Minnesota Gophers football and basketball games.

On the occasion of WCCO Radio's 40th anniversary in 1964, William J. McNally, then chairman of the board, said, "The sun has never shown more brilliantly on WCCO Radio than it does today, and every prospect is that its brightest days still lie ahead." It is a statement as true today as it was then.

◆   ◆   ◆

For 30 years, until his death in 1961, Cedric Adams was among the region's most popular radio and newspaper personalities.

WCCO-TV

Channel 4 went on the air July 1, 1949, with a total staff of 26, three studios, one film camera, and one studio in the old Radio City Theater building in downtown Minneapolis. It matured as the medium matured, evolving from a novice producer of local entertainment to a sophisticated provider of local, regional, and national news and information.

In the beginning Channel 4 wasn't WCCO at all. The station operated as WTCN-TV until the 1952 merger with WCCO Radio that formed the parent organization, Midwest Radio and Television, Inc. William J. McNally became chairman of the board, Robert Ridder president, F. Van Konynenburg, vice-president and general manager—and television began to come of age in the Twin Cities.

The networks were still formative organizations in the 1950s; local stations originated much of their own entertainment programming. The first live full-color program to be broadcast locally on Channel 4 was "Axel and His Dog" in October 1954. Several years later a young local actor named Dave Moore went on camera with his first 10 p.m. newscast, beginning a tenure that would span more than a quarter of a century (weatherman Bud Kraehling, a member of that early team, was one of the station's original employees). In the past decade some 16 WCCO-TV reporters, photographers, and producers have gone on to network ranks.

The honors came quickly and often, beginning when the Radio Television News Directors Association named WCCO-TV the "Outstanding News Operation of the Nation" in 1955, the first of more than a half dozen national RTNDA honors. The George Foster Peabody Award was presented to

An illustration of WCCO-TV's new studios along Nicollet Mall and 11th Street.

• • •

WCCO-TV in 1961 and in 1975, making Channel 4 the only television station in Minnesota to receive broadcasting's highest and most significant award twice. In 1980 WCCO-TV was the only local station in the country awarded a national Emmy. There have also been more than a few Sigma Delta Chi and Alfred I. du Pont-Columbia University honors.

As television evolves beyond a simple provider of entertainment and information, WCCO-TV is changing as well, now under the leadership of W. T. Doar, Jr., James M. Rupp, and Ronald N. Handberg. Locally owned in an era of corporate broadcasting, WCCO-TV news operation includes three bureaus: Minneapolis, St. Paul, and Washington, D.C. In 1982 it began serving the Upper Midwest on the new Westinghouse-ABC Satellite News Channel, which combines 18 regional commercial television stations into a 24-hour-a-day

cable news service. WCCO-TV also supplies programming to Minnesota Cable Systems with a two-channel cable news and weather service. One channel provides a 24-hour news service, while the second channel provides the latest in weather information.

For more than 30 years WCCO-TV has become identified with broadcast excellence. A new era will begin in early 1983 when Channel 4 moves into new studios along the Nicollet Mall as perhaps the single most honored local television station in the country.

• • •

The WCCO building (formerly Radio City Theater) was remodeled in 1956.

WARDEN OIL COMPANY

A.L. "Al" Warden, founder and president of Warden Oil Company.

When A.L. "Al" Warden was 19, he left the family farm to make his fortune in the big city of Minneapolis. His entire bankroll back in 1922 amounted to $145, $90 of which he immediately invested in an aged three-quarter-ton Republic truck to start Warden Haulage Company. Summers he delivered furniture for the Hartman Company; winters he hauled coal for Pittsburg Coal.

In 1924 he was hired by the Gray brothers (Lee, Roland, and Russel, who later started Grayco) to gather the used oil they burned as fuel oil in their steam-cleaning boiler. He had moved up to a Model T Ford truck by then, and the mechanical aptitude he had gained on the farm and working with his trucks planted a nagging idea. Why burn a product that still had a lot of good lubrication in it? Left in a barrel, oil would settle clear, so he knew there must be a way to re-refine used oil—all he had to do was invent it.

To gain technical background, he took night classes in petroleum chemistry at the University of Minnesota. He constructed a homemade lab in the basement laundry room of his apartment building and, after many tries, came upon the acid clay process (a process actually invented several years before in Kansas City, but unknown to him during his experiments).

Warden Oil Company was launched in 1927—in a shack at 187 Humboldt Avenue North, near the Leef Brothers Overall Laundry which had succeeded the Gray brothers as a customer for the fuel oil he still hauled. Once Warden had his re-refining process cooking, the days of burning up good lubricating oil were behind him forever.

Back then the wise car owner changed oil about every thousand miles, which presented Warden with a ready-made opportunity. Weekends cars would line up for blocks to have their old oil drained and replaced with fresh. The drained oil Warden promptly re-refined and sold again. Farmers often brought dressed poultry and meat to trade for the oil they needed for their carefully maintained machinery. Even during the Depression the small company kept itself going, selling oil for 10 cents a quart and meeting a payroll for operators who worked for 45 cents an hour.

By 1940 Warden was calling on so many outstate accounts that he bought a company airplane, a Piper Cub Cruiser, often delighting customers by taking them up for a ride. Too old to be a pilot during World War II, Warden flew for the Minnesota Civil Air Patrol and later took a U.S. Navy commission, serving as an oil tanker expediter to speed badly needed fuel supplies from a port in southern France to U.S. Army units in Europe.

Warden Oil today is much as it has always been—a small, close-knit organization which re-refines and custom mixes oil for customers ranging from small farmers to major railroads and airlines.

•   •   •

The original home of Warden Oil (with Al Warden center), where motorists came for an oil change. Today the shack serves as a warming shed for yard workers. The sign on the wall offers five gallons of oil for $1.75.

PATRONS

The following individuals, companies, and organizations have made a valuable commitment to the quality of this publication. Windsor Publications and the Greater Minneapolis Chamber of Commerce gratefully acknowledge their participation in *City of Lakes: An Illustrated History of Minneapolis.*

Albitz Design, Inc.
Alexander & Alexander Inc.*
American Linen Supply Company*
Arthur Andersen & Co.*
Apache Corporation*
BankAmerica International
Batten, Barton, Durstine & Osborn, Inc.
Beckman Produce
Bennett-Ringrose-Wolsfeld-Jarvis-Gardner, Inc.
Benson Optical Company*
Blue Ox Restaurant
The Boisclair Corporation
Boker's Inc.*
Bor-Son Construction Companies*
Burgess-Beckwith Division of Burgess Publishing Company*
CPT Corporation*
Campbell-Mithun*
Carlson Companies, Inc.*
Cedar Lake Farm
Century Manufacturing Company*
Continental Machines*
Convergent Systems, Inc.
Dayton Hudson Corporation
Dayton's*
Deloitte Haskins & Sells*
Derickson Company*
Donaldson Company, Inc.*
Dorsey & Whitney*
Dyco Petroleum Corporation*
Eberhardt Company*
Ettel & Franz Company
FMC Corporation/Northern Ordnance Division

Faegre & Benson*
Fairview Community Hospitals*
Fingerhut*
First Bank Minneapolis*
Fisher Paper Box Company*
Fist Brokerage Co.
E. C. Forbes, Forbes Marketing Group
Garland's Inc.
General Mills*
Grain Terminal Association*
Gray, Plant, Mooty, Mooty & Bennett*
Greater Minneapolis Chamber of Commerce*
S.J. Groves and Sons Company*
Harris-Billings Co.
Mildred G. Hemmingsen
Honeywell*
Hopkins House*
Horton Manufacturing Co., Inc. (Horton Industries Inc.)*
Hubbard Broadcasting (KSTP)*
International Multifoods*
InterNorth, Inc.*
Inter-Regional Financial Group*
Investors Diversified Services*
Johnson & Rauch, Inc.
Harold V. Knutson
Kwik Sew Pattern Co., Inc.
Litton Microwave Cooking Products*
Daryl Losey, Realtor
Lutheran Brotherhood*
MSI Insurance
Marquette National Bank*
Marsh & McLennan*
Medtronic, Inc.*
Metro Metals, Inc.
Minneapolis Star & Tribune Company*
Minnesota Gas Company*
Minnesota Twins*
Modern Merchandising, Inc.*
Monson/Ueland Architects, Inc.
Munsingwear*
Napco*

Nash Finch Company*
National Car Rental System, Inc.*
National City Bank of Minneapolis*
Nordquist Sign Co.
North Memorial Medical Center*
Northern Pump Company*
Northland Aluminum Products, Inc.*
Northland Development Company of Minneapolis, Inc.
Northrup King Company*
Northwestern National Bank of Minneapolis*
Northwestern National Life Insurance Co.*
Nortronics Company, Inc.*
Oxford Development Minnesota, Inc.*
Pako Corporation*
Parker Hannifin Corp.
Peat, Marwick, Mitchell & Co.*
Pillsbury*
Prudential*
Radisson Hotels*
St. Mary's Hospital*
Skarnes Incorporated*
Soo Line Railroad Company*
Stephens Buick Co.
Super Valu Stores, Inc.*
Target Stores*
Tennant Company*
Thermo King Corporation
The Thunderbird Motel*
Touche Ross & Co.*
Upper Midwest Industries, Inc.
The Valspar Corporation*
Warden Oil Company*
WCCO Radio*
WCCO-TV*

•   •   •

*Partners in Progress of *City of Lakes: An Illustrated History of Minneapolis.* The histories of these companies and organizations appear in Chapter 5, beginning on page 273.

AFTERWORD

As Minneapolis looks to the future, it faces a situation that it has not confronted before in its history. In the past, growth was measured solely in the quantitative expansion of the major industries that operated within the city. Recently, however, the view of such activity has shifted to a more sophisticated perspective, with emphasis upon quality rather than simple quantity. The decline in the population of Minneapolis since 1950 is a good example of this shift. Viewed with alarm in the 1960s, the population decline has been interpreted more favorably as of late, as economic disaster has not followed hard on its heels.

The decline of population in Minneapolis reflects, in part, the movement of people and industry away from the cities of the Midwest and East to the Sun Belt cities of the South and West. It also reflects the rapid development of suburbs around Minneapolis, as industries and people have left the inner city for the space of the surrounding area. A "leapfrog" effect can be discerned in this process, as the commercial and industrial areas of the city of Minneapolis are surrounded by residential areas, which give way to the industrial and business belt in the suburbs, which in turn give way to more residential areas, and which finally fade into the surrounding farmlands. This process of outward expansion was early feared to presage the decline of the Minneapolis city center, but over the years the city's central commercial district has retained its premier position in the metropolitan region as measured by its share of retail sales, banking and finance concentrations, and office space. With the continued development of the business district in the late 1970s and early 1980s, this primary position appears to be insured for some time to come. While the removal of some businesses to the suburbs has meant the loss of some jobs and people, then, the overall picture is one which stimulates optimism.

The results of the partial exodus have been to enhance the quality of the urban environment, as population density has been reduced and as industrial crowding on limited space also has been reduced. Unemployment remains higher in the city than in the surrounding regions, however, but the rate of unemployment remains below the national figures. Average incomes within the city are also slightly below the averages for the metropolitan region, but they remain competitive with other urban areas around the nation. The growing emphasis upon highly-skilled workers needed by employers in the city and suburbs has also enhanced the overall picture, as the general levels of education and skill of the work force have increased in response to this need.

The abrupt rise in the cost of energy in the 1970s has had a great impact upon patterns of work and life in Minneapolis and presents a major obstacle to future progress. Energy conservation on the part of government, industry, and the citizenry, however, is being practiced on a greater scale with each passing year and already has had a strong effect. Experimentation with new forms of architecture, techniques to increase the productivity of existing energy sources, research to develop new sources (especially solar power), and relative absence of energy-intensive industries located in the area indicate that the future may be brighter than many observers first suspected.

While faced with problems, then, Minneapolis has reason to be optimistic about the future. Its greatest strength, however, remains its people. The inhabitants of Minneapolis have an urban environment that is the envy of many other cities. Conscious of this fact, Minneapolitans are willing and able to strive to maintain and improve their condition. Neighborhood associations are strong and active, working to overcome particular local problems, while interest in the city as a whole and its improvement is not diminished. Controversies do rage occasionally and are often heated, as is evidenced by the conflict which developed over the decision to locate the domed Hubert H. Humphrey Stadium in downtown Minneapolis. Such controversies indicate the degree of civic involvement in such decision-making, however, rather than permanent discord and divisiveness. This characteristic involvement and belief in the effectiveness of democratic participation on the part of the citizenry reflects the continued vitality of the city's heritage and is its strongest asset in coming to grips with the vagaries of the future.

SUGGESTED READING

The decennial Census of the United States provides a convenient starting place for examining the history of urban places in the United States, and in the case of Minneapolis this material is supplemented by the decennial census of the state of Minnesota, which was taken in the middle of the interval of the national counts. The various publications of the Census Bureau also provide invaluable information about the growth of industry, standards of living, and social and cultural characteristics of the inhabitants.

General histories of the city of Minneapolis have been done at various periods, but the most substantial were completed in the early part of the 20th century. A late 19th-century effort was Isaac Atwater's *History of the City of Minneapolis* (New York, 1893). Horace B. Hudson's compendium, *A Half Century of Minneapolis* (Minneapolis, 1908) is another valuable work and includes substantial biographical sketches on most of the members of the city's social and business elite. E. Dudley Parsons' *The Story of Minneapolis* (Minneapolis, 1913) was another notable effort, as were Marion D. Shutter's *History of Minneapolis* (Chicago, 1923) and Ruth Thompson's *The Twin Towns at the Falls of Saint Anthony* (Minneapolis, 1926). *Minneapolis: The Story of a City,* compiled by the Writers' Project of the Works Projects Administration in 1940, is another valuable, comprehensive effort.

Because of their proximity to one another, Minneapolis and St. Paul have been the subject of several comparative histories. Eva Gale's *A Tale of Twin Cities* (Minneapolis, 1889) was one of the first of these efforts, along with *A Tale of Two Cities, Minneapolis and St. Paul Compared* (Minneapolis, 1885). Calvin F. Schmid's *Social Saga of Two Cities* (Minneapolis, 1937) is one of the best of this particular genre. Thomas J. Abercrombie's "Tale of Twin Cities," in the *National Geographic's* November 1980 edition keeps the metaphor alive for almost an entire century.

The economic history of Minneapolis has received a great deal of attention from historians. Mildred L. Hartsough's *The Twin Cities as a Metropolitan Market* (Minneapolis, 1925) is a particularly valuable work. Lucile M. Kane's *The Waterfall That Built a City: The Falls of Saint Anthony in Minneapolis* (St. Paul, 1966), is a definitive explication of the role of the waterpower of the falls in the city's development. Merrill E. Jarchow's "King Wheat," in *Minnesota History* (March 1948) presents an interpretation of Minnesota agriculture, and Charles B. Kuhlmann's "The Influence of the Minneapolis Flour Mills Upon the Economic Development of Minnesota and the Northwest," in *Minnesota History* (June 1925), despite its age, presents a fascinating picture of the relationships between the city's hinterland and its primary industry. Charles Rumford Walker's *American City: A Rank-and-File History* (New York, 1937) presents a leftist interpretation of the city's economic rise and focuses in depth upon the labor troubles which afflicted the city

in 1934. Publications of the Federal Reserve Bank in Minneapolis, along with the publications of the Minneapolis City Planning Commission and various agencies of the state of Minnesota concerned with economic development, are extremely useful for the post-World War II period. Don Larson's *Land of the Giants* chronicles the development of Minnesota's large corporations from their origins in the 19th century when appropriate and includes the large firms that have played roles in the history of Minneapolis. Unfortunately no comparable work deals with the major contributions of small business to the vitality of the city's history.

The political history of Minneapolis and Minnesota has also received a great deal of attention from eminent political historians as well as political scientists. Volume III of William Watts Folwell's *A History of Minnesota* (St. Paul, 1926) is an excellent point of reference for understanding the major issues and personalities that dominated the city and state's politics. Arthur Naftalin's various writings, such as "The Tradition of Protest and the Roots of the Farmer-Labor Party" in *Minnesota History* (June 1956), are also extremely useful, as are the writings of G. Theodore Mitau. Special topics in the political history of the city have been treated in detail by various scholars, as is seen in June Drenning Holmquist's "Convention City: The Republicans in Minneapolis, 1892," which was published in *Minnesota History* in June of 1956. A particularly incisive treatment of the political history of Minneapolis in essay form is to be found in Gustav Rolf Svendsen's *Hennepin County History: An Illustrated Essay* (Minneapolis, 1976). Fred W. Friendly's *Minnesota Rag*, published in 1981, is a recounting of the landmark Supreme Court case of *Near* v. *Minnesota* but is also a dramatic representation of Minneapolis during the turbulent 1920s and 1930s.

The history of ethnicity and immigration in Minneapolis and the general evolution of community have been developed extensively. Numerous memoirs of original pioneers such as John H. Stevens, Thomas B. Walker, Charlotte O. Van Cleve, and others, as well as the autobiographies of prominent immigrants such as Andreas Ueland's *Recollections of an Immigrant* (New York, 1929), provide interesting insights and rich detail. Pioneer immigration historians with roots in Minnesota and Minneapolis, exemplified by Theodore C. Blegen, have done extensive research on the Scandinavian groups that figured so prominently in the city's history. The history of the Jews in Minneapolis and the rest of the state has been treated in W. Gunther Plant's *The Jews in Minnesota: The First Seventy-Five Years* (New York, 1959), while the role of Samuel N. Deinard has been explored by Michael G. Rapp in an article in *Minnesota History* in 1973. The remarkable community of the Bohemian Flats was the subject of a WPA history that was published in 1940. Few published materials are available on the history of smaller immigrant groups in

the city, but the Slavic groups, blacks, and Native Americans have been the subjects of many professional studies conducted by graduate students and staff at the University of Minnesota. Histories of these groups also abound in the native tongues of the foreign immigrants, and many are collected in the Immigration History Research Center of the University of Minnesota at its St. Paul location.

There are several recent works dealing with Minneapolis that are of general interest. Journalist Barbara Flanagan's *Minneapolis* (New York, 1973) is informative, as is Lawrence Brings' slightly dated centennial effort, *Minneapolis: City of Opportunity* (Minneapolis, 1956). Sue E. Holbert and June Holmquist's *A History Tour of 50 Twin City Landmarks* (St. Paul, 1966) is another useful piece. Jean Ervin's works, *The Twin Cities Explored* and *The Twin Cities Perceived*, especially the latter, are particularly incisive efforts. David A. Lanegran and Ernest R. Sandeen's *The Lake District of Minneapolis: A History of the Calhoun-Isles Community* (St. Paul, 1979), is a well-executed historical sketch of one of Minneapolis' most pleasant areas.

• • •

ACKNOWLEDGMENTS

I am indebted to several individuals and institutions in the preparation of this history, directly and indirectly. The Hennepin County Historical Society, which has been busy for several decades preserving the history of Minneapolis and the surrounding county, is foremost among these. The Minneapolis Heritage Preservation Commission, which is charged with delineating and preserving the city's historic buildings and sites, is of more recent vintage, but its work, too, has greatly facilitated this study.

The development of history in Minnesota, in all its guises, owes an ultimate debt to the Minnesota Historical Society. Under the guiding hand of Mr. Russell Fridley for the past quarter century, the society continues to collect historical materials of all sorts and to engage in and support historical investigation in Minneapolis and elsewhere in the state. My former supervisor at the society, Mrs. June Holmquist, director of Research and Publications, greatly stimulated my own interest in Minnesota history, and her editorial maxims have guided me through this and several other projects.

Last but not least I wish to thank Professor Hyman Berman of the Department of History, University of Minnesota, for his guidance and inspiration. A longtime student of Minneapolis history and Minnesota history generally, Professor Berman's work and writings greatly facilitated the organization and execution of this volume.

Appreciation is also due the Minnesota Tourism Division (Dept. of E.P.D., 480 Cedar St., St. Paul, MN 55101), which provided some of the color photographs used in this volume. — Joseph Stipanovich

INDEX

Numbers in italics indicate illustrations.

Joseph Stipanovich received his Ph.D. in history from the University of Minnesota in 1978. A specialist in the social and economic history of the United States in the 20th century, he has published two previous books on American immigration history, as well as a dozen articles and reviews in various historical journals in the United States and Europe. Dr. Stipanovich was formerly employed by the Minnesota Historical Society as a research historian, and was director in 1978 and 1979 of the Historical-Cultural Survey of the Minnesota Iron Mining Regions, a project that was co-sponsored by the State of Minnesota and the Minnesota Historical Society. The author is currently the director of research and world trade activities for the economic development division of The Greater Minneapolis Chamber of Commerce.

Dick Schaaf, who researched and wrote the "Partners in Progress" section, is the managing editor of *Training: The Magazine of Human Resources Development* published in Minneapolis. A sought-after and prolific writer whose 200 articles have appeared in many regional and national publications, Mr. Schaaf has been extensively published in *Corporate Report,* Minneapolis' distinguished business publication.

Harold Chucker, the editorial consultant for the book, is a writer who specializes in economic commentary. Mr. Chucker was formerly the editor of the *Minneapolis Star*'s editorial page.

Phil Waters, the book's designer, lived in Minneapolis from 1974 through 1978 and graduated with honors from the studio arts program at the University of Minnesota. In 1976 he received the first Studio Arts Department Annual Award. Born in Springfield, Massachusetts, he now resides in Santa Monica and works as a designer and photographer throughout California.

Los Angeles: A City Apart, by David L. Clark (1981)

Heart of the Commonwealth: Worcester, by Margaret A. Erskine (1981)

Out of a Wilderness: An Illustrated History of Greater Lansing, by Justin L. Kestenbaum (1981)

The Valley and the Hills: An Illustrated History of Birmingham and Jefferson County, by Leah Rawls Atkins (1981)

River Capital: An Illustrated History of Baton Rouge, by Mark T. Carleton (1981)

Chattanooga: An Illustrated History, by James W. Livingood (1981)

New Haven: An Illustrated History, edited by Floyd Shumway and Richard Hegel (1981)

Albany: Capital City on the Hudson, by John J. McEneny (1981)

Kalamazoo: The Place Behind the Products, by Larry B. Massie and Peter J. Schmitt (1981)

Mobile: The Life and Times of a Great Southern City, by Melton McLaurin and Michael Thomason (1981)

New Orleans: An Illustrated History, by John R. Kemp (1981)

Regina: From Pile O'Bones to Queen City of the Plains, by William A. Riddell (1981)

King County and its Queen City: Seattle, by James R. Warren (1981)

To the Setting of the Sun: The Story of York, by Georg R. Sheets (1981)

Buffalo: Lake City in Niagara Land, by Richard C. Brown and Bob Watson (1981)

Springfield of the Ozarks, by Harris and Phyllis Dark (1981)

Charleston and the Kanawha Valley, by Otis K. Rice (1981)

At the River's Bend: An Illustrated History of Jackson County, by Richard D. McKinzie and Sherry Lamb Schirmer (1982)

Dallas: An Illustrated History, by Darwin Payne (1982)

Heart of the Promised Land: An Illustrated History of Oklahoma County, by Bob L. Blackburn (1982)

Winnipeg: Where the New West Begins, by Eric Wells (1982)

Rhode Island: The Independent State, by George H. Kellner and J. Stanley Lemons (1982)

Calgary: Canada's Frontier Metropolis, by Max Foran and Heather MacEwan Foran (1982)

Greensboro: A Chosen Center, by Gayle Hicks Fripp (1982)

Norfolk's Waters: An Illustrated Maritime History of Hampton Roads, by William L. Tazewell (1982)

Metropolis of the American Nile: An Illustrated History of Memphis and Shelby County, by John E. Harkins (1982)

Beaumont: A Chronicle of Promise, by Judith W. Linsley and Ellen W. Rienstra (1982)

Boise: An Illustrated History, by Merle Wells (1982)

Broome County Heritage: An Illustrated History, by Ross McGuire and Lawrence Bothwell (1982)

Hartford: An Illustrated History of Connecticut's Capital, by Glenn Weaver (1982)

Raleigh: City of Oaks, by James Vickers (1982)

The Story of Evansville, by Kenneth P. McCutchan (1982)

Duluth: An Illustrated History of the Zenith City, by Glenn N. Sandvik (1982)

The Valley and its Peoples: An Illustrated History of the Lower Merrimack River, by Paul Hudon (1982)

The Upper Mohawk Country: An Illustrated History of Greater Utica, by David M. Ellis (1982)

Chicago: Commercial Center of the Continent, by Kenan Heise and Michael Edgerton (1982)

Corpus Christi: The History of a Texas Seaport, by Bill Walraven (1982)

Cape Fear Adventure: An Illustrated History of Wilmington, by Diane Cobb Cashman (1982)

The Lehigh Valley: An Illustrated History, by Karyl Lee Hall and Peter Hall (1982)

At the River's Bend: An Illustrated History of Jackson County, by Richard D. McKinzie and Sherry Lamb Schirmer (1982)

Headline and text type set in Goudy by Auto-Graphics. Printed on 70 lb. acid-free Warrenflo and bound by Walsworth Publishing Company.